I10793359

IMAGES
of America

ALGOMA TOWNSHIP

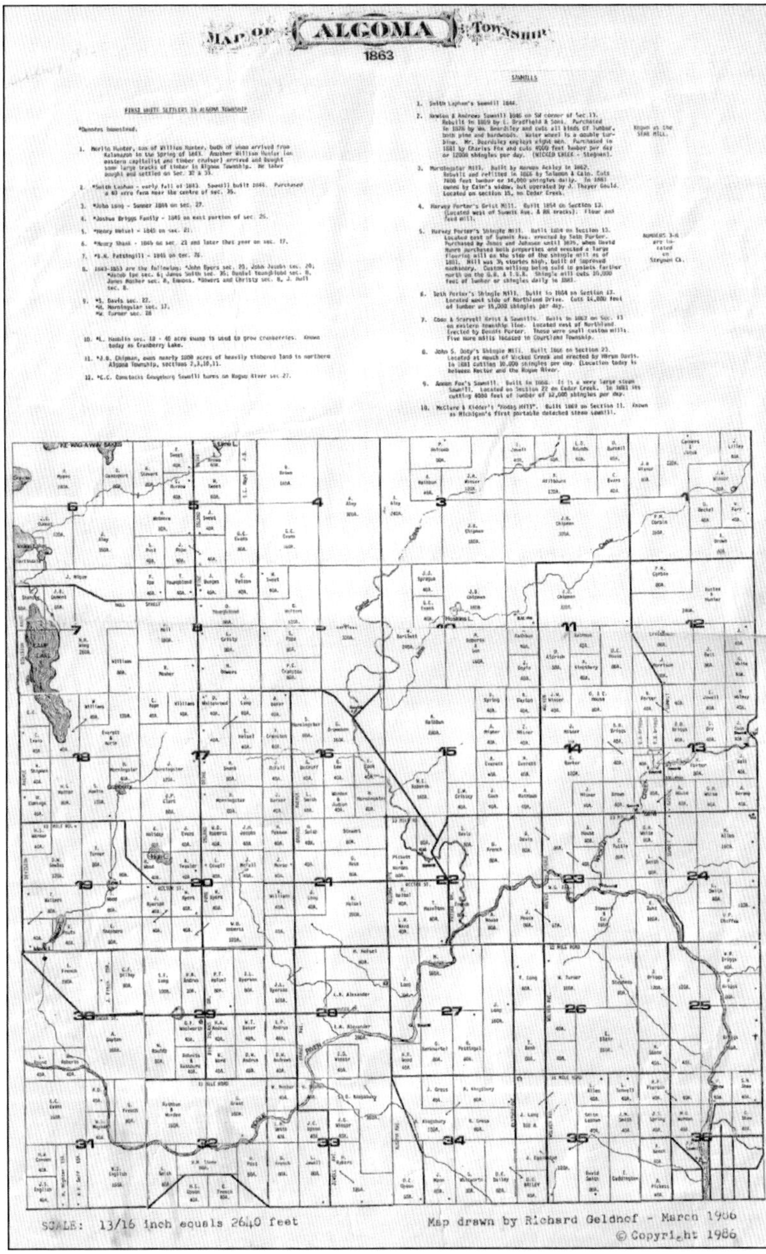

This map of Algoma Township is provided as a guide for the rest of the book. Published in 1986, it gives some reference to the many early homesteaders and sawmills of Algoma Township in 1863, approximately 15 years after the township was established. Additionally, the rivers and lakes of Algoma Township are visible here.

On the Cover: An Algoma Township road building crew poses for the camera. The crew leader and organizer is road commissioner James Madison "Matt" Davis (first row, third from the left). The photograph was donated to the Algoma Township Historical Society by Lorrain Pennington. (Courtesy of Algoma Township Historical Society.)

IMAGES
of America

ALGOMA TOWNSHIP

Bethany Hart with the
Algoma Township Historical Society

ARCADIA
PUBLISHING

ISBN 978-1-4671-1416-5

Published by Arcadia Publishing
Charleston, South Carolina

Printed in the United States of America

Library of Congress Control Number: 2014958790

For all general information, please contact Arcadia Publishing:
Telephone 843-853-2070
Fax 843-853-0044
E-mail sales@arcadiapublishing.com
For customer service and orders:
Toll-Free 1-888-313-2665

Visit us on the Internet at www.arcadiapublishing.com

To the people who have made Algoma Township their home, and especially for those who have preserved the history of our township

Contents

ACKNOWLEDGMENTS

The Algoma Township Historical Society (ATHS) was established in 1986. Since that time, hundreds of historical artifacts and photographs have been donated to be preserved and displayed. First and foremost, thanks to those who have contributed to the society—without your donations, there would be no book. Secondly, but equally as important, thanks to the hardworking volunteers and members of ATHS who have cataloged and preserved these items over the years. Without the documentation accompanying the images in the collection, this book would not have been possible. Unless otherwise noted, all images appear courtesy of the ATHS.

The ATHS quarterly newsletter has also been an invaluable resource in completing this book. Thank you to all of the writers, interviewers, and compilers who have made it possible to gather and disseminate the wealth of historical knowledge about our area four times a year since 1989. Thank you Print Metro for working with us for the past 10 years.

I would like to thank Jacel Egan and Emilia Monell for their assistance in beginning my journey with Arcadia Publishing. Thank you to Julia Simpson, who has been an understanding editor and guide as I make my first foray into authorship.

Julie Sjogren and Laural Walkons, president and treasurer of ATHS, respectively, thank you for believing in me when I came to you with the idea for this project and for your hours of assistance sorting through and helping me find the right photographs. Thanks also to Dick and Judy Helsel, Tom Hoskins, and Carole Holden Christensen, who have been invaluable in editing and allowed us to use their photographs in this project.

Thanks to Becky Veydt, who pushed me to pick up just one more project for agency class.

Thank you to my grandmother Irene Rosell Lamphear, for writing down your memories and inspiring my interest in the history of Algoma.

Finally, thank you to my mother, Heidi, for your love and encouragement, assistance scanning, and continued support as I attempt to launch.

Introduction

One of 21 townships in Kent County, Michigan, Algoma Township is approximately six miles north of Grand Rapids. The land is comprised of 36 square miles of rolling terrain that at one point was covered with pine but is now mostly sandy soil. The Rogue River and several of its tributaries, including Cedar Creek and Stegman Creek, run through the township, as does US Route 131 and White Pine Trail State Park. In the northern part of Algoma lies a narrow waterway, approximately one mile long, known as Camp Lake.

The nearby towns of Cedar Springs, Rockford, and Sparta are not part of Algoma Township but are nonetheless important to the community. The towns tend to overshadow Algoma's independent identity as residents need to frequent one of these communities for most business and everyday needs as well as to attend public school. Even without a town center, though the township has a population of 9,932 according to the 2010 census, there is still a rich underlying local history in Algoma.

The steamer *Algoma*, after which the township was later named, was launched in 1845. It traveled the Grand River between Grand Rapids and Grand Haven and carried both passengers and freight. Algoma means "field, or hill, of wild roses" in a local Native American language. Residents of the area petitioned the Michigan Legislature to be designated as a township in the fall of 1848, and the legislature officially did so on March 15, 1849.

Smith Lapham became Algoma Township's first supervisor three weeks later. Lapham was the first permanent settler in the early 1850s after settling in the community in 1843 with his wife, Katherine Gilbert. Other early settlers included John Mosher, William Chrissey, Andrew House, Albert Picket, Merlin Hunter, Henry Hensel, Henry Shank, John Davis, and George Curtis. The Algoma Township Historical Society (ATHS) has no pictorial documentation of most of these men, only stories of their hard work in making Algoma Township their home.

Hardworking people are what make Algoma truly unique. Before the focus was on farming, it was a logging community with the Caine (or Morningstar) Mill, Comstock Mill in Gougeburg, and Porter's Shingle Mill near Wicked (now Stegman) Creek serving the area. Many small communities in west Michigan were established using timber for logging as a resource. Loggers in the Algoma area told legends of the "Hodag," a creature with the head of an ox, feet of a bear, back of a dinosaur, and tail of an alligator, standing 40 feet tall.

When the township had its own K–8 schools (until the 1970s, Algoma Central, Block, Burchtown/Burchville, Chalmers, Edgerton, Foxville, Gougeburg, Hull, and Morningstar schools), various family names in the community were used, including at times the previous owner of the land the school stood upon, like Hull or Foxville Schools. Many of these schools have vanished, but Foxville School was reimagined as Maranatha Baptist Church, and Chalmers School (which was first a fire station for Algoma Township) now serves the Algoma Township Historical Society (ATHS) as a meeting place and as a museum for displaying artifacts and photographs, including many from the fire department that previously used the building.

Groups like the Algoma Grange No. 751, established around 1903, were key in bringing the community together in Algoma Township. The Grange hosted dances and other get-togethers in their hall. Other groups started by residents, such as the Jolly Rouges, the Foxville Friendship Club, and the Sunshine Circle, also improved the community as much as national organizations like 4H and the Grange.

Algoma Township is the home to a few famous Michiganders. Julia Davis Moore, the "Sweet Singer of Michigan," was a poet and pioneer storekeeper in the community. Hammered dulcimer player Chester "Chet" Parker, who was part of the folk revival of the 1960s, also got his start in Algoma Township.

As the community grew over time, farming became the main economic engine. In Algoma Township, there are a few centennial farms, where families have maintained ownership of the same land for at least 100 years. The James Bowler, Henry Helsel, Hannah Rawson, Goeller/Woodhull, and Powell families have received such recognition. Many of the farming families have also left their mark on the community in another way: the names of roads. Roads were sometimes built by men in the area who did so to help pay off taxes, so Algoma Township has some named Rector, Fonger, Pennington, and Jewell to reflect the residents who lived here.

At one point, Algoma Township did have a village. A deed/abstract was found showing the date of November 20, 1856, and it listed Village of Algoma Center. Also, in the 1860s, the historic community of Edgerton grew near what was known as Porter's Station, a depot and small junction for the Grand Rapids and Indiana Railroad. Oscar House suggested the name Edgerton based on the town in Illinois from which he originated. Two general stores and a post office also sprung up in the area, as did a few churches. A tornado in 1965 completely destroyed many of the buildings. The businesses were not rebuilt, and the chance that Algoma Township would have a proper town ended. Today, all that remains is a sign designating the historic community.

In the recent past, Algoma Township has achieved a few milestones. The township celebrated its sesquicentennial in 1999 with a picnic, ice cream social, display of historical artifacts, and a Little League baseball game. Two sites in Algoma have garnered historical designations by the State of Michigan. In 1885, James Ward House, as commissioned by the Grand Rapids & Indiana Railroad Company, built a large stone culvert over Stegman Creek (known as Wicked Creek at the time) to complete a railroad grade. The culvert, located on Summit Avenue north of 13 Mile Road on the west side of the road, was named a Civil Engineering Landmark in 2006 with a sign erected at the site. The "Rainbow Arch Bridge" at Pine Island Drive was built from 1922 to 1924 and is one of only three concrete through arch bridges that still exist in Michigan. The bridge was designated a historical site and a sign erected in 2014.

Algoma Township has one cemetery that is operational, and erected on the property through a joint effort between Algoma Township and Algoma Township Historical Society is a memorial to remember both Algoma Township veterans and the former Swedish Baptist Church (then Algoma Baptist Church) that stood on the site (demolished in 2004). The monument is surrounded by a plaza with engraved bricks with names of military veterans. The memorial park was dedicated in 2009.

The people of Algoma work hard to maintain a sense of community through preserving and treasuring the memories and artifacts of the past so that present and future generations will be guided toward a bright future.

One

People and Families

Algoma became a township because of people—those who came before laid the foundation of today's community. Citizens transformed the land from forests to farms to homesteads to neighborhoods. Algoma residents act as neighbors, always willing to lend a helping hand. Many of the families represented here have lived in the area for generations, and Algoma is shaped by their influence.

The township has also been home to many heroes. While not all military veterans could be included in this book, the Algoma community is grateful for their willingness to fight and sacrifice on behalf of the country.

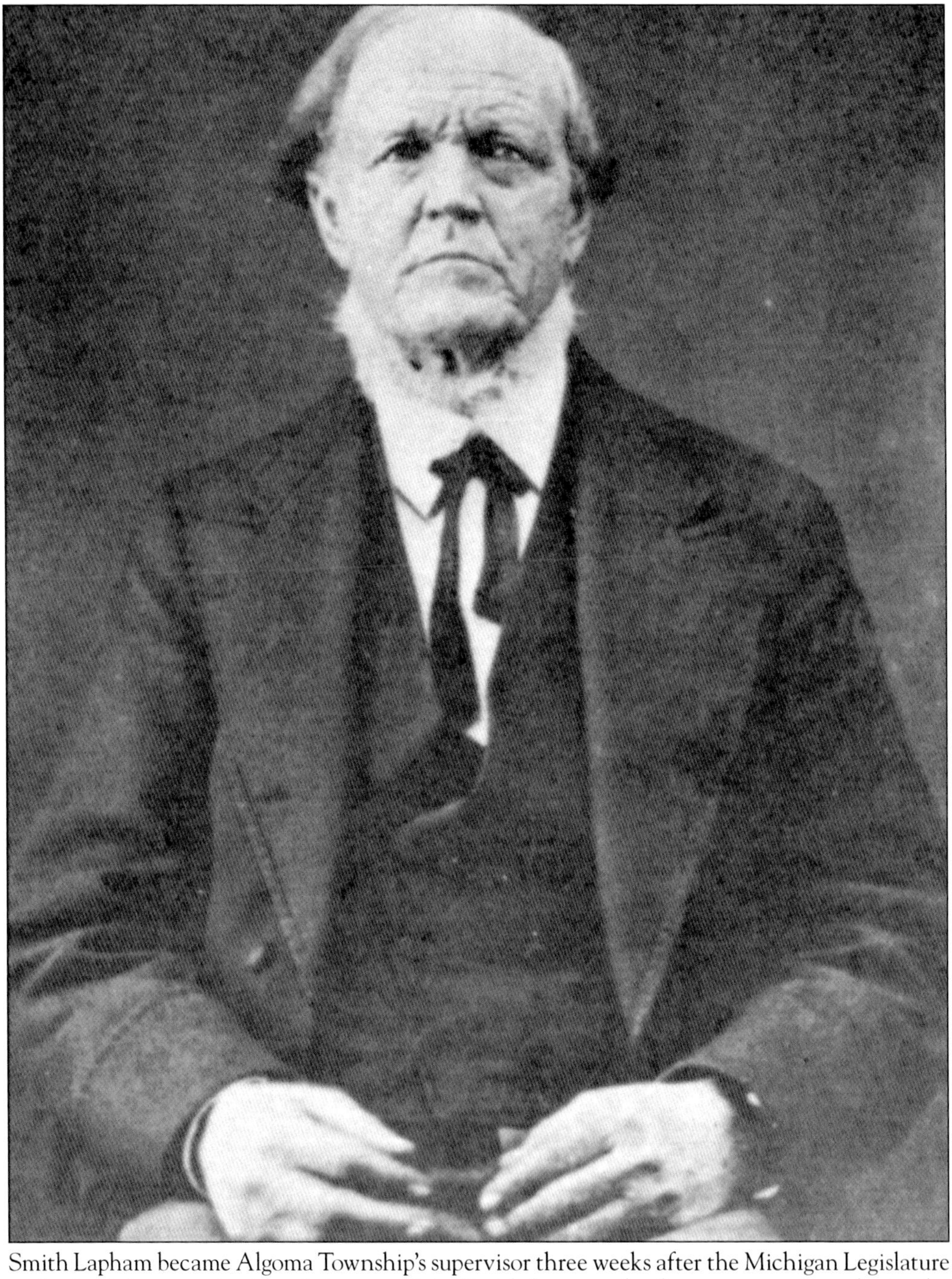

Smith Lapham became Algoma Township's supervisor three weeks after the Michigan Legislature authorized the organization of the township. Smith became the first permanent settler in the early 1850s after settling in the township in 1843 with his wife, Katherine Gilbert. He owned 40 acres south of 11 Mile Road and east of Wolven Avenue.

Theo Davis Pennington was the daughter of early settlers James Madison "Matt" and Maggie Davis. Pennington traveled around the country as a light opera singer with the Dunbar Opera Company, which was later renamed the American Light Opera Company. She starred in a variety of productions in the 1930s, including *The Bohemian Girl* (which she is in costume for here), *The Mascot*, *The Chocolate Soldier*, and *Robin Hood*. (Donated to the ATHS by Loraine Pennington.)

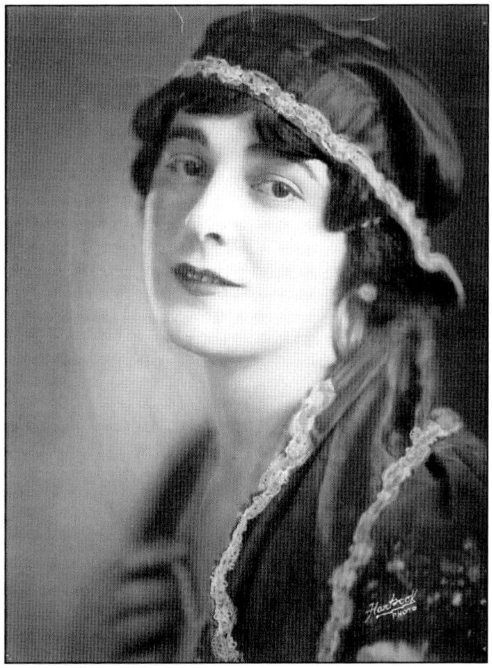

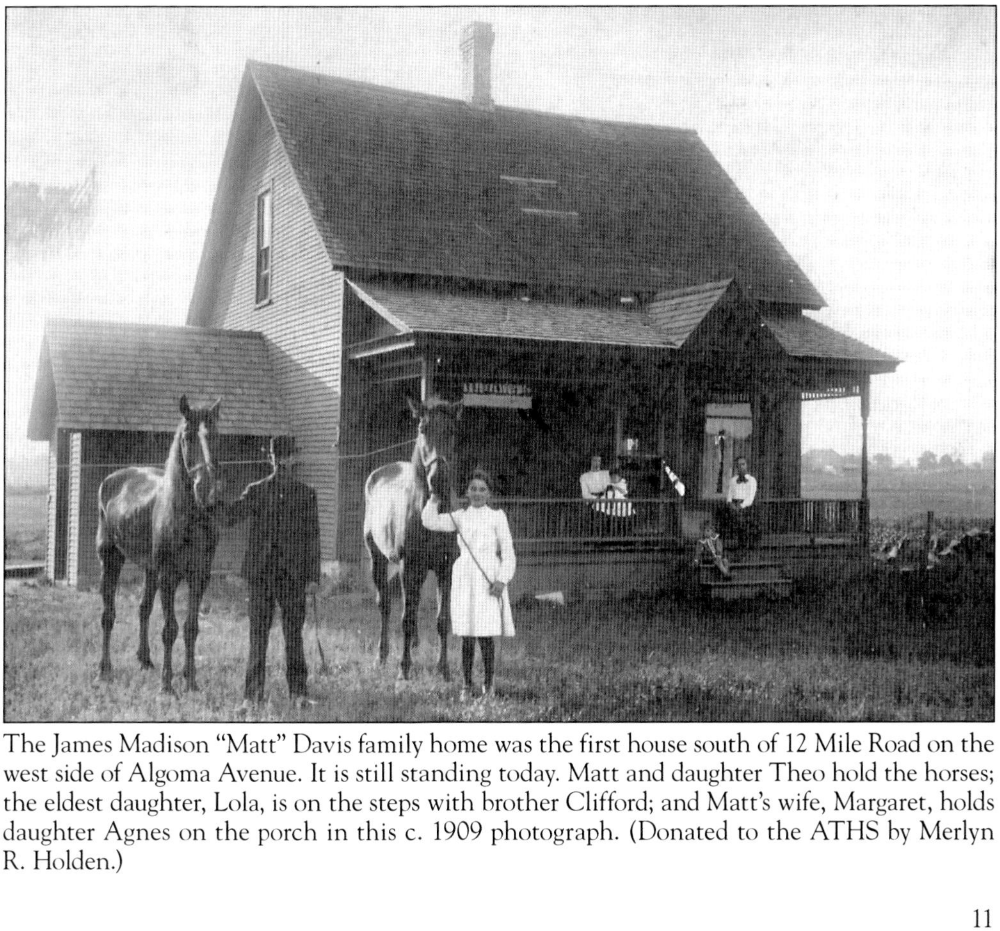

The James Madison "Matt" Davis family home was the first house south of 12 Mile Road on the west side of Algoma Avenue. It is still standing today. Matt and daughter Theo hold the horses; the eldest daughter, Lola, is on the steps with brother Clifford; and Matt's wife, Margaret, holds daughter Agnes on the porch in this c. 1909 photograph. (Donated to the ATHS by Merlyn R. Holden.)

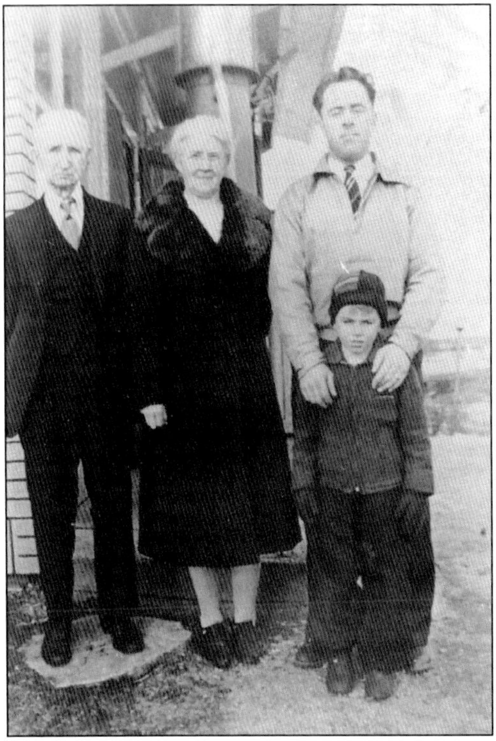

From left to right, A.W. Putman, his daughter Jessie Putman Helsel, Jessie's son Wayne Helsel, and Wayne's son Gordon Helsel stand outside of Reed's Store, also known as Helsel's Store. The store, owned by Jessie and her husband, Ernest, was about 600 feet east of Reed's Station in the Edgerton area. (Donated to the ATHS by Wayne Helsel.)

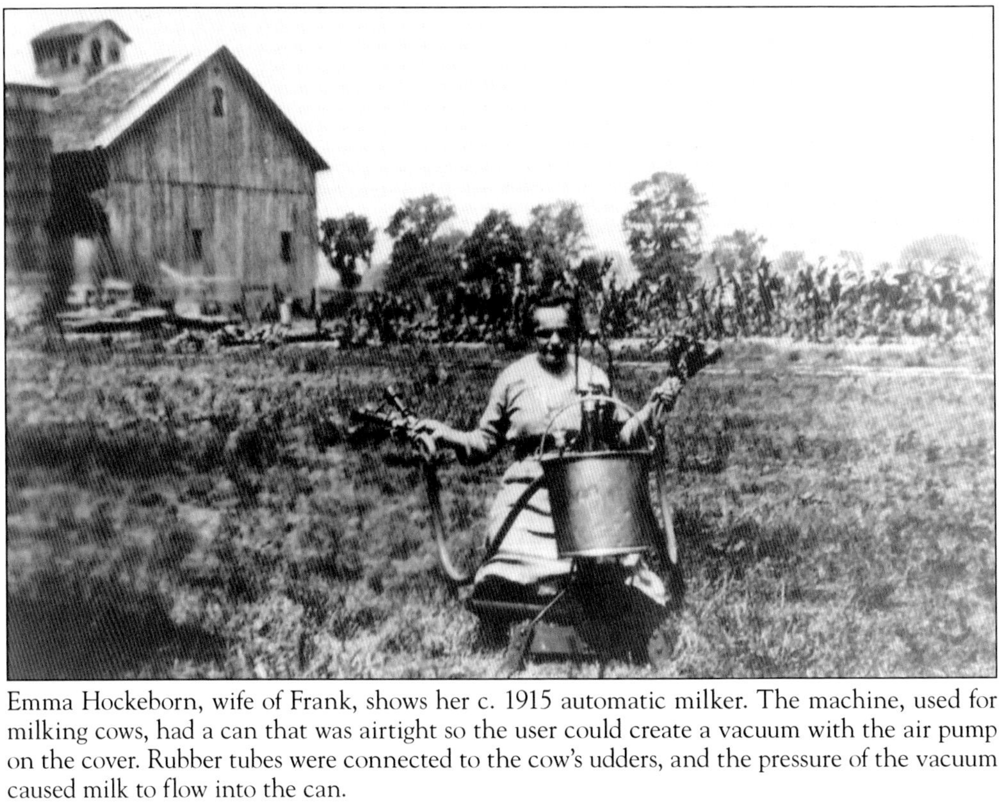

Emma Hockeborn, wife of Frank, shows her c. 1915 automatic milker. The machine, used for milking cows, had a can that was airtight so the user could create a vacuum with the air pump on the cover. Rubber tubes were connected to the cow's udders, and the pressure of the vacuum caused milk to flow into the can.

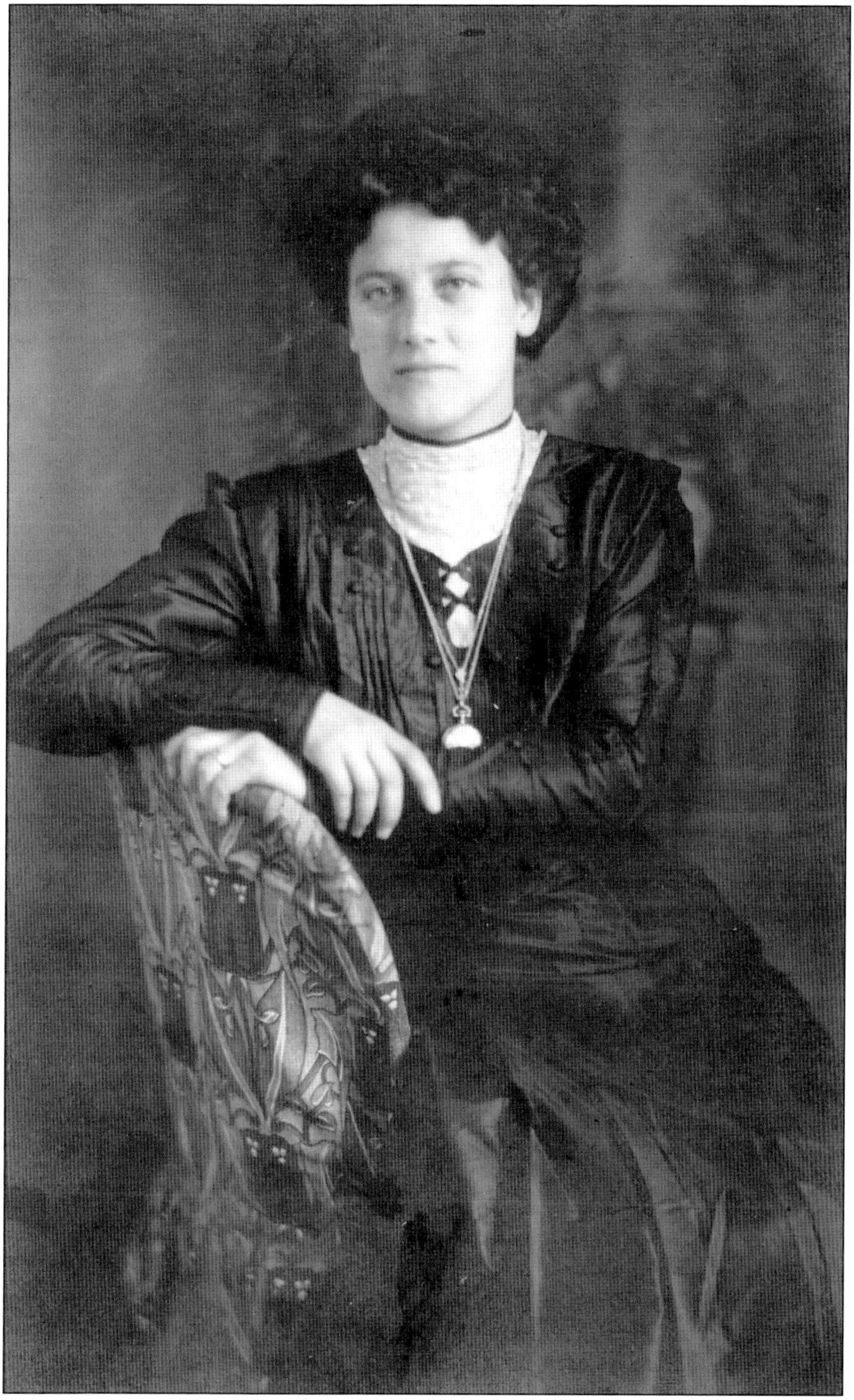

Orpha Dunn never married, but she loved children. She taught at Gougeburg School for more than seven years. She also taught at Cedar Springs and at Shank School in Courtland. Unfortunately, after a failed romance in the mid-1930s she committed suicide by dousing a straw pile and herself with gasoline and lighting a match.

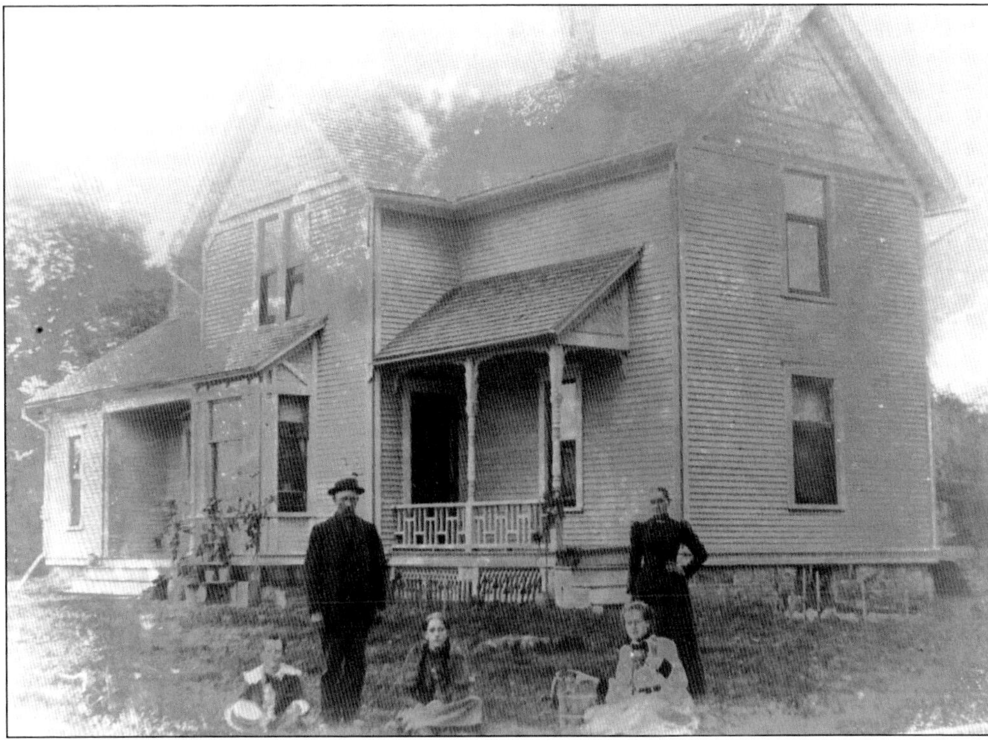

Christian and Mary Powell are the great-grandparents of the present owners of the Powell farm. This photograph shows them, along with their children, in front of the 80-acre farmstead they bought in 1884 at 10433 Algoma Avenue. The boy on the left is Jacob, grandfather of the current owners.

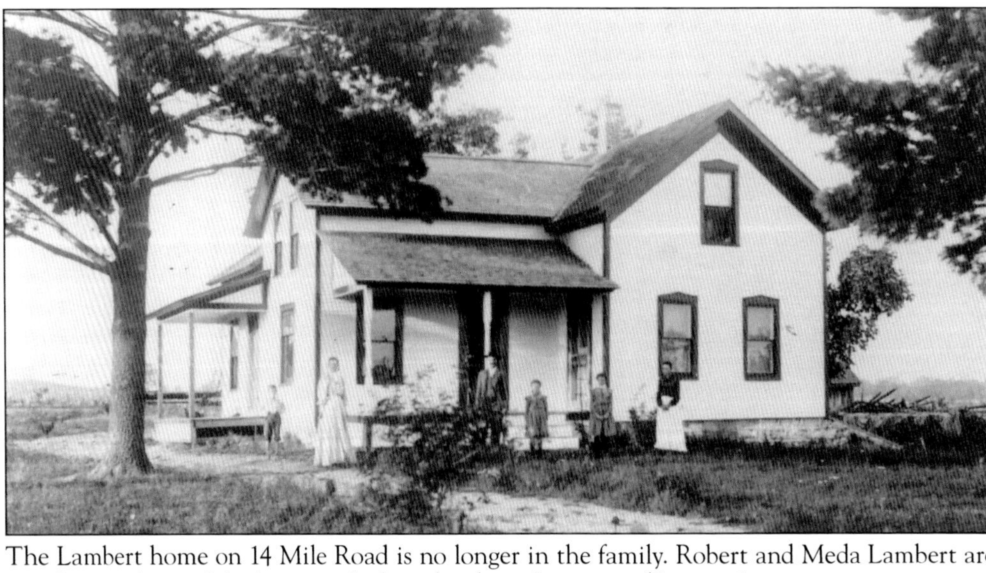

The Lambert home on 14 Mile Road is no longer in the family. Robert and Meda Lambert are seen here in front of the home with their daughters Lorena and Loreta. Lorena went on to marry Victor Johnson and had one daughter, Ireta Johnson Kraft. Loreta went on to marry Clifford Johnson (no relation to Victor) and had a son, Ward, who married Delora Lundin, and a daughter, Evelyn, who married Franklin Wegal.

Kendric and Minnie (Porter) Holden are pictured here in 1937. Minnie was the daughter of Seth and Rebecca Porter, owners of Porter's Mill, located on Stegman (once known as Wicked) Creek in Porter Hollow. Kendric and Minnie lived on the east side of Algoma, just north of Indian Lakes Road. They were the parents of Gladys Althea Holden Colby (Forrest), Austa Holden Bowler (William James), Lynn Holden (Lola M. Davis), and Lorna Holden Deboer (John).

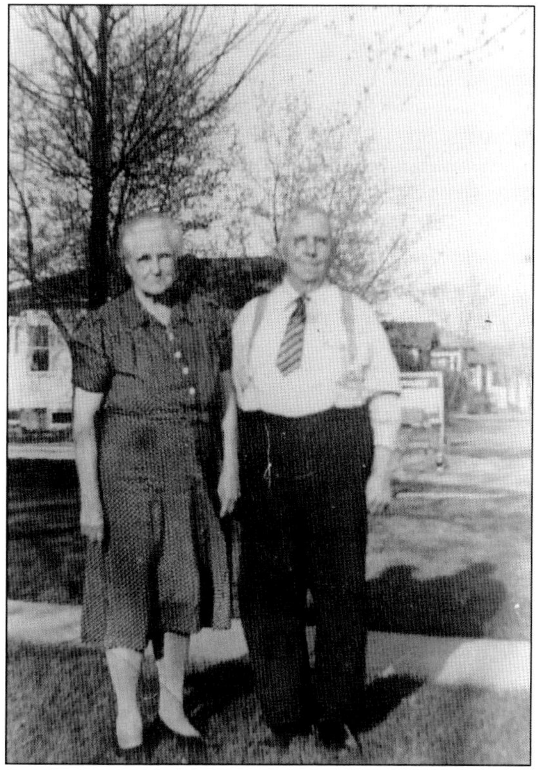

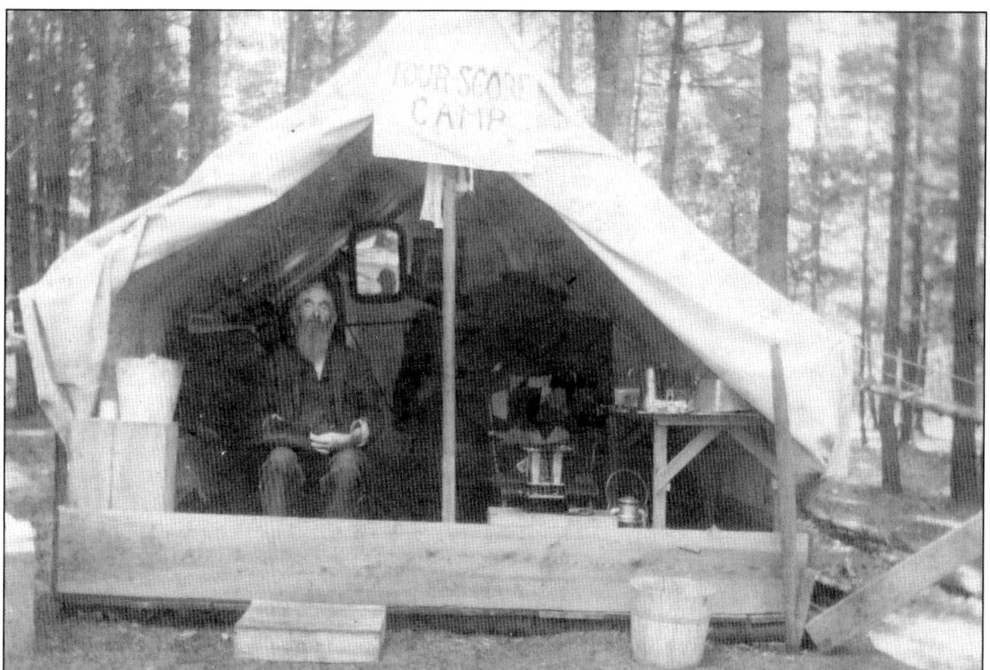

C.A. Kelly owned a dry goods and grocery store at the corner of Pine Island Drive and Fonger Street before Fonger's Store was built in its place. In dealing goods from his store, he used his covered wagon for journeys in the area. He is pictured here sitting outside his tent at Camp Lake.

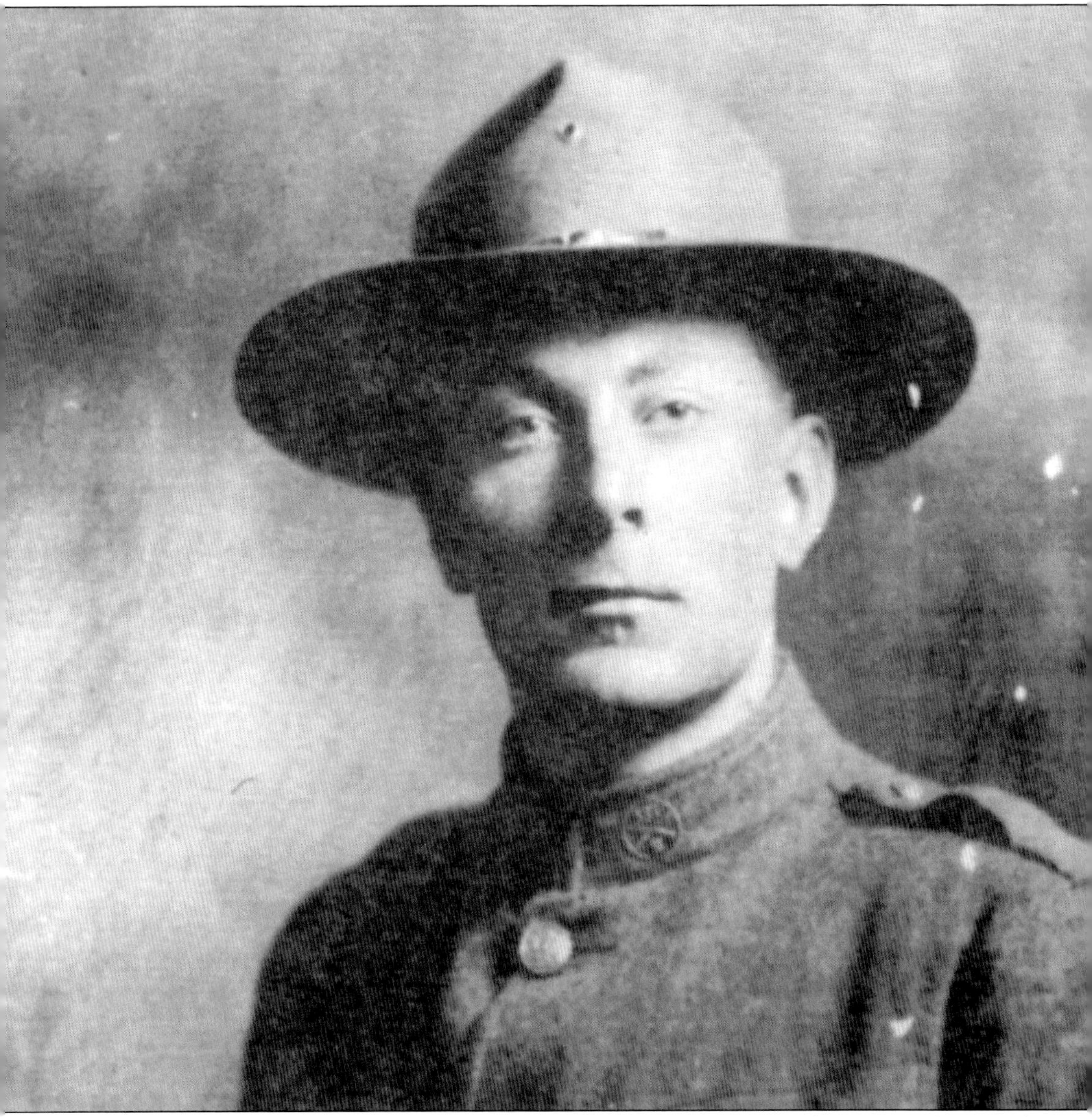

Pvt. Harvey R. Armstrong fought in World War I. He spent time on the Russian front in the north, where he did see some fighting with the 339th Infantry Regiment. Prior to that, he spent time in both England and France doing drills and handling supplies after seven months of training at Camp Custer, near Battle Creek.

Harry V. Pinckney moved to the corner of Rector and Grange Avenues with his brother Harvey A. in 1918. They attended Gougeburg School together. Harry worked and traveled with John Mosher and his threshing machine. Due to ill health, Harry was discharged from the Jefferson Barracks in Missouri after two years.

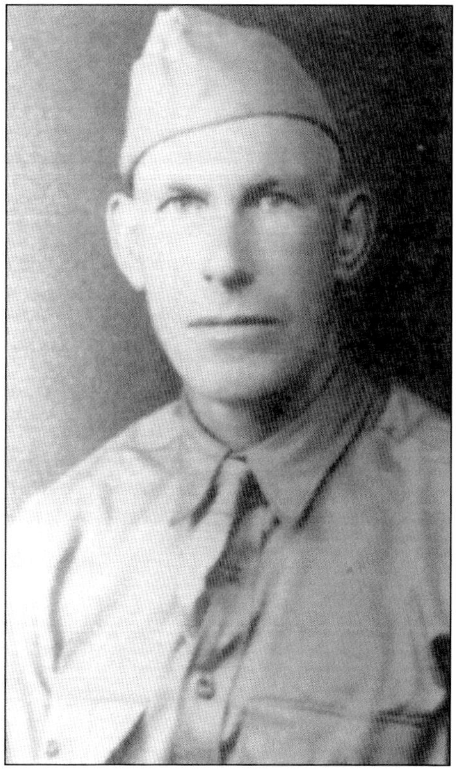

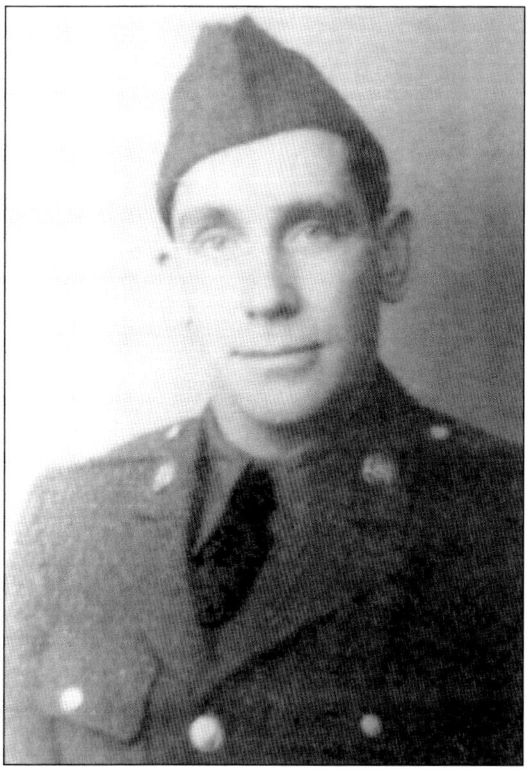

Harvey A. Pinckney spent most of his life in Algoma Township but with the Army traveled overseas to Normandy with the 28th Division, 112th Regiment during World War II. Shrapnel injured his foot, and his hospitalization began in France, but he traveled to England, Staten Island, Billings General Hospital at Fort Benjamin Harrison in Indianapolis, Indiana, and Fort Custer annex of Percy Jones Hospital in Battle Creek, Michigan, where he was discharged.

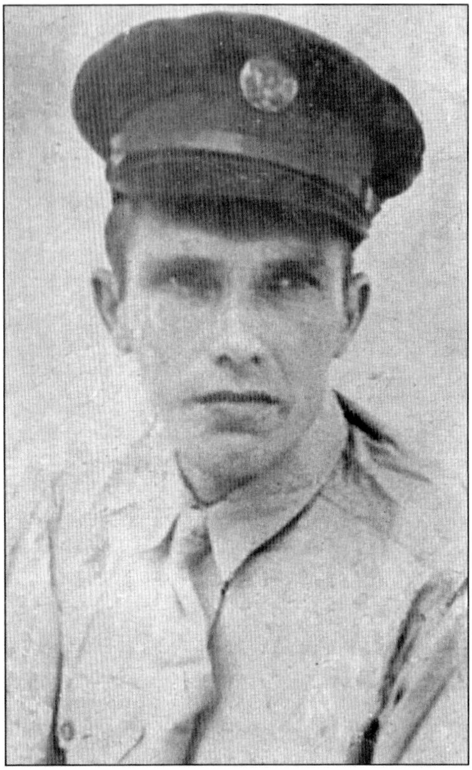

S.Sgt. John C. Sjogren was Kent County's first Medal of Honor recipient for "taking tremendous risks, overcoming bitter resistance and never hesitating in his relentless advance." Sjogren was instrumental in battle at John's Mountain in the Philippines on May 23, 1945. He lobbed grenades into machine-gun nests, injuring his hands and back when Japanese forces retaliated. He killed 43 enemy soldiers, allowing the Filipino and American forces to advance.

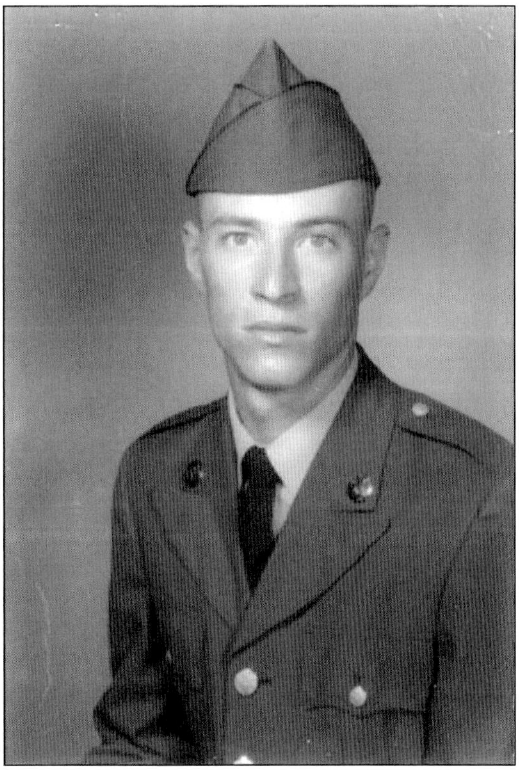

Jimmy Roger Murrell was born to Ralph and Carrie Murrell on September 24, 1950, the eldest of their 11 children. He enlisted in 1969 after graduating, married Jean Hanson in 1970, and welcomed son Jeff later that year. Jimmy served with the 101st Airborne Screaming Eagles in Vietnam following his deployment in March 1971. He was a sergeant when he was killed in action on July 2, 1971.

Delbert Jay Waid, born in 1926, served in the Navy during World War II in the Pacific Theater. He received three Service Stars for his service. Following his service, Delbert moved to Michigan and married Betty Matthews in 1947. They had six children. Delbert passed away in 2009.

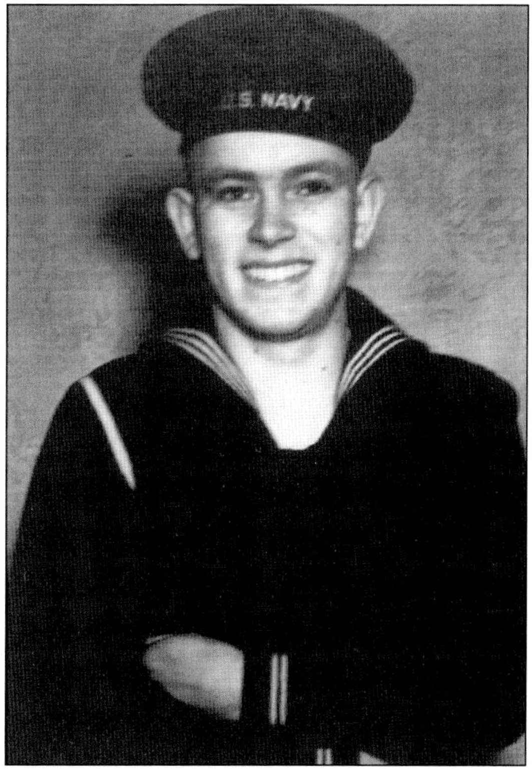

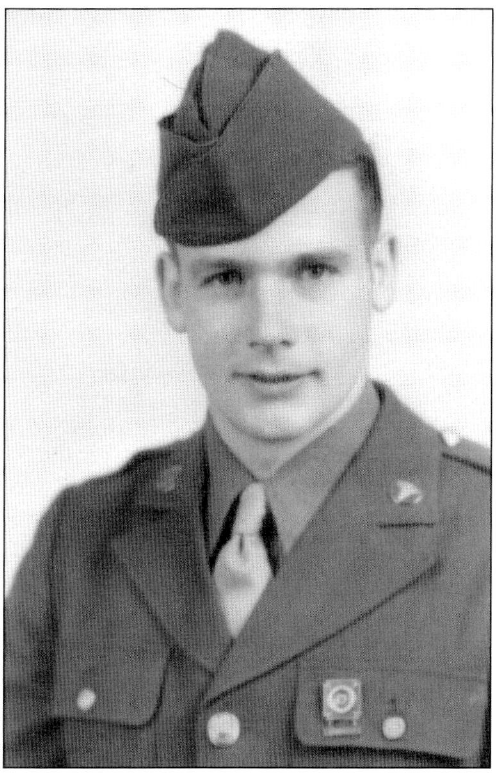

William Brown served in the US Army during World War II. He met and married his wife, Agnes, at Knapp Street Reformed Church, where he was a faithful attendee. Their children are Richard Brown, Linda Olcheske, Sue Dombrowski, and Sallyann Fellows. He worked at American Packaging Corporation for 30 years and was a 4-H leader for the Foxville Club of Kent County.

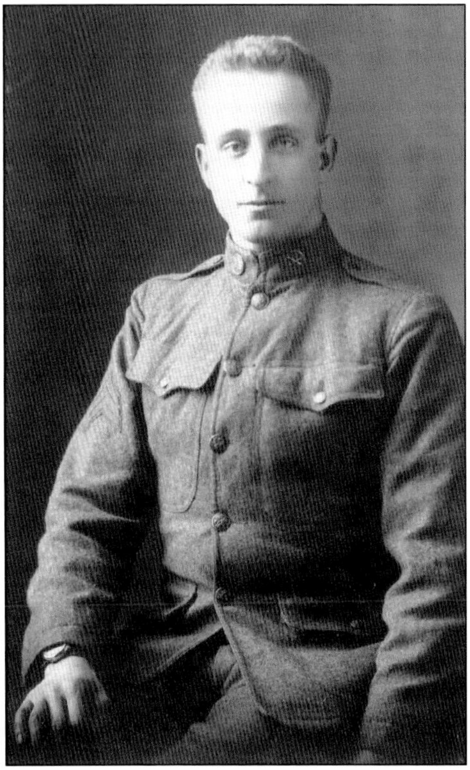

Robert Fonger, son of Tom and Ella Fonger, married Charlotte Culver in 1922. They bought a country store, with living areas, from George Orr. They had three children: Reva, Ruth, and Carl. Robert was stationed at Fort Custer, Michigan, during World War II; he did not go overseas, because he had contracted influenza.

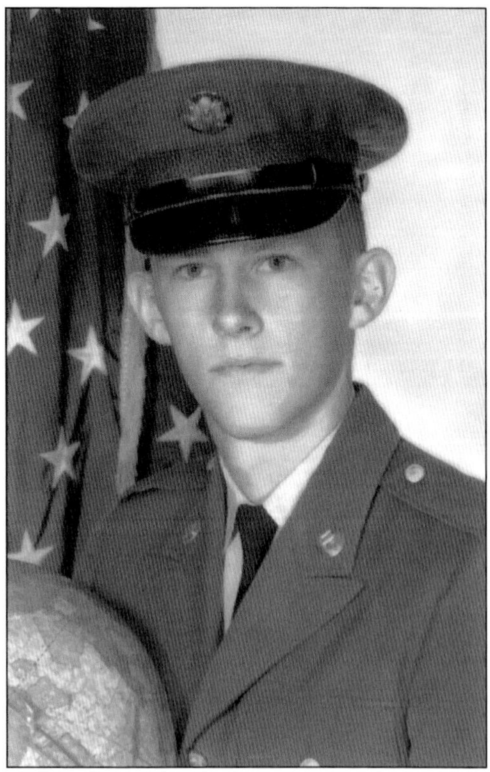

Daniel Louis Behm, born in 1948, was the only son of Louis and Kathleen Behm. He had six sisters. The family moved to Algoma Township in the 1950s, and Daniel graduated from Kent City High School in 1968. In 1970, after 18 months in the Army and a year in Vietnam, he was killed in action at age 21.

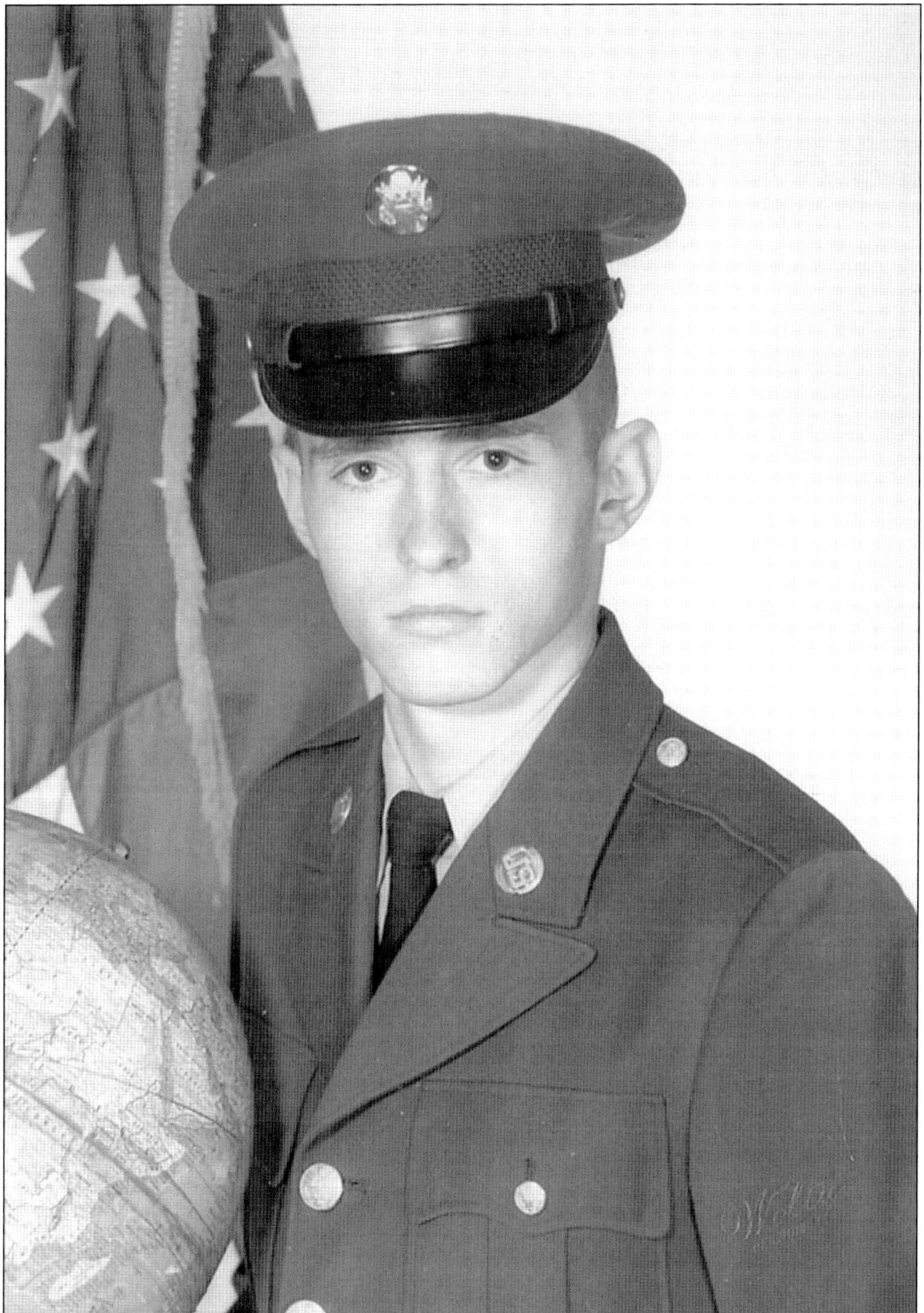

Craig Edward Yates was born in 1950 to Roland and Marian Yates. In 1968, Craig volunteered for the Army after graduating from Sparta High School. He served in the 82nd Airborne Division and the 505th Infantry Division. Craig was killed in Vietnam in May 1969.

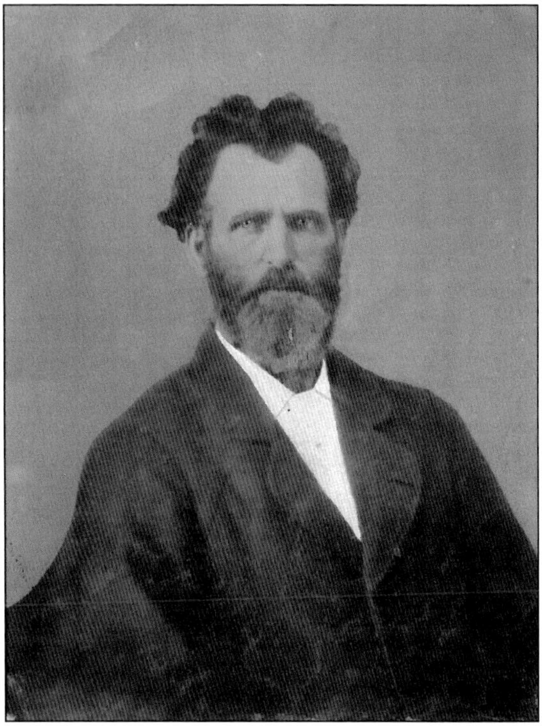

Henry Helsel was born in Washington County, Pennsylvania, and moved with his parents, John and Elizabeth (Byers) Helsel, to Ohio when he was two years old. Henry married Julia Helsel (his first cousin) in Ohio in 1845 and traveled to Algoma Township that year with Henry and Harriet Shank. Henry and Julia had four sons. After Julia's death in 1854, he married Sarah Deer, and they had eight children.

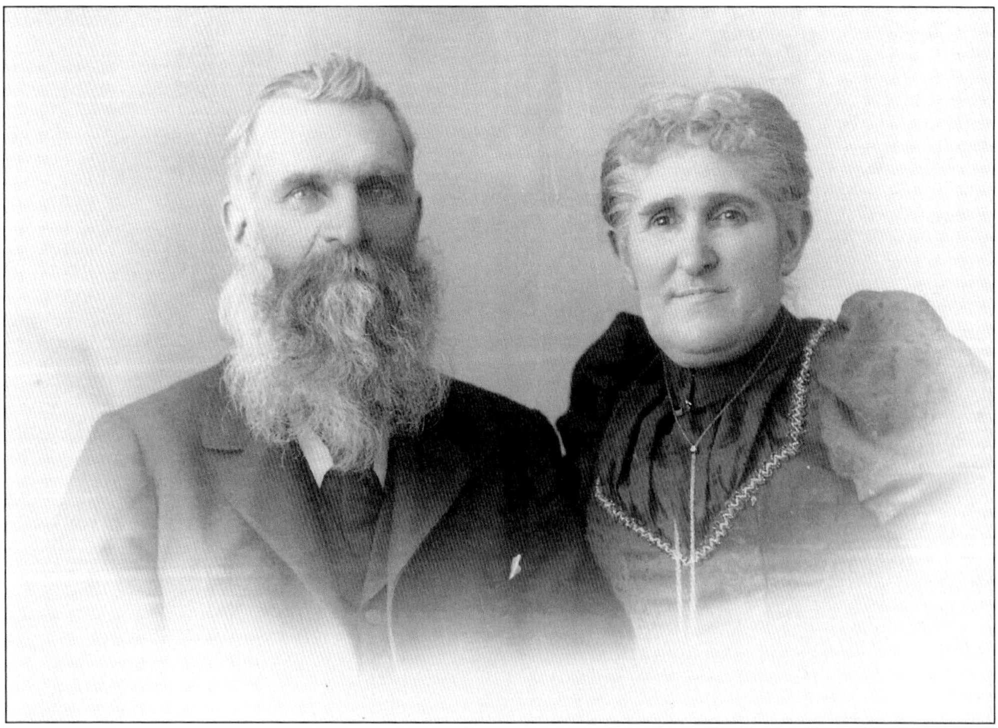

William Botruff was the eldest of Adam and Barbara Hammer Botruff's nine children, born in 1838. He married Lavina Morningstar, daughter of Jacob and Mary Helsel Morningstar, in 1861. They had seven children together. William died in 1912.

Noah, eldest son of John and Elizabeth Helsel, was born in Somerset County, Pennsylvania. He married Harriet Leonard in Trumbull County, Ohio, in 1838. They moved to Algoma Township after 1860 and lived on the northeast corner property at what is now Algoma Avenue and 12 Mile Road. He built the red barn at that site.

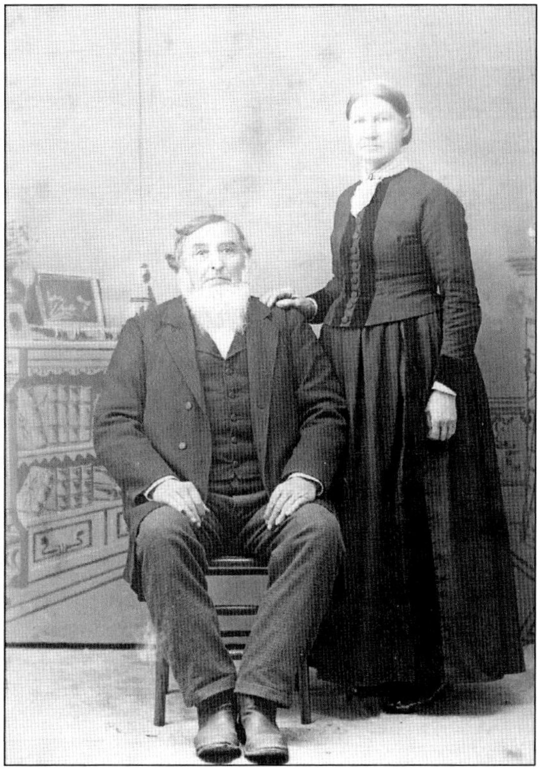

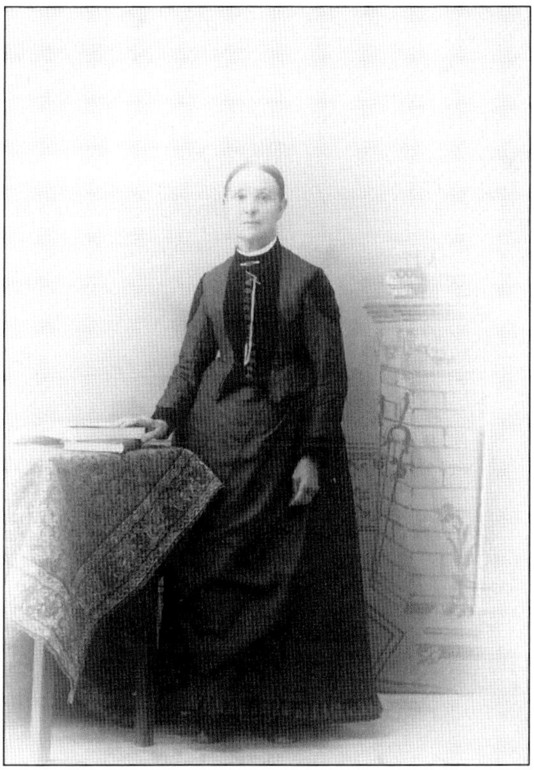

Mary, daughter of John and Elizabeth Helsel, married Jacob Morningstar, and they had at least 10 children: Louisa (b. 1842), Lavina (b. 1844), William H. (b. 1847), John (b. 1849), Levi (b. 1852), Lewis (1853–1907), Hiram (b. 1856), John (b. 1858), Sarah (1859–1924), and Charles (b. 1862). Jacob died in 1863, and Mary married Louis "Whitebread" Weisbrotte.

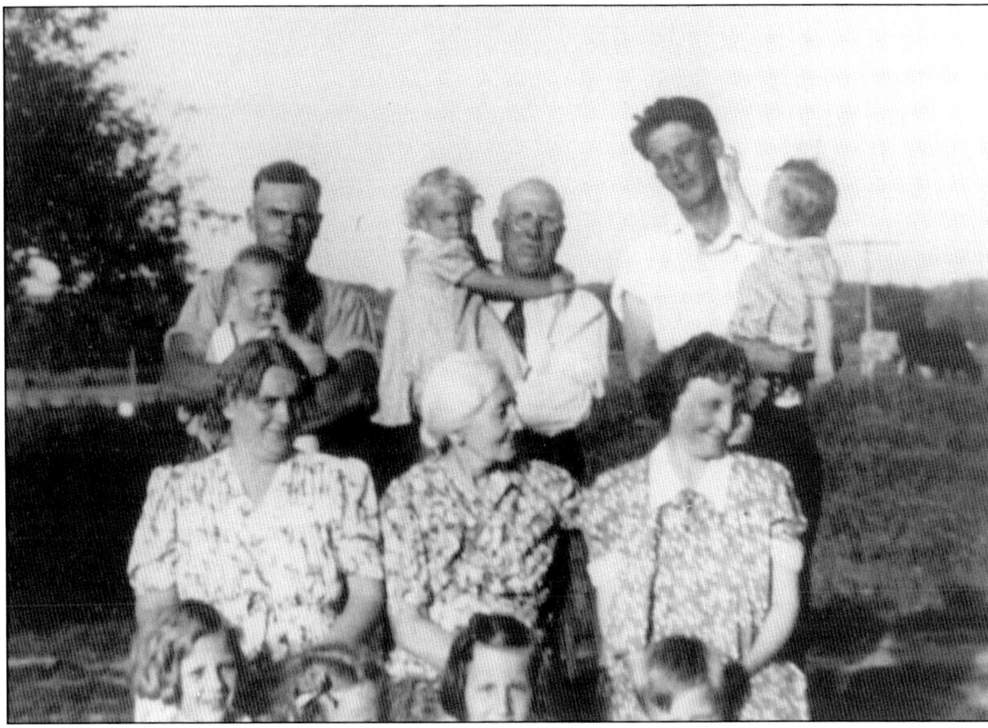

Here, the Magoon family poses for a photograph. From left to right are (first row) Elsie Magoon, Pat Magoon, Inez Magoon, and Bob Bennett; (second row) Dorothy Magoon, grandmother Grace Chaffee, and Arvilla Dines; (third row) Clare Magoon holding son Clare Magoon Jr., Glen Chaffee holding granddaughter Lillian Magoon, and Roy Dines holding Rose Marie.

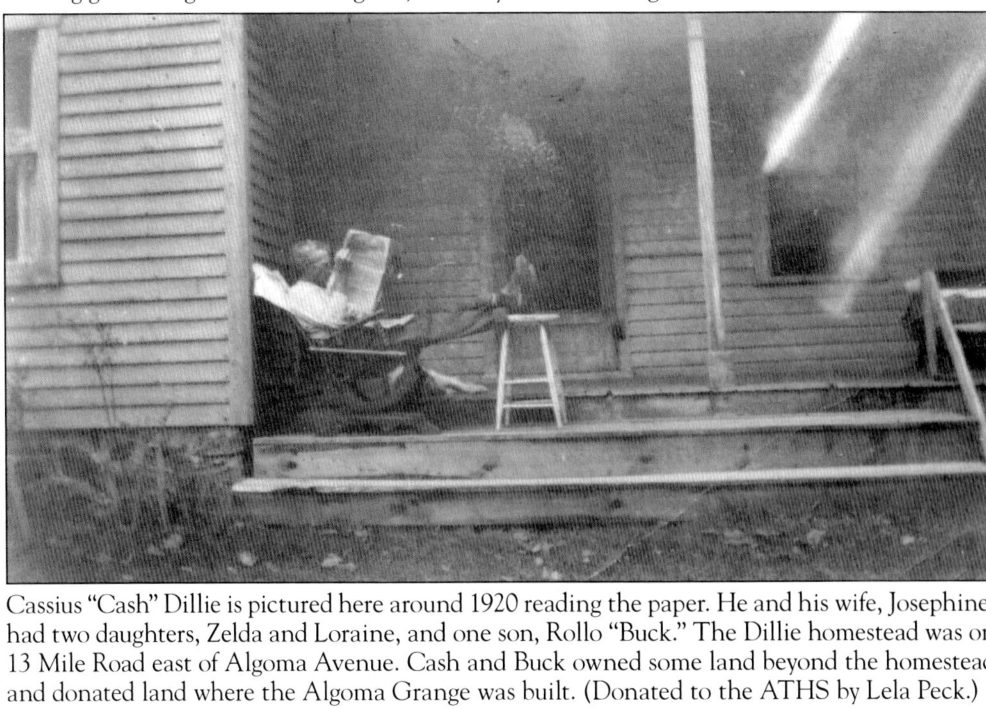

Cassius "Cash" Dillie is pictured here around 1920 reading the paper. He and his wife, Josephine, had two daughters, Zelda and Loraine, and one son, Rollo "Buck." The Dillie homestead was on 13 Mile Road east of Algoma Avenue. Cash and Buck owned some land beyond the homestead and donated land where the Algoma Grange was built. (Donated to the ATHS by Lela Peck.)

Lola Davis and Lynn Holden were married June 1, 1912, at the Davis residence at 9861 Algoma Avenue, the first house south of 12 Mile Road on the west side of the road. They later purchased the farm from Lola's father, James Madison "Matt" Davis, widower, on May 24, 1929. Lola and Lynn had one son, Merlyn, born on April 25, 1916.

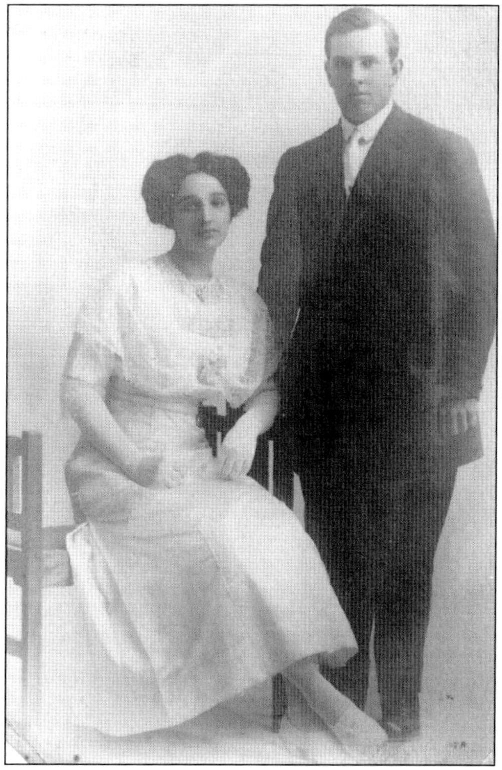

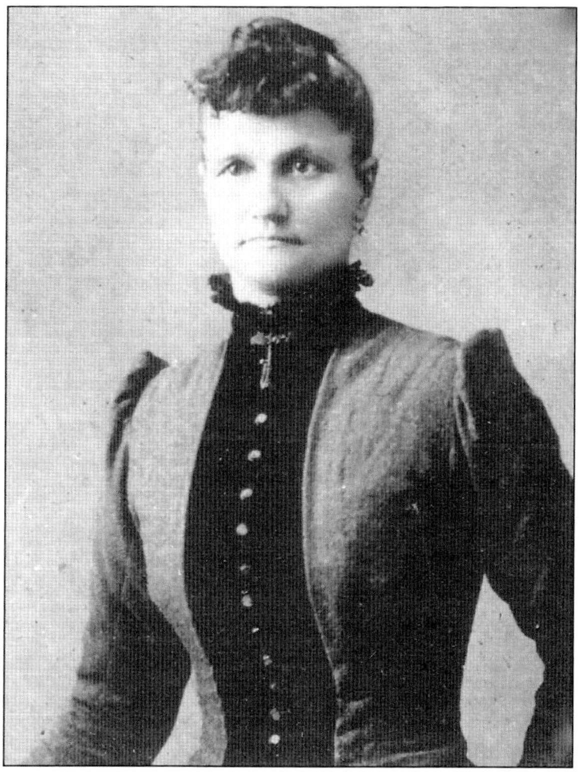

Nancy Hughs (pictured) married Cyrus Glass, with whom she had a daughter, Christena Glass (b. 1872). Christena later married Cleon Helsel. Nancy's second marriage, in 1888, was to Darius Helsel. The couple had no children, but Nancy helped raise Ernie and Benjamin, sons of Darius's earlier marriage to Alice (Botruff) Helsel. Ernie was seven years old and Benjamin was four years old when Darius and Nancy married.

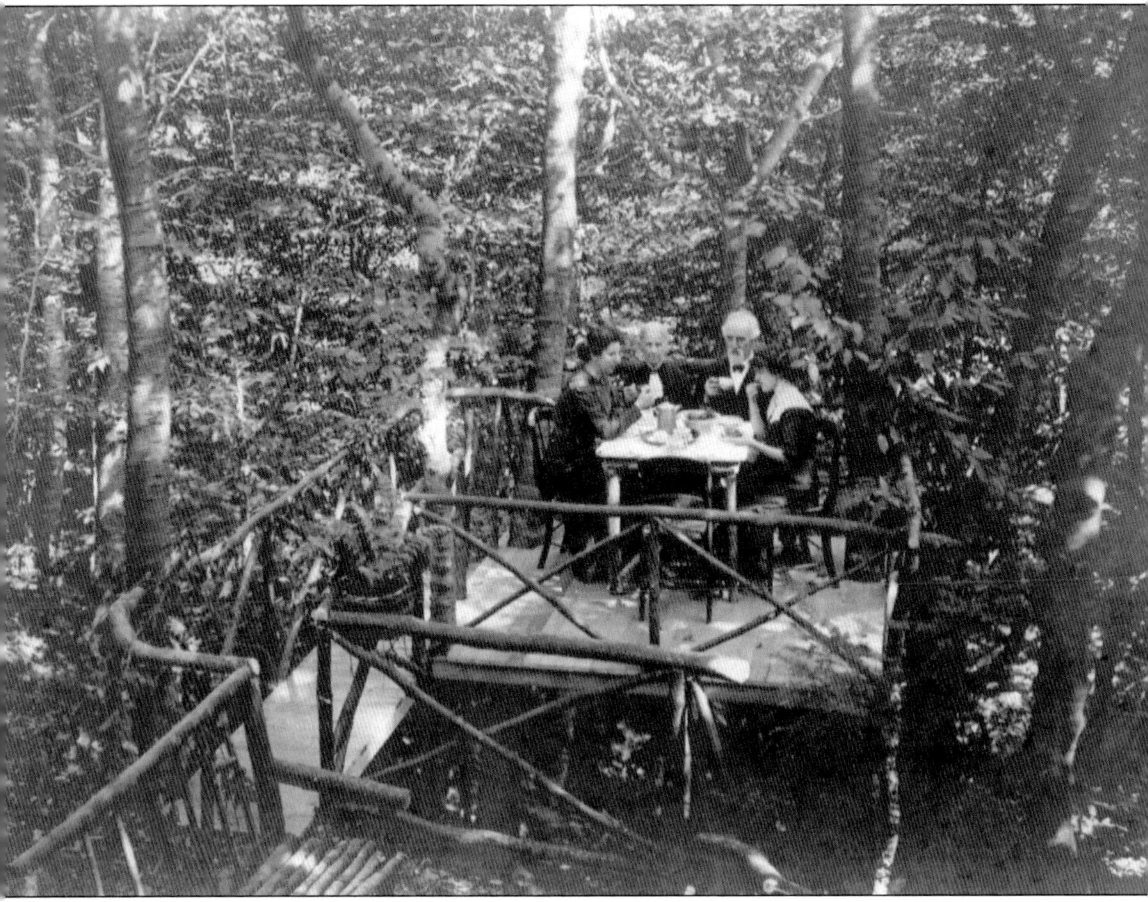

Harlow Field (1869–1949) was the father of Marvin and Mildred Field. This outdoor picnic deck, somewhere in northern Michigan, must have had an interesting view since it was raised in the air. Note the elegant dishware the family is using for an outdoor meal.

Fred and Ethel Pope Teesdale were both born and raised in Algoma Township. They had 13 children together. Fred worked for Forrest Montgomery building roads in the Algoma Township area, and he also did some blacksmithing. Ethel passed away in 1942, while Fred passed away in 1947.

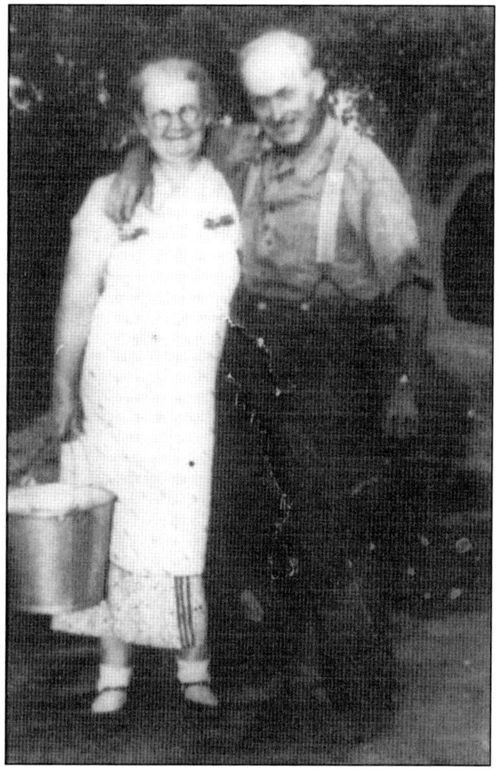

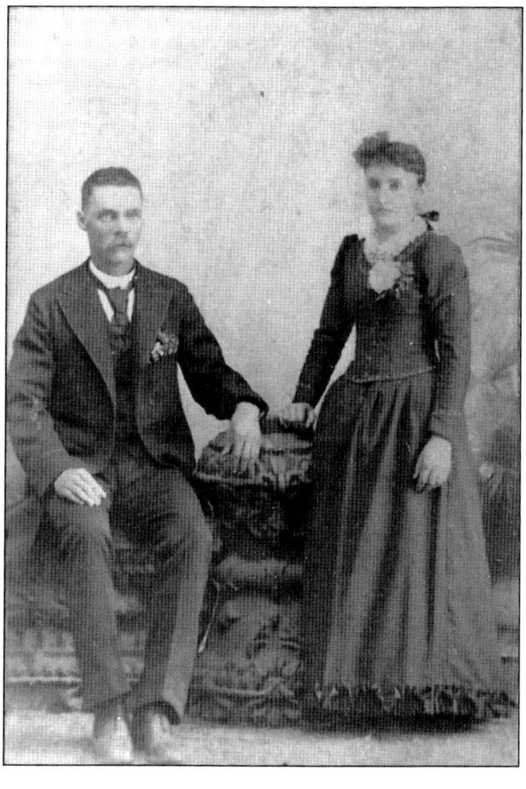

Joseph Henry Hoskins was born in Canada in 1860. At age 12, his family moved to Kansas with a team of oxen. They stayed there for a short time before moving to Algoma Township. Joseph married Jennie Uplinger, and they lived on and farmed 40 acres at the northeast corner of 14 Mile Road and Edgerton Avenue. The Hoskins barn still stands there today.

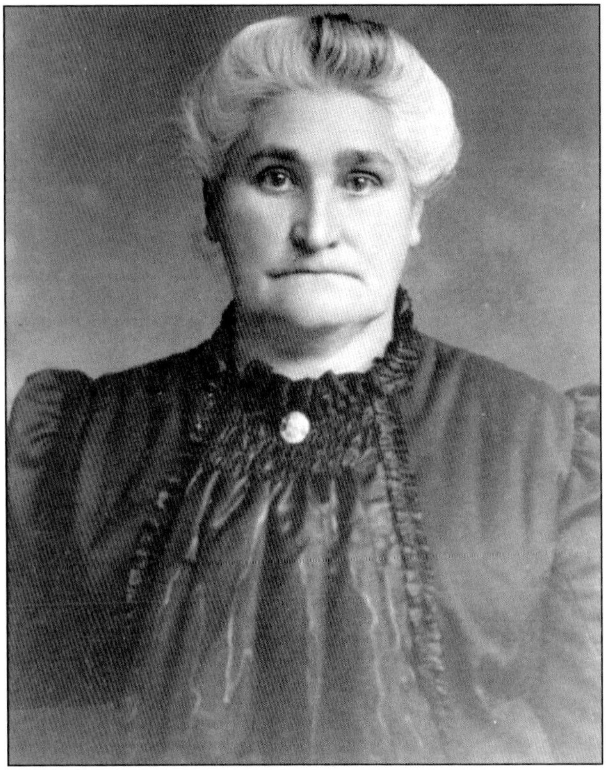

Julia (Davis) Moore was known as the "Sweet Singer of Michigan." She published five books of poetry in her lifetime. *Sentimental Song Book*, published in 1876, was her best-known work. Julia gave formal readings of her poetry, sold individual poems for special occasions, and copyrighted her music. Born on December 1, 1847, Julia moved to Algoma Township at age 10. She began writing poetry in her teens about everyday happenings. Because death, especially that of children, was a common frontier occurrence, Julia specialized in funeral odes. She lost 4 of her own 10 children in their younger years. Mark Twain alluded to Julia's work in his *Following the Equator.* Twain quoted Julia frequently, and she was famous enough nationally that following her death in 1920 the *Boston Herald* produced a long obituary about her.

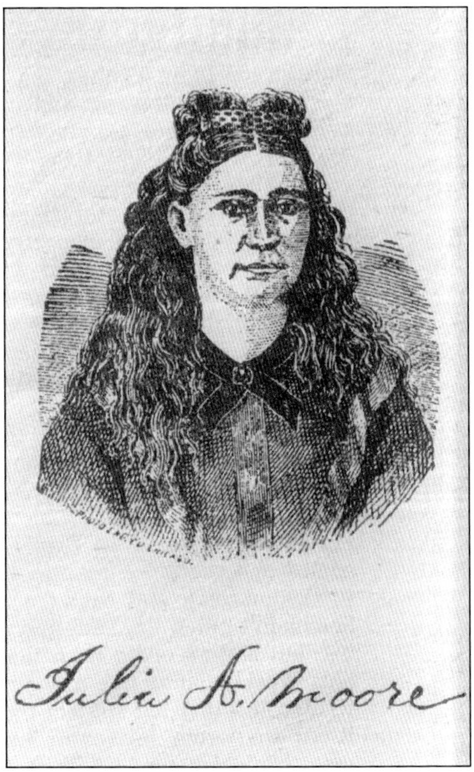

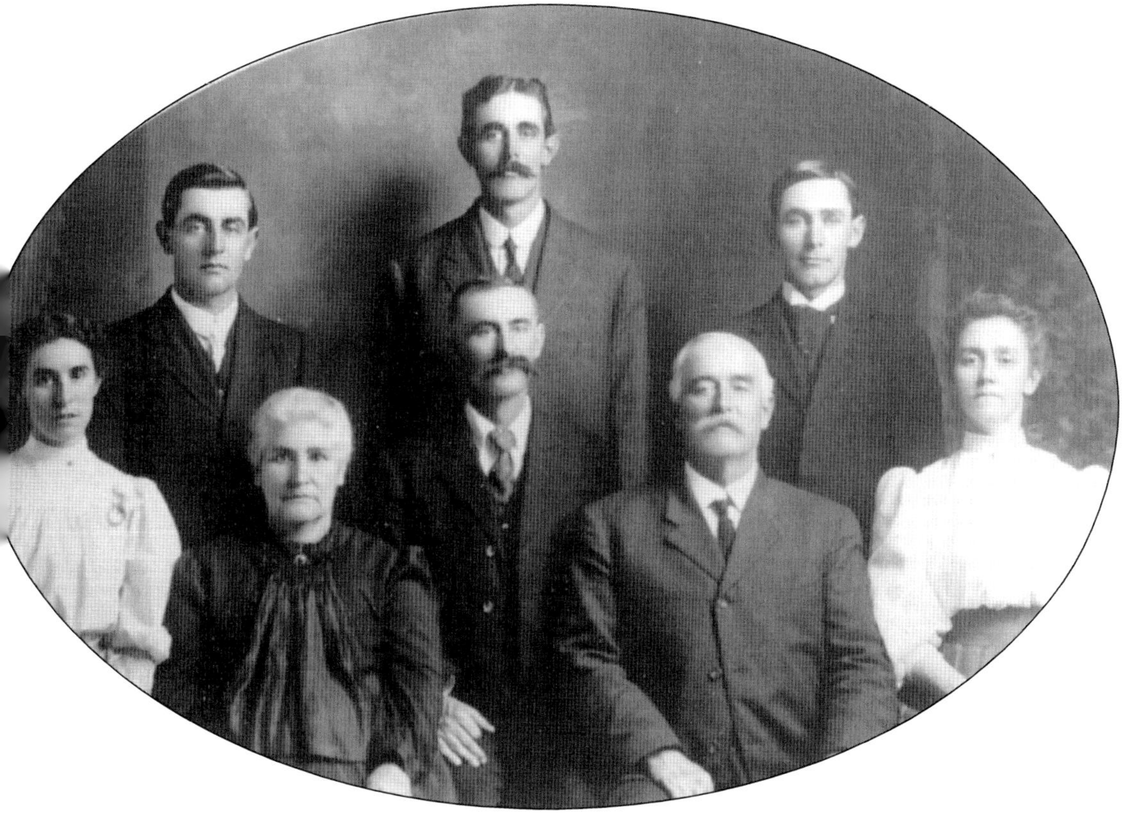

The Moore family poses for a photograph between 1880 and 1885, before Frederick and Julia Moore moved away from Algoma Township. Pictured from left to right are (first row) Ida Moore Hanthorne, Julia Davis Moore, Frederick Franklin Moore Jr., Frederick Franklin Moore, and Ada Moore Burns; (second row) Clyde Moore, Earnest Everett "Bert" Moore, and Claude Moore.

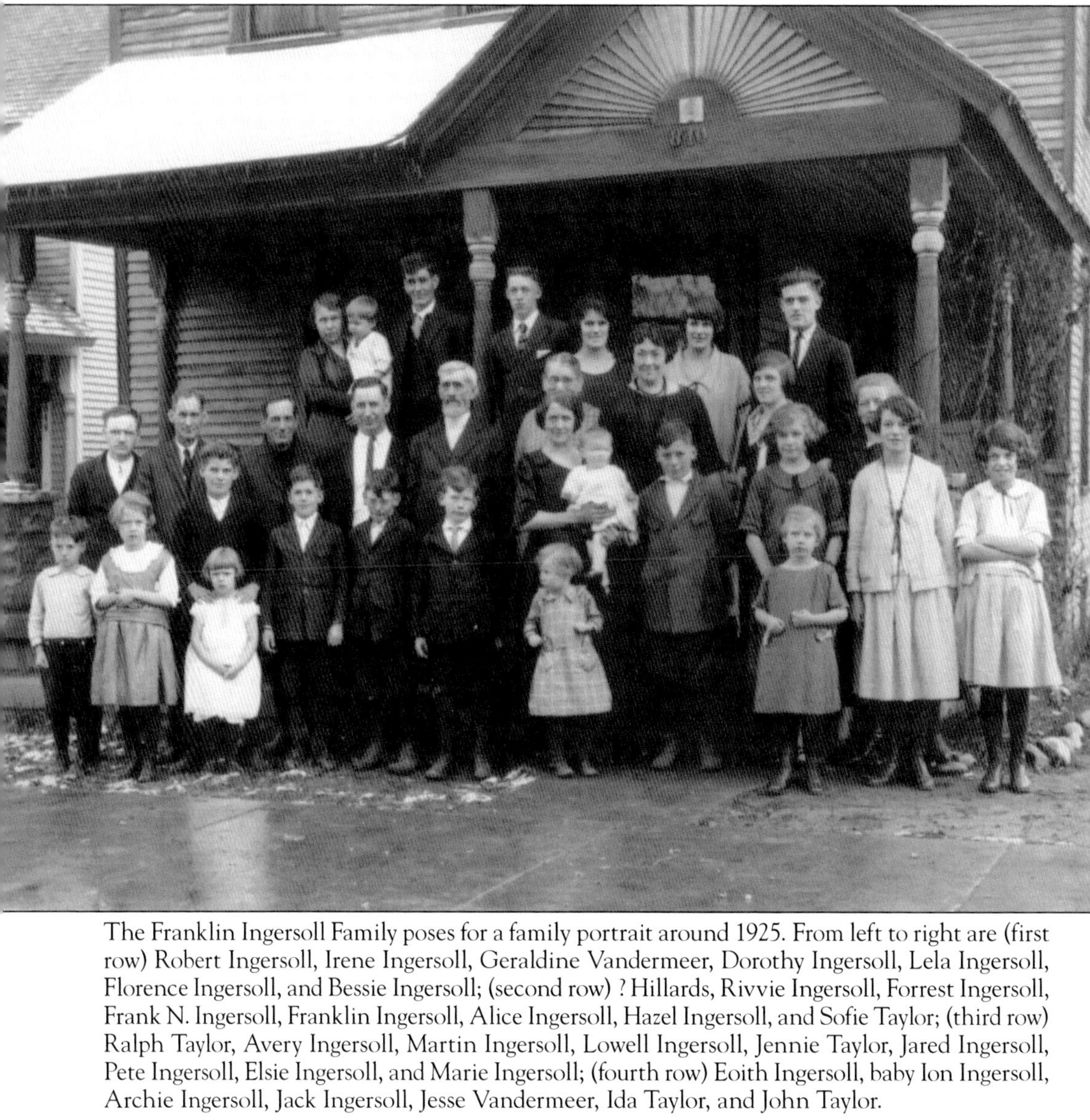

The Franklin Ingersoll Family poses for a family portrait around 1925. From left to right are (first row) Robert Ingersoll, Irene Ingersoll, Geraldine Vandermeer, Dorothy Ingersoll, Lela Ingersoll, Florence Ingersoll, and Bessie Ingersoll; (second row) ? Hillards, Rivvie Ingersoll, Forrest Ingersoll, Frank N. Ingersoll, Franklin Ingersoll, Alice Ingersoll, Hazel Ingersoll, and Sofie Taylor; (third row) Ralph Taylor, Avery Ingersoll, Martin Ingersoll, Lowell Ingersoll, Jennie Taylor, Jared Ingersoll, Pete Ingersoll, Elsie Ingersoll, and Marie Ingersoll; (fourth row) Eoith Ingersoll, baby Ion Ingersoll, Archie Ingersoll, Jack Ingersoll, Jesse Vandermeer, Ida Taylor, and John Taylor.

Alice "Kitty" (Toms) Vinton, known as Doc Vinton, is seen here with a dog and a child. She was the only doctor in the area in the early 1900s. She drove a Model T to meet with patients whenever they needed attention, and she charged them based on what they could pay. Mildred May Bristol Darling lived with Doc Vinton while teaching at Koon School.

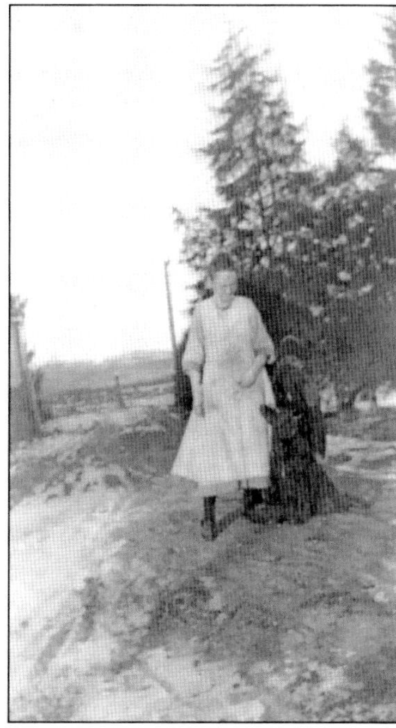

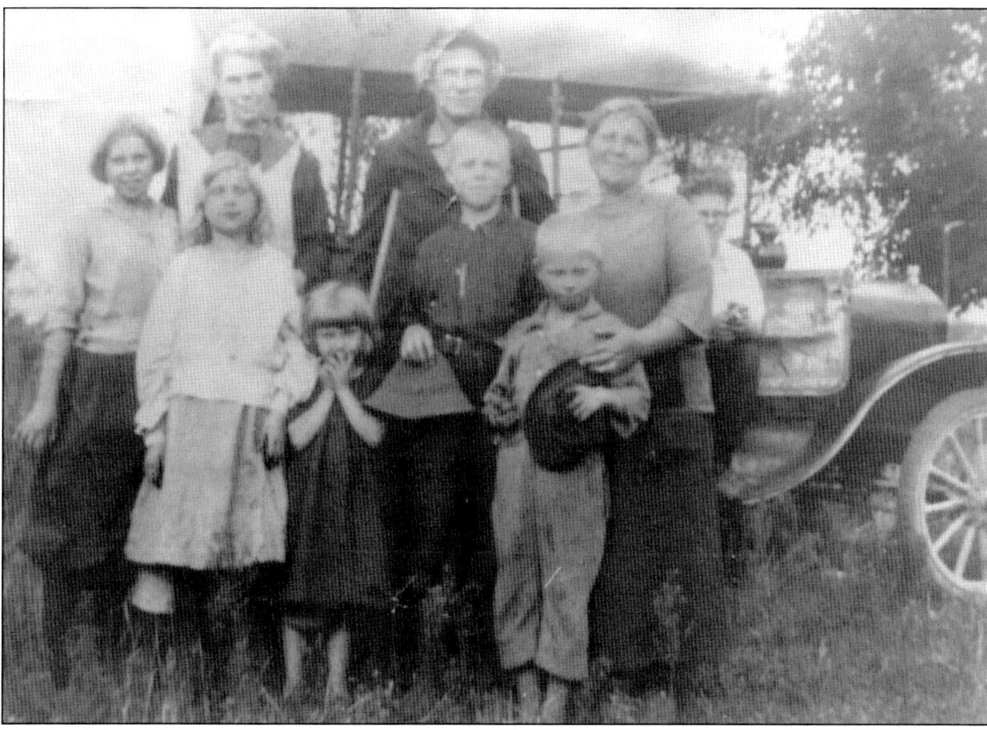

Hoskins Avenue, located between 14 Mile Road and Old Indian Lakes Road in northeastern Algoma Township, was named in honor of the John Hoskins family. They lived on their farm about seven-tenths of a mile southwest of Burchtown. Family members pictured here include, from left to right, (first row) Fannie and Fredrick; (second row) Sarah, Vera, Richard, Fannie Hoskins, and Seymour and his Model T car; (third row) aunt Lizzie Hoskins and John Hoskins.

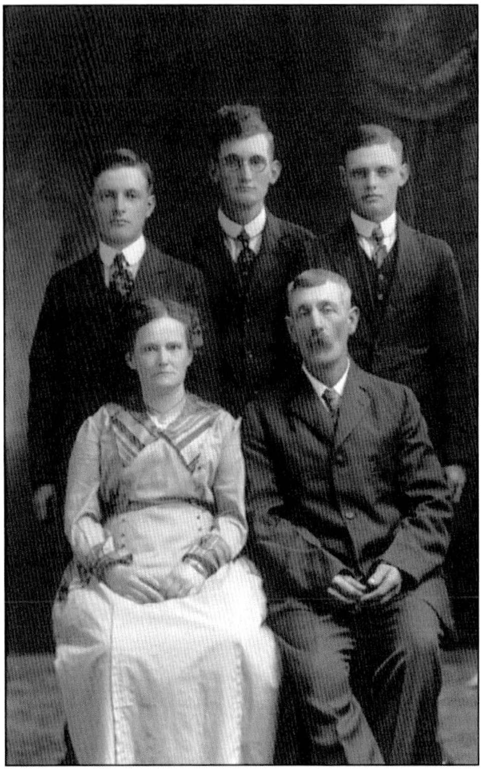

The Culp house was on Algoma Avenue on the south side of Cedar Creek. The house was later moved to 14 Mile Road east of Grange Avenue. The Culp family members pictured here are, from left to right, (seated) Clara (Rawson) Culp and Elmer Culp; (standing) Dewey Culp and brothers Everett and Harley.

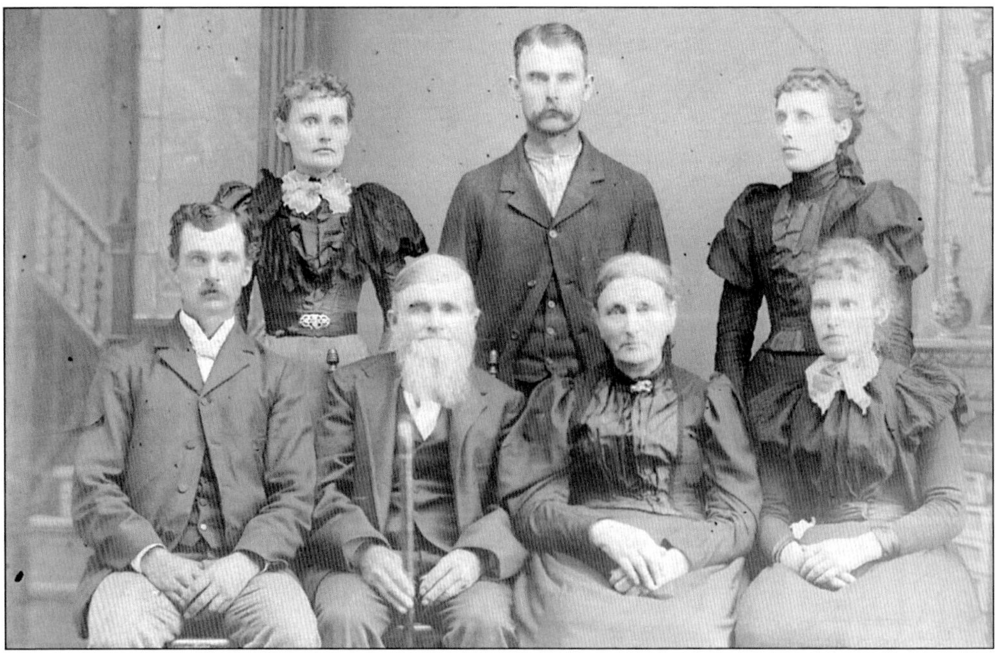

Pictured here is the Rawson family. They are, from left to right, (seated) John Rawson, Harley Rawson, Hannah (Wait) Rawson, and Clara (Rawson) Culp; (standing) Anna (Rawson) Crites, Henry Rawson, and Abbie (Rawson) Helsel. George, Lena, and Minnie Rawson, children of Harley and Hannah, are not pictured; they died before the family came to Michigan from Ohio.

Jeremiah was the third son of Henry and Julia Helsel, born in 1850 in Algoma Township. He married Mary Ellen Farnham (born 1853, died 1924) in 1872 in Algoma Township. Jeremiah died in 1923.

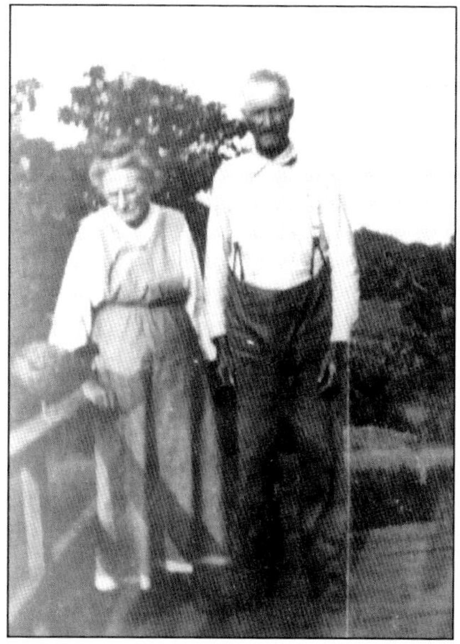

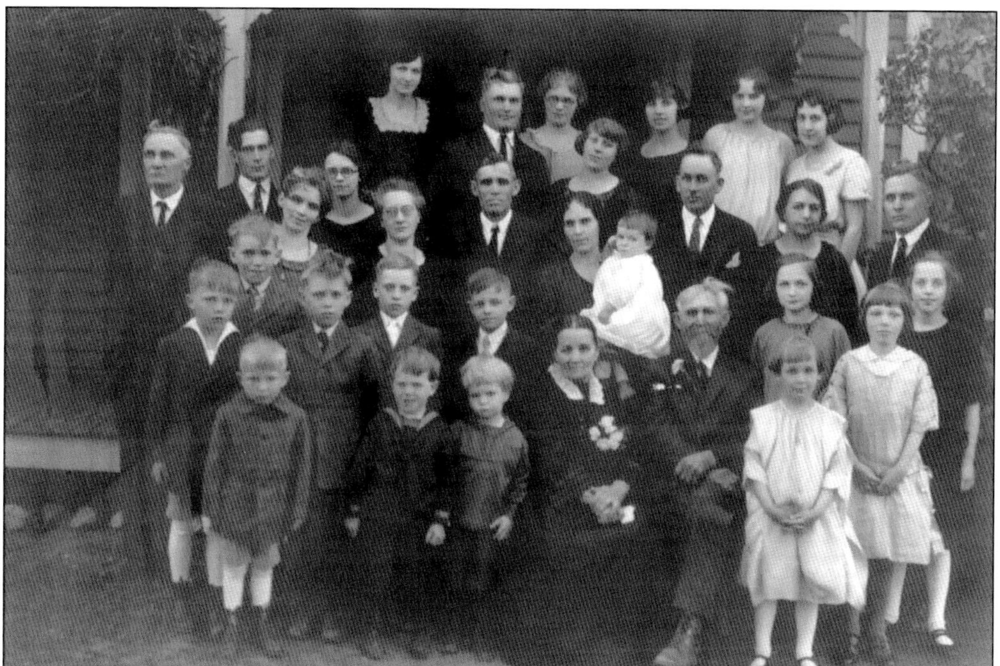

Pictured here on May 7, 1923, is the Erickson clan. In no particular order are Laura Erickson, Edward Erickson, Lillian (Anderson) Sjogren, Elsie (Erickson) Friske, Edith (Friske) Erickson, Gertrude (Anderson) Ericson, Emma (Erickson) Lund, Carl Sjogren, Vincent Erickson, Anna (Sjogren) Erickson, Edith (Erickson) Rosenlund, Albin Erickson, Selma (Peterson) Erickson, Ethel (Knapp) Peterson, Ernest Peterson, Ameia (Erickson) Sorenson, Axel Erickson, Ellsworth Peterson, Roswell Peterson, Marvin Erickson, Gordon Erickson, John Erickson, Sylvia (Anderson) Erickson, Esther (Steed/Lang) Sjogren, Florence (Anderson) Erickson, John Carleton Sjogren, Norman Edward Sjogren, Willard Erickson, Burton Erickson, Emma (Erickson), and Ellanette (Murnin) Peterson.

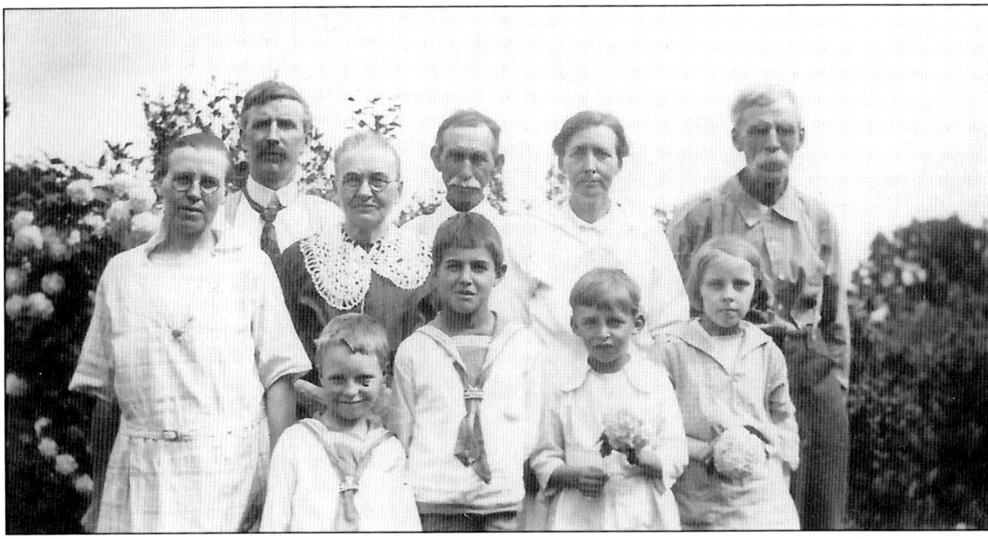

The Jakobsen family has gathered for a photograph. From left to right are (first row) Ernie Davis, Don Davis, Henry Hoskins, and Dorothy Hoskins Smith; (second row) Gyda Jakobsen Davis, William Davis, Maren Jakobsen, Gustav Jakobsen, Alvilde Jakobsen Hoskins, and Isaac Hoskins. (Courtesy of Tom Hoskins.)

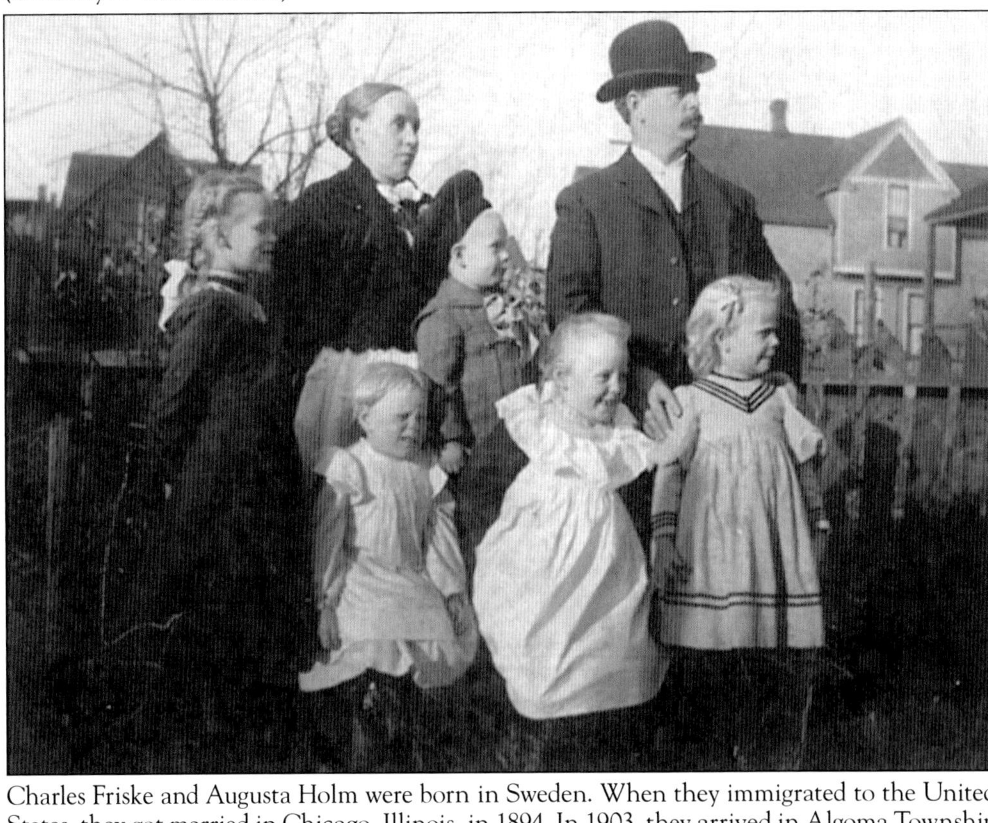

Charles Friske and Augusta Holm were born in Sweden. When they immigrated to the United States, they got married in Chicago, Illinois, in 1894. In 1903, they arrived in Algoma Township with their children: Grace, Irene, Elsie, Helen, Carl, and Milton. They settled on Friske Drive near Cedar Creek. Two more daughters were born there: Ruth and Marion.

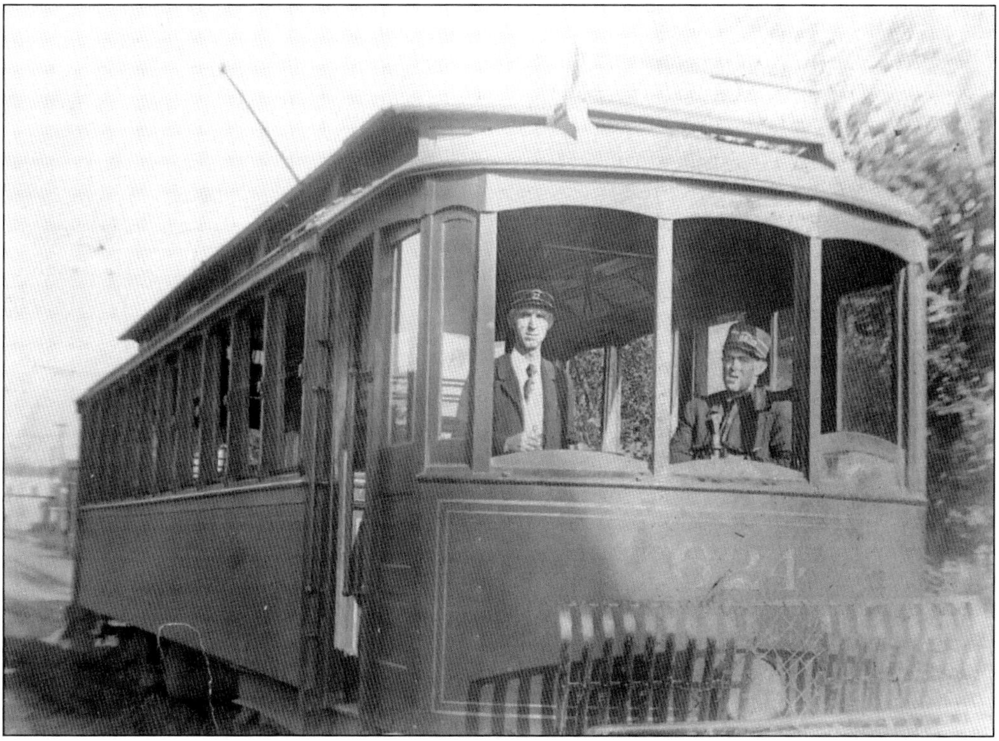

Ernest (1881–1965) and Benjamin (1884–1964) were the sons of Darius and Alice (Botruff) Helsel. They became railroad conductors in Kansas City. Ernie returned to Algoma Township to run a store, called Reed's Station because the Toledo, Saginaw and Muskegon Railway ran just to the north of the store across Pine Island Drive. Ernie renamed the business Helsel's Store.

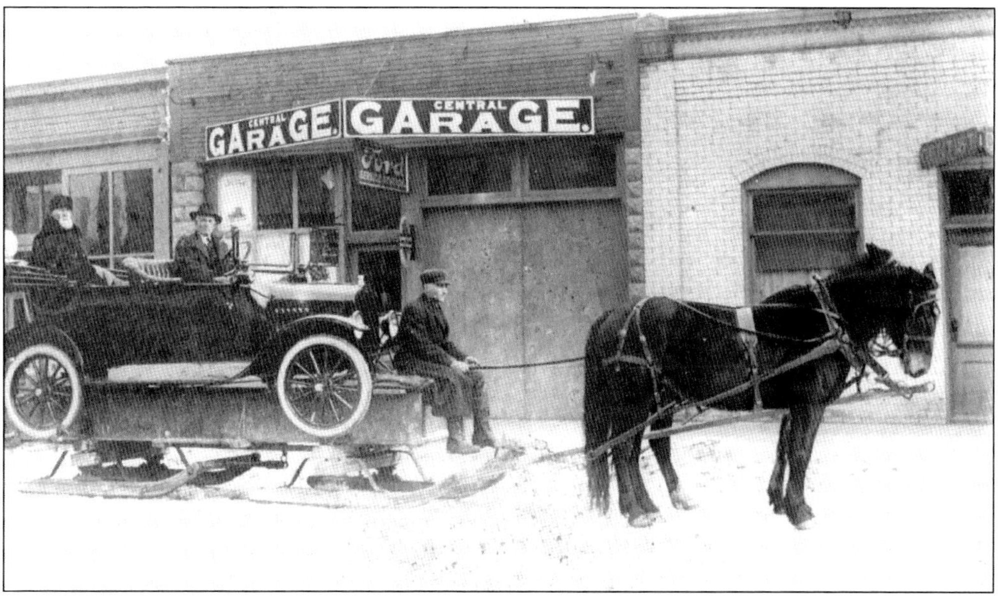

Ray E. Helsel bought this car at the Ford dealership in Cedar Springs. Automaker Henry Ford was visiting the dealership and is pictured here in 1917 in the driver's seat of the new car. Ray is driving the horses, and his father, Noah F. Helsel, is in the back seat. At the time, the car cost $500.

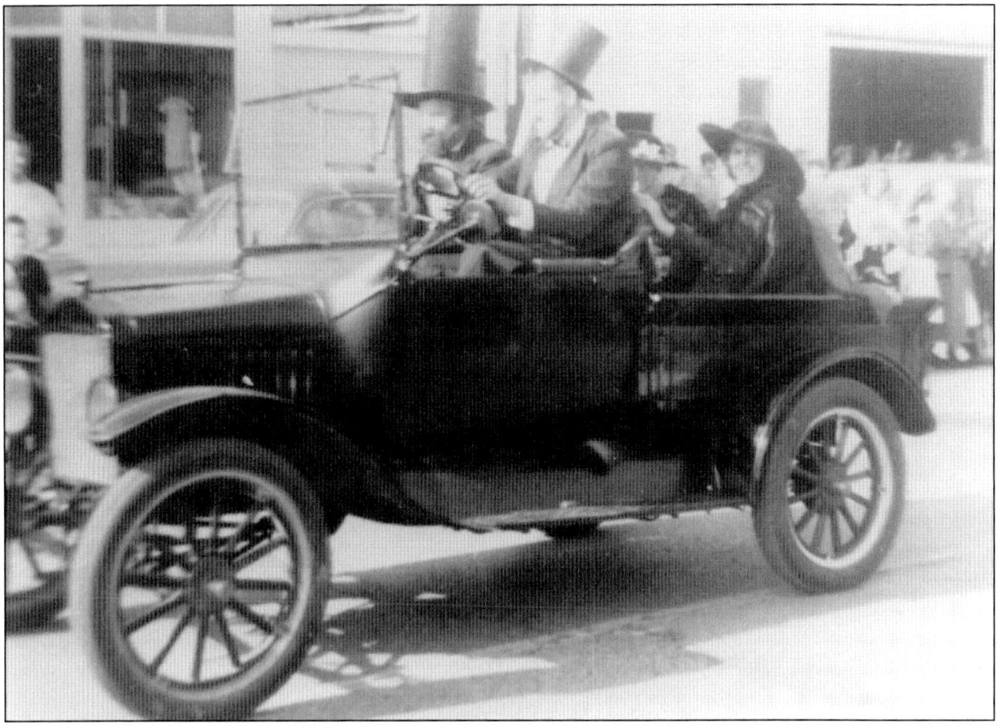

In 1956, Cedar Springs held the Centennial Farmers Day Parade. Bruce Armstrong drove his 1917 Model T in the parade. The passenger in the front seat is Calvin Covey. Eloise Armstrong Covey and Bernice Armstrong are in the back seat.

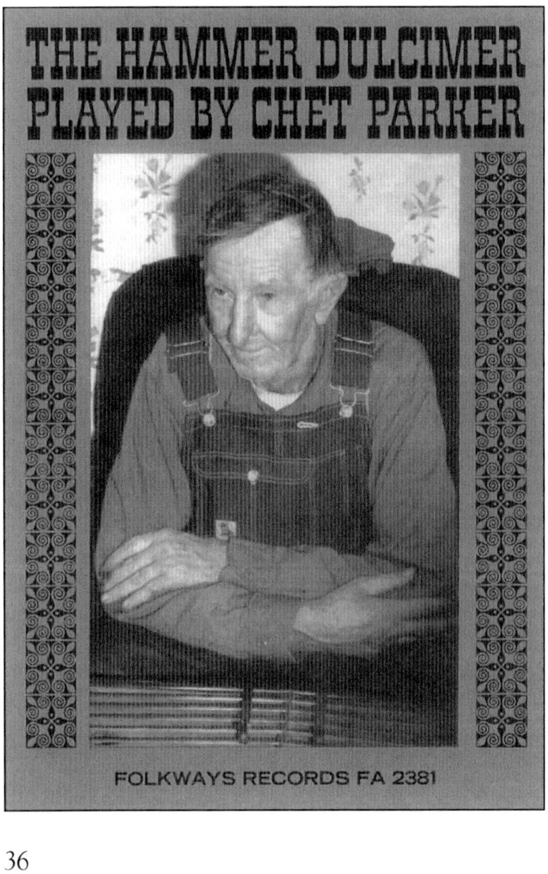

Chet Parker, born in 1891 in Edgerton, was a famous hammer dulcimer player. He began playing the instrument in 1900 and then built his own hammer dulcimer in 1904. This is the one he played in the dance band he formed in 1910. The band played dances for about 50 years.

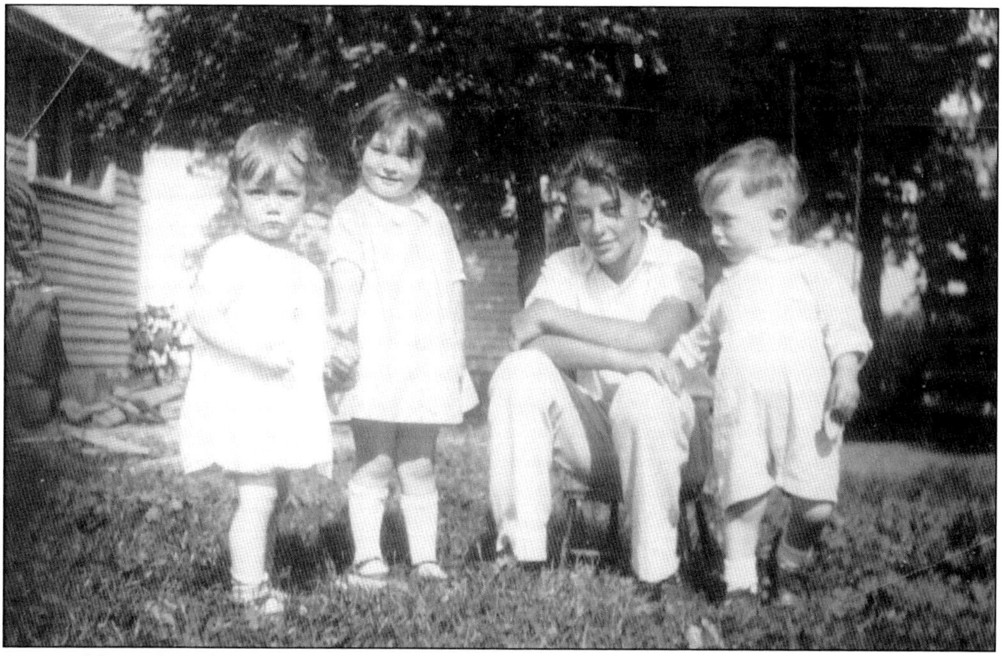

Pictured here from left to right are Connie (the niece of Maude Davis) at almost two years of age, Eleanor Davis at three and a half years of age, Elmo Pennington in his teen years, and Roger Davis at just over two years of age.

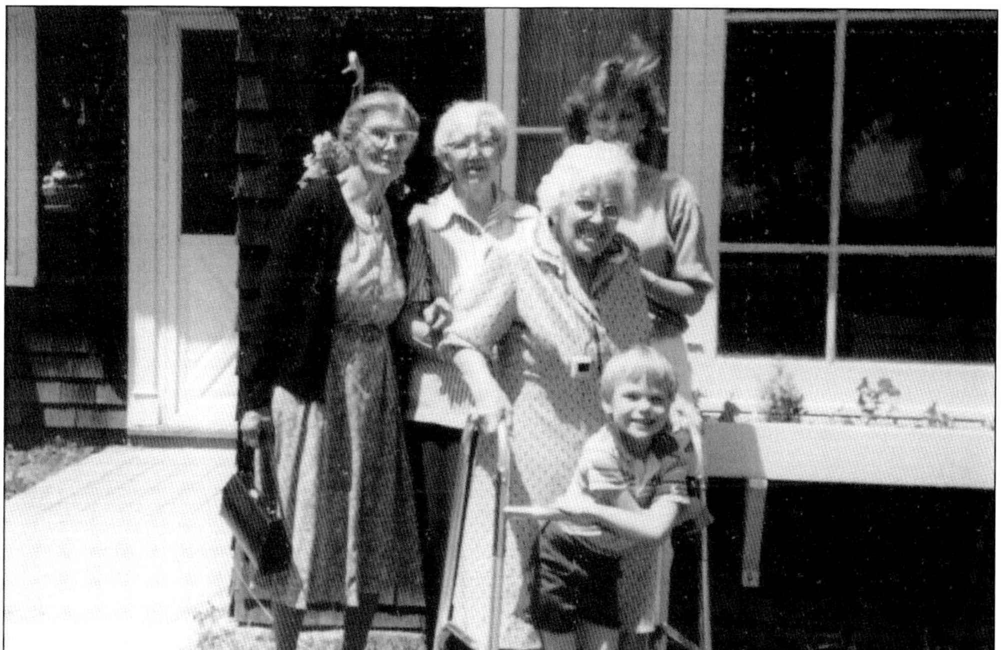

Leota M. Hamilton was born on April 1, 1896. She married Maurice A. Rector on December 30, 1916. In the early 1950s, the couple planted the pines east of Friske Drive and west of Cedar Creek. Leota is pictured here (far left) with Grace VanSchurr, Elsie Erickson, Beverly Sjogren Maler, and Chad Maler.

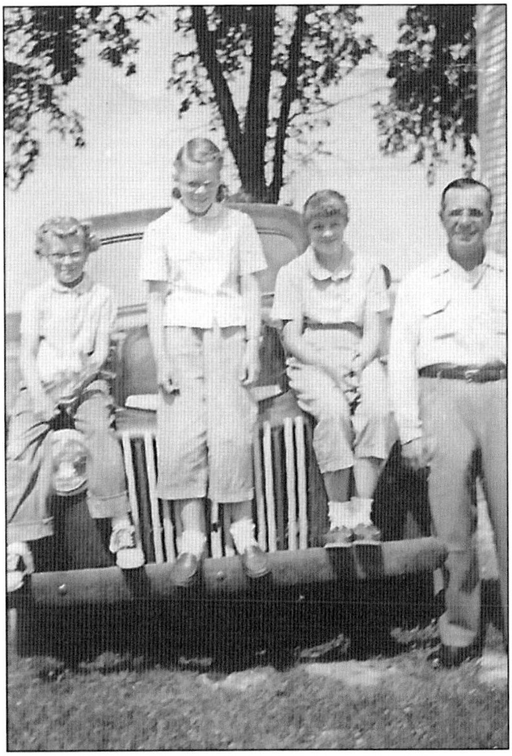

From left to right, Ruth, Carole, and Julia Holden are seen with their father, Merlyn, in front of their farmhouse at 3201 12 Mile Road in May 1953. Merlyn farmed both his land and his parents' (Lynn and Lola Holden) 80 acres. The girls always helped with milking and other farm chores. (Photograph by Della Osborne Holden, wife and mother.)

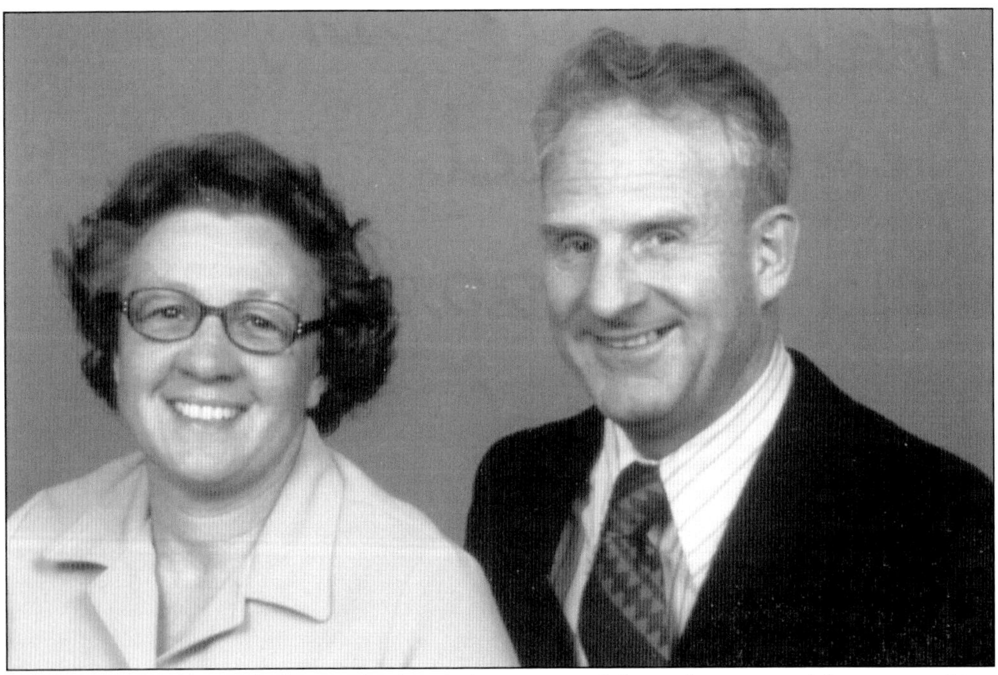

Paul Nielson and his wife, Jean Wheeler Nielson, ensured the replacement of the sign marking the historic community of Edgerton, which was never incorporated as a village. Replaced in 1995, the sign had been missing for approximately 30 years. Much of downtown Edgerton was destroyed in April 1965 by a very bad tornado that killed six people.

Two

Schools and Churches

Two of the most important institutions that bring people together in Algoma Township are the schools and the churches. The community has been strengthened by the interactions these have places fostered throughout the years.

The schools of Algoma Township included Gougeburg, Chalmers, Edgerton, Block, Hull, Foxville, Burchtown (or Burchville), Morningstar, and Algoma Central. They were often founded near the areas around sawmills or train depots. Although elementary and middle school students of Algoma no longer attend these schools, they are funneled to districts of surrounding towns as they are for high school.

The churches of Algoma Township include United Brethren Church, Algoma Baptist Church, Edgerton Methodist Episcopal Church, and Maranatha Baptist Church. Remaining today are Algoma Baptist Church, Camp Lake Baptist Church, Grace Evangelical Church, and Maranatha Baptist Church. These places of worship allowed residents to interact and worship together and create a community of neighbors.

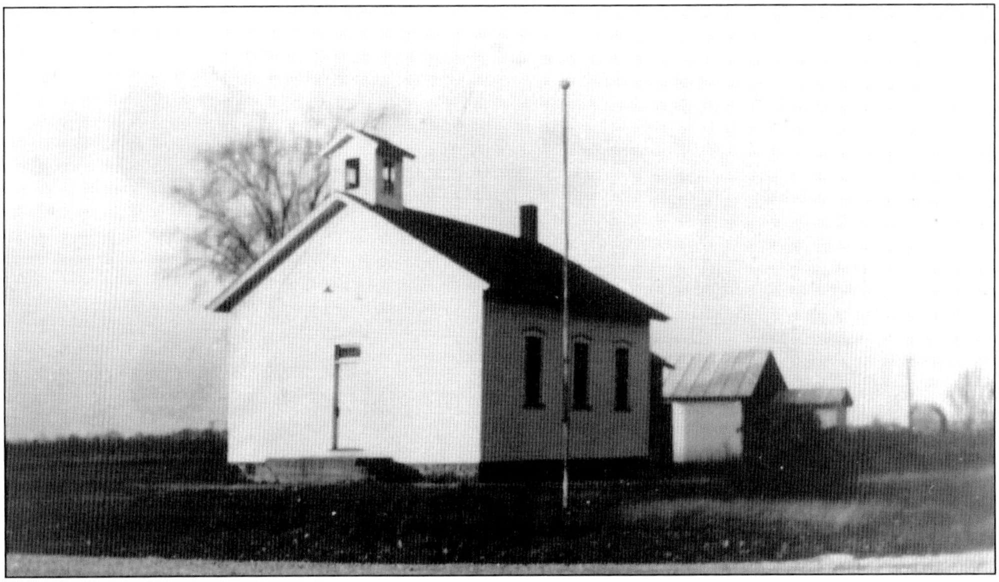

Gougeburg School was located on the southwest corner of Algoma Avenue and 12 Mile Road in section 28. As recorded in the Abstract of Title from the Kent County Register's Office on December 29, 1856, the land for School District No. 3 was donated by Henry Shank and his wife on December 18, 1852. The description identifies the land as "9 R square in NE cor for School Purposes." The school, built in 1852, later was named after the settlement half a mile down the road, east of Algoma Avenue at Fonger Street.

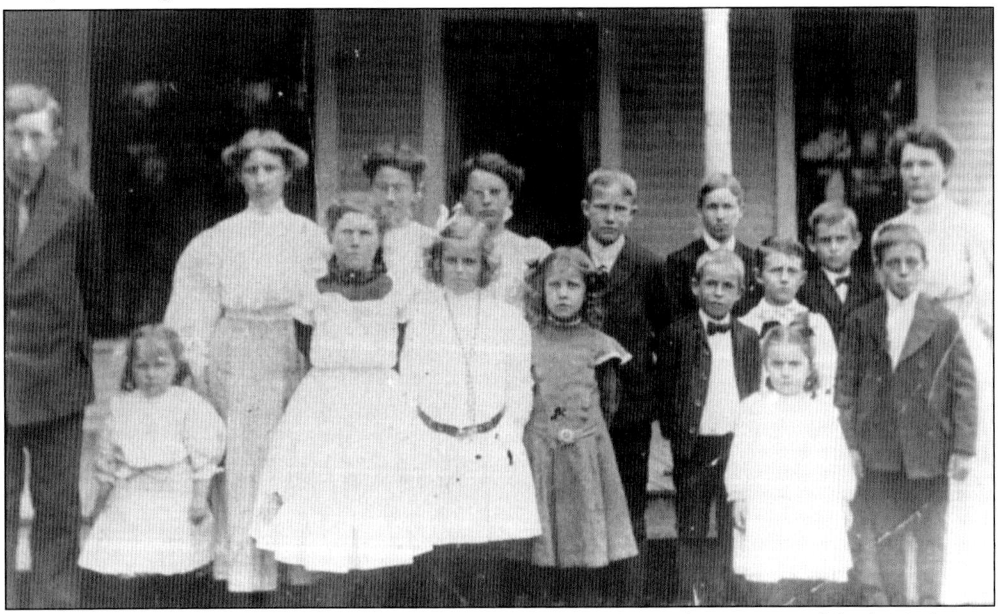

Gougeburg School students were invited to the John Tuttle residence in Rockford, Michigan, seen here around 1900. Ella Tuttle was their teacher, who in later years was known as Ella Tuttle Faber. Pictured from left to right are (first row) Lorraine Dillie, Hattie Truax, Edna Peterson, Zelda Dillie, Walfred Peterson, Marvin Field, Harry Minion, and Mildred Field; (second row) Vern Hayton, Ester Pardy, Ruth Jewell, Theo Davis, Rolla Dillie, Marvin Peterson, Arvid Peterson, and Tuttle.

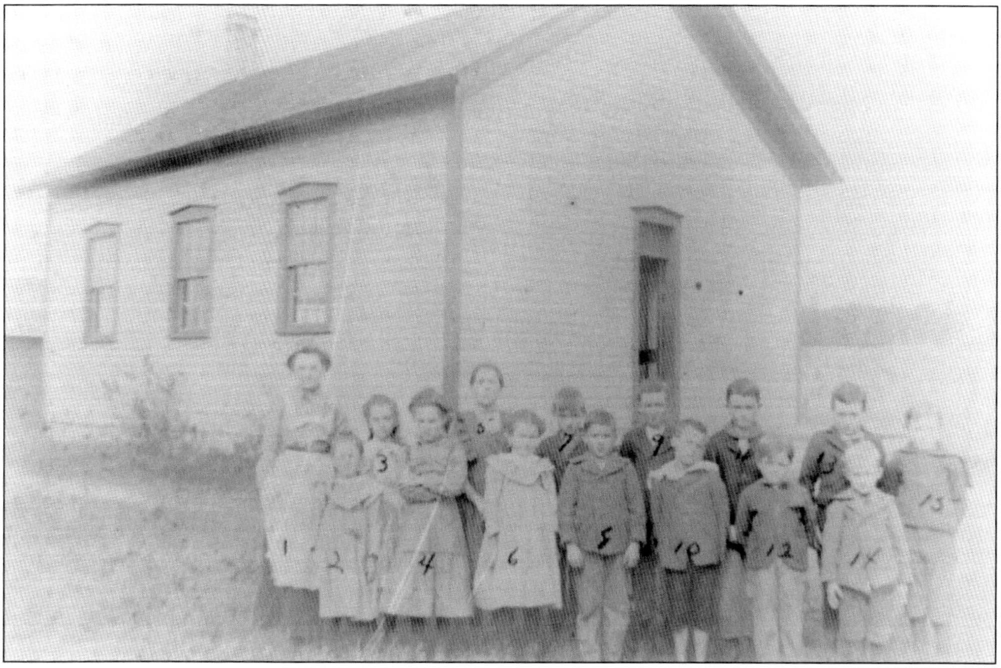

This photograph of Gougeburg School shows the class during the 1900–1901 school year. Pictured from left to right are (first row) Mamie Jewel, Lelia Rector Ives, Ruth Jewell, Maurice Rector, Benton Fretenberg, Jesse Helsel, and Harry Turner; (second row) teacher Mabel Colby, Hazel Richards, Maude Baldwin, Delbert Rhinehart, Clarence Teesdale, Henry Helsel, Ray Helsel, and Harry Turner.

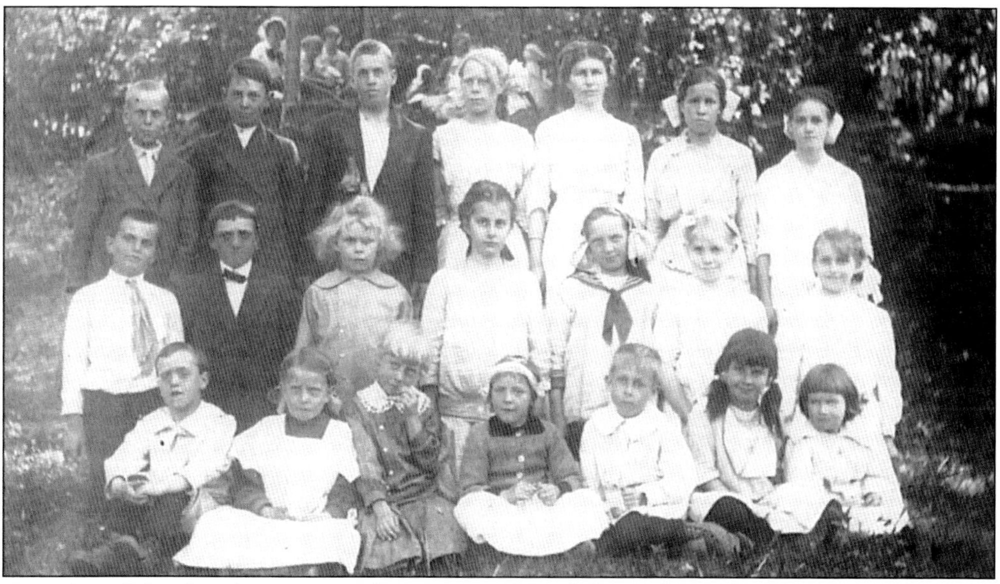

Gougeburg School students are seen here in 1913. From left to right are (first row) Clifford Lundin, Florence Peterson, Marion Friske, Dorothy Lundin, Agnes Davis, an unidentified boy, Wava Jewell, and unidentified; (second row) Richard Jewell, Roy Lundin, Ruth Friske, Mildred Field, Lorraine Dillie, Mildred Peterson, and Lillian Sjogren; (third row) Milton Friske, Clifford Davis, Carl Friske, Helen Friske, and teacher Blanch Buzzard, Zelda Dillie, and Evelyn Lundin.

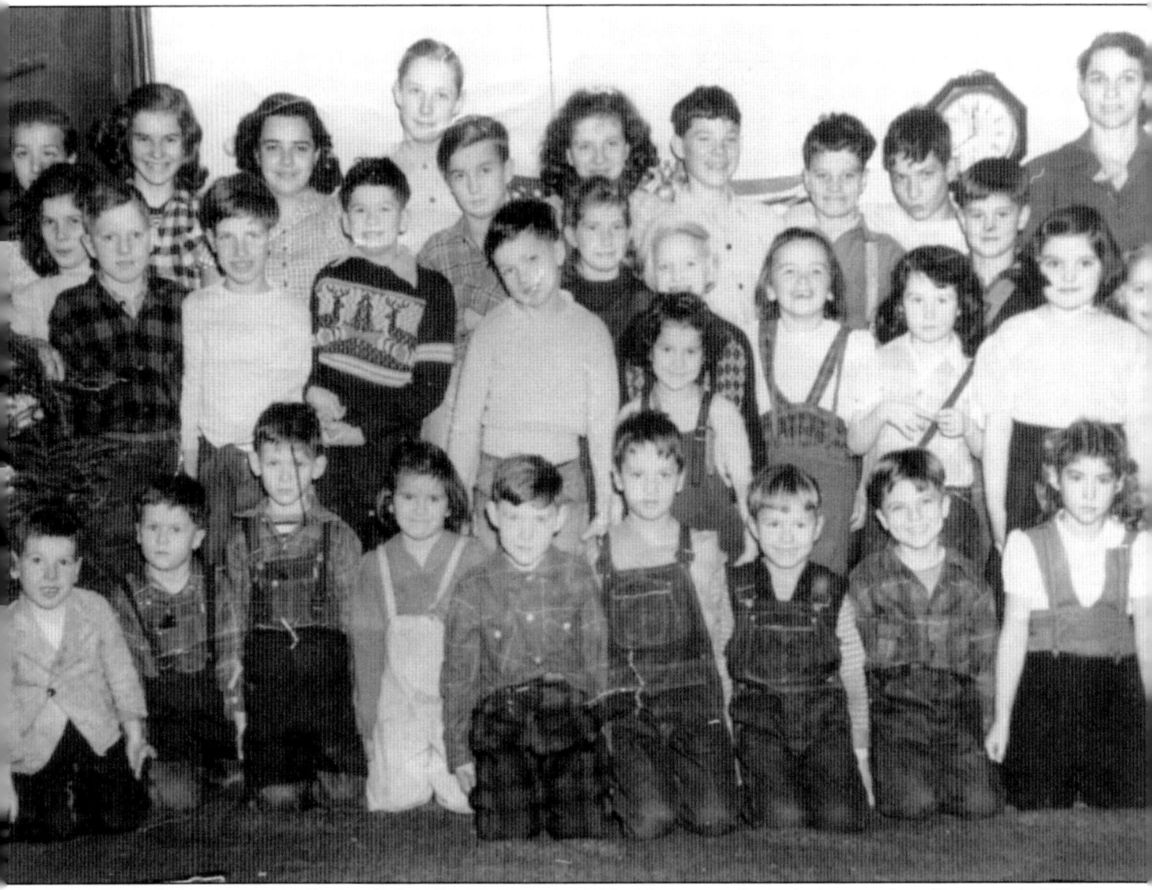

Students from Chalmers School are seen in 1946. They are, from left to right, (first row) Albert Gunnett, Elmer Schultz, Frank Schultz, Kathy Colby, Jack O'Gorman, Leon Ingersoll, Edward Ingersoll, Kennis "Kent" Dixon, and Jean Cavanaugh; (second row) Shirley Denton, Gail Taylor, Ken Hoaglin, George Denton, unidentified, Donnie Cavanaugh, June Bristol, Sandy Denton, Judy Colby, Charlene Wiggins, Ruth Ann Kent, and Carol Bristol; (third row) Bertha Maciejewski, Evelyn Ring, Shirley Bradley, Duane Bradley, Dean Truac, Joyce Hoaglin, Ron Denton, Norman Nestor, Clarence "Bud" Hoadlin, John Nestor, and teacher Mildred Ring.

The former Village of Algoma Center, later named Gougeburg, was comprised of a group of houses used by families working for C.C. Comstock's mill. Henry Shank, a pioneer of Algoma Township, donated the land upon which Gougeburg School, District No. 3, was built in 1852. This image shows students at the school, along with their teacher, in January 1953.

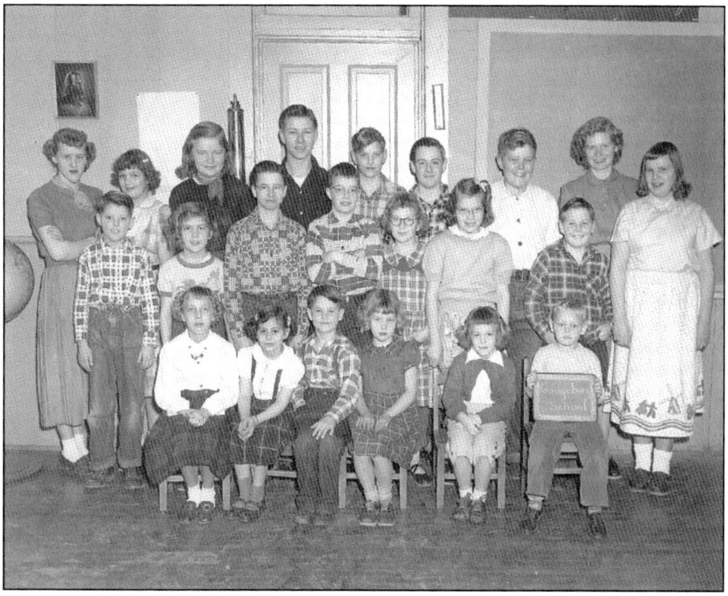

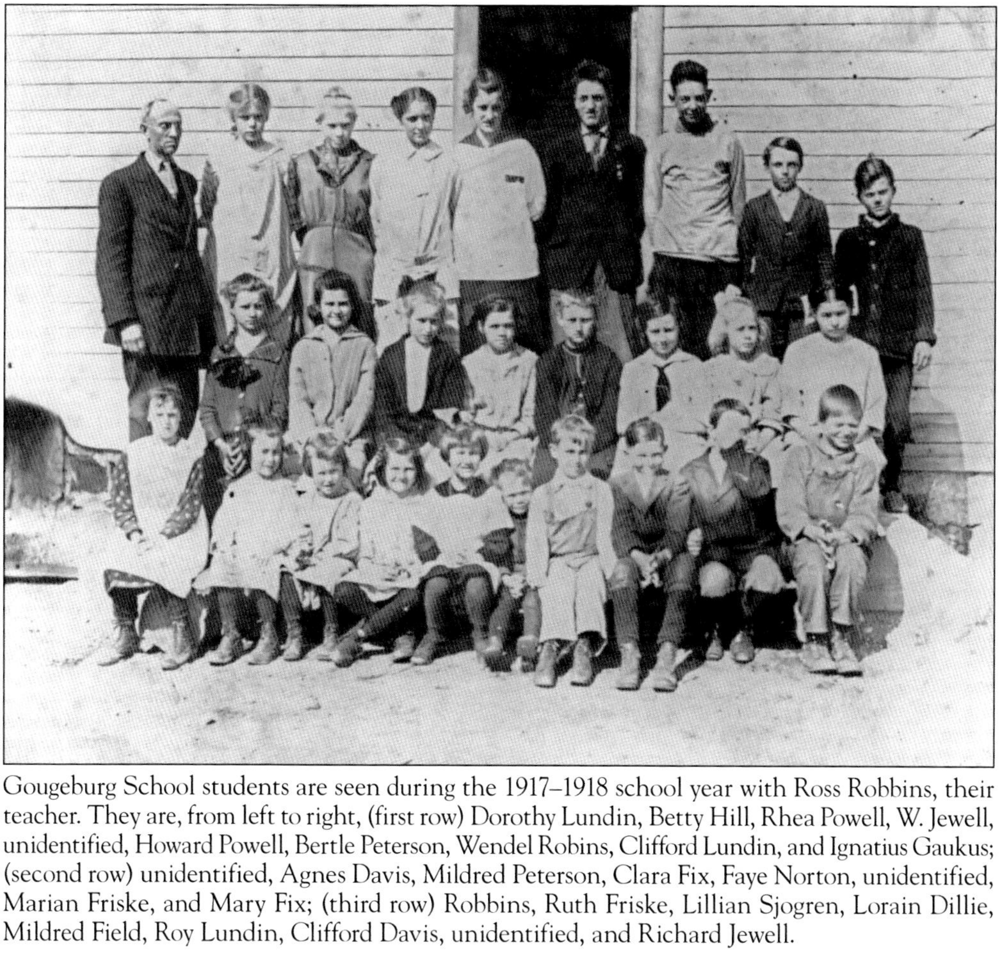

Gougeburg School students are seen during the 1917–1918 school year with Ross Robbins, their teacher. They are, from left to right, (first row) Dorothy Lundin, Betty Hill, Rhea Powell, W. Jewell, unidentified, Howard Powell, Bertle Peterson, Wendel Robins, Clifford Lundin, and Ignatius Gaukus; (second row) unidentified, Agnes Davis, Mildred Peterson, Clara Fix, Faye Norton, unidentified, Marian Friske, and Mary Fix; (third row) Robbins, Ruth Friske, Lillian Sjogren, Lorain Dillie, Mildred Field, Roy Lundin, Clifford Davis, unidentified, and Richard Jewell.

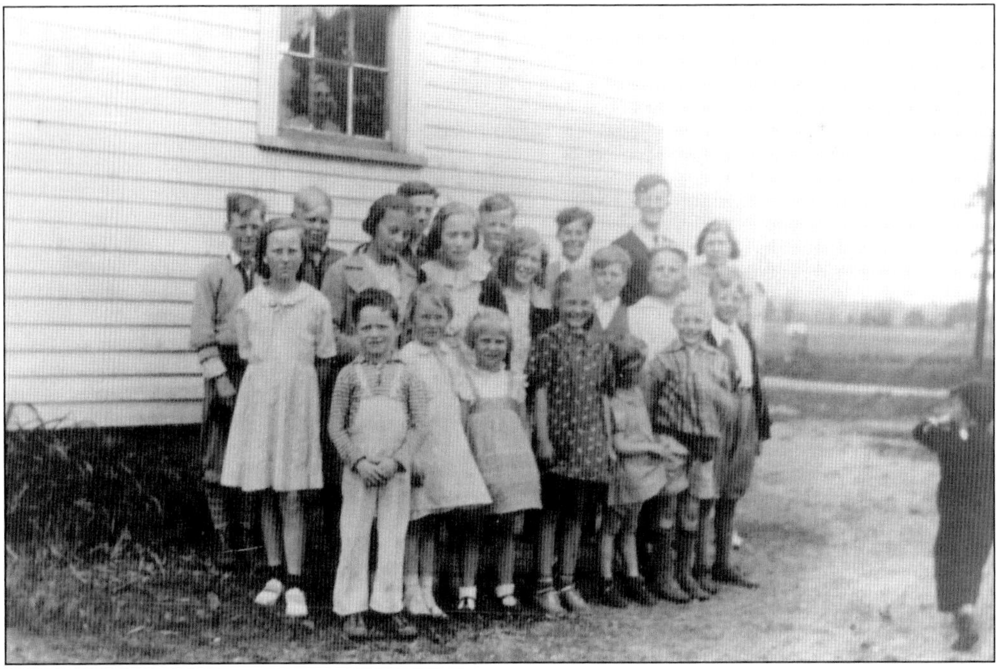

Students of Gougeburg School pose for a group photograph around 1936. From left to right are (first row) Jack Dufort, Norma Powell, Carolyn Friske, Dolorus Jewell, an unidentified girl, Jerry Anderson, and unidentified; (second row) Elaine Powell, Ruth Helsel, Betty Jane Howard, Lois Pinckney, Arnold Bishop, Carl Lambert Friske, and teacher Florence Guege; (third row) Russell Powell, Robert Erickson, unidentified, Marvin Powell, unidentified, and Marvin Field Jr.

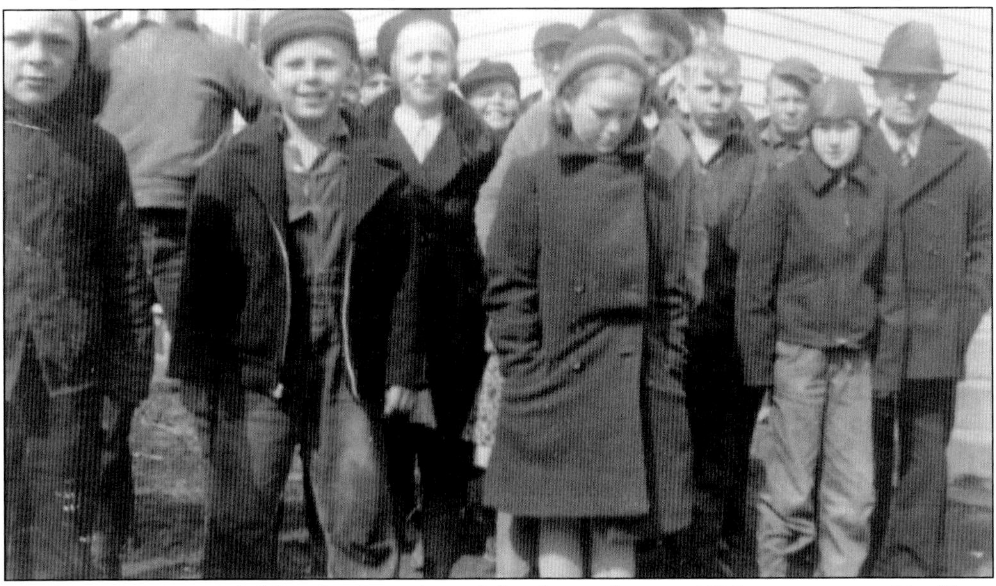

The first 4-H meeting held at the Gougeburg School, seen here in 1938, was organized by Keats Vining of 4-H Kent County. Pictured from left to right are (first row) Roger Pennington, Carl Friske, Elaine Powell, Bruce Armstrong; (second row) unidentified, Betty Jane Howard, unidentified, Chuck Erickson, and K.K. Vining; (third row) two unidentified, Robert Erickson, Marvin Field (cap half cocked to left), and Russ Powell.

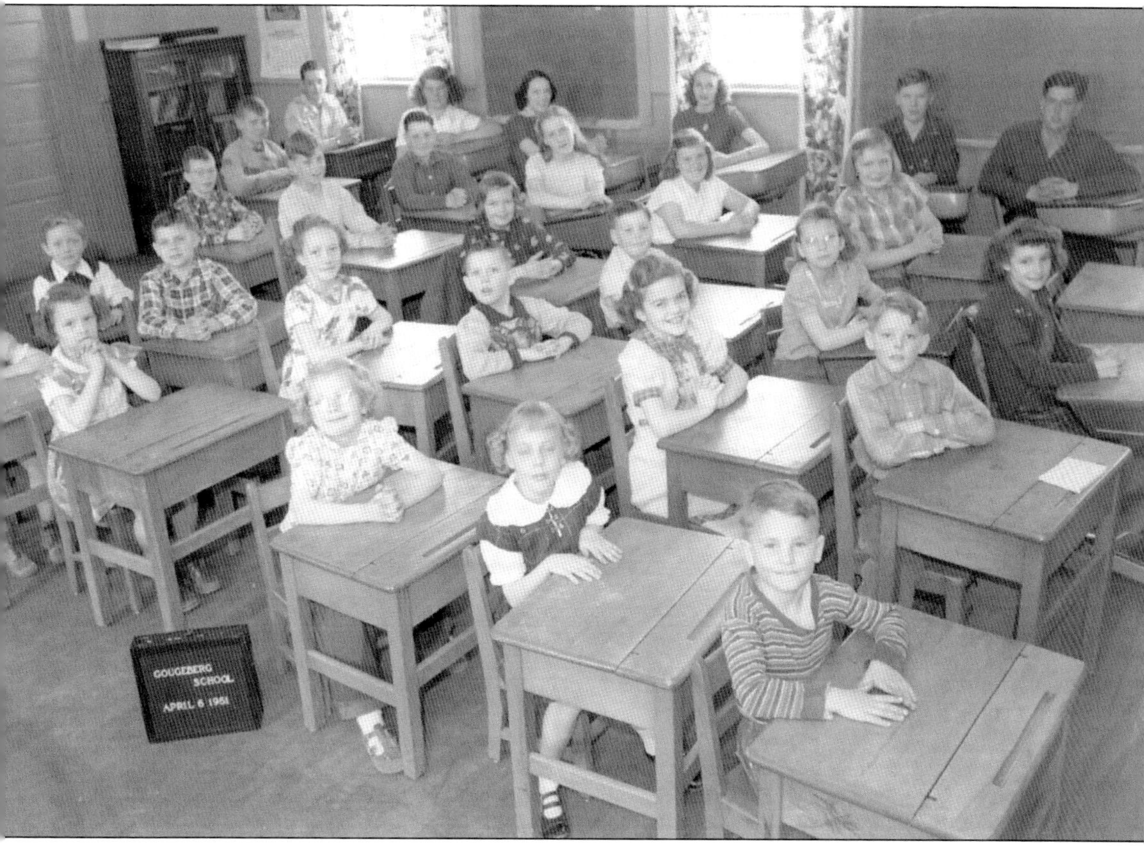

Mrs. Hough's class is seen here on April 6, 1951, at Gougeburg School. Pictured from left to right, front to back, are Linda Dakens Patterson, Judy Rogers, Ruth Ann Holden Plambeck, Judith Turner Brookover, Jerry Manning, Don Graham, Ronald Rogers, Louann Sherrod, David Willett, Donna Lee Sherrod, Donald Maning, Jim Long, Earl Manning, Julia Holden Pyne, Ronald Teesdale, Carole Holden Christensen, Barbara Packer, Leo Dakens, Tom Teesdale, Ruth Knox Robinson, Patsy Becker, Donna Dakens Empie, Vernon Sherrod, Virginia Dakens Young, Delora Lundin Johnson, Lois Wainwright, Donald Becker, and Randy Smith.

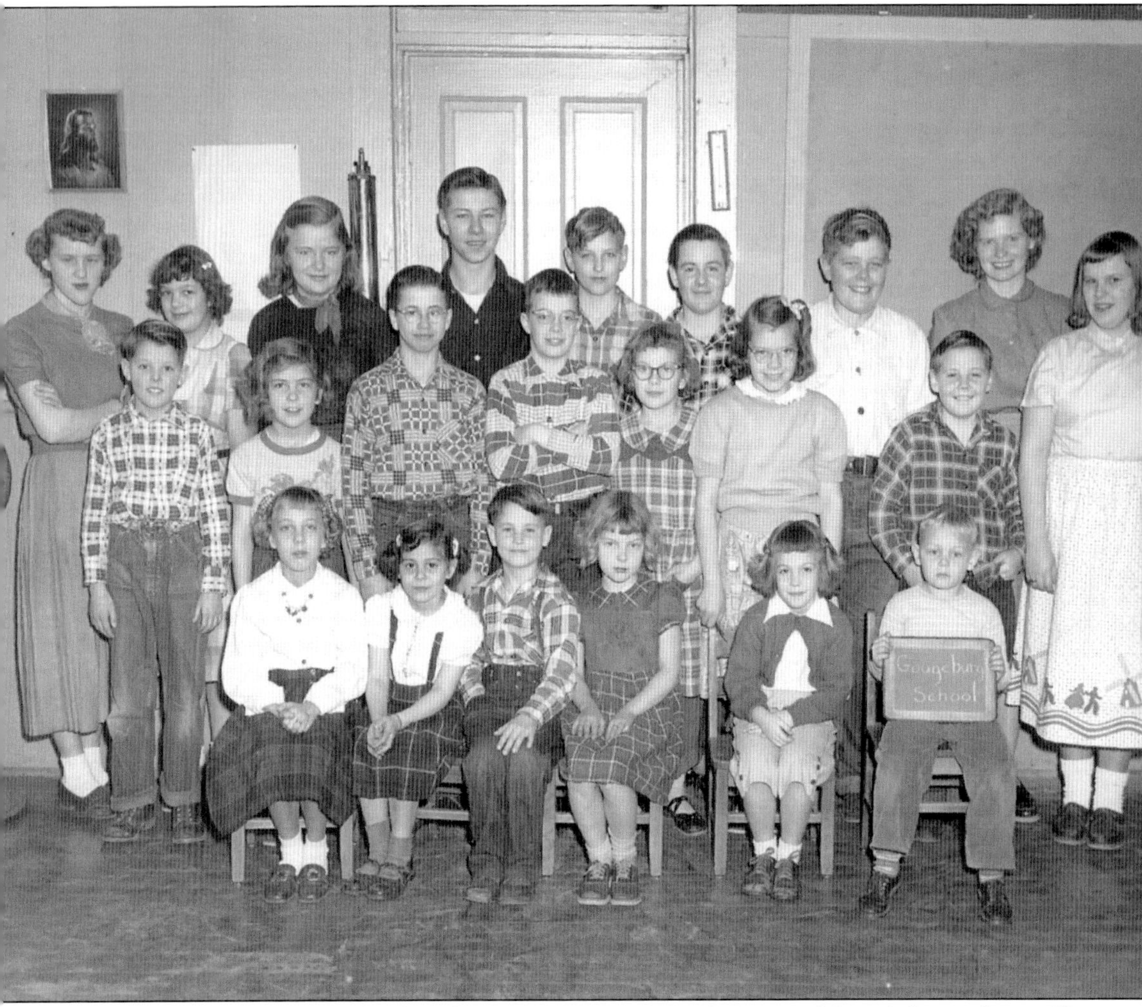

These are Gougeburg School students seen in January 1953. Pictured from left to right are (first row) Judith Turner, Sandy Teesdale, Jerry Manning, Lorene Dakens, Christine Long, and Wayne Wainright; (second row) Don Manning, Linda Dakens, Raymond Demick, James Long, Ruth Ann Holden, Carole Holden, Ron Teesdale, and Patsy Becker; (third row) Ruth Knox, Julia Holden, Donna Dakens, Lyle Lapree, Earl Manning, Tom Teesdale, Leo Dakens, and teacher Beverly Haskins Reyner. Absent from the photograph this day are Steven Powell, Allen Norman, and Pamela Teesdale.

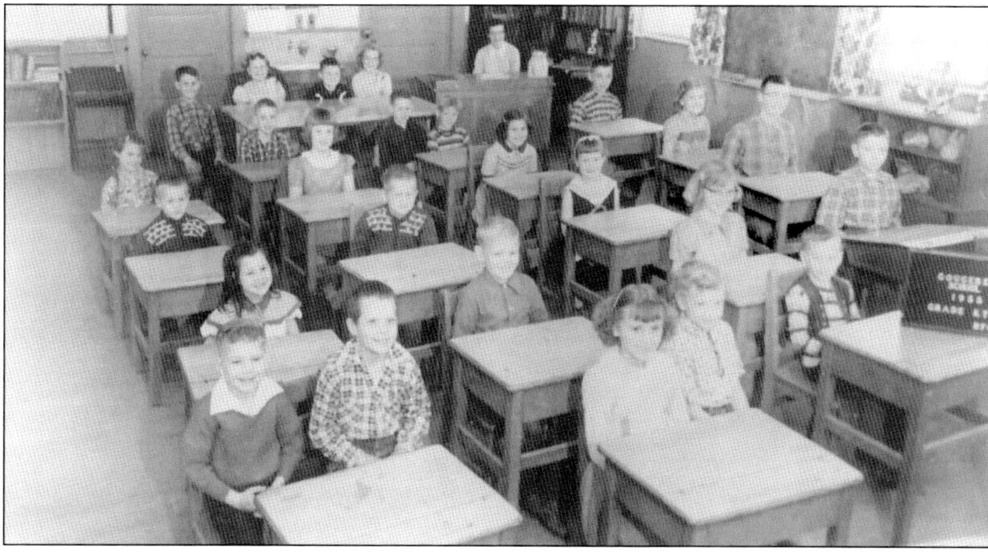

Gougeburg School students pose for the camera in 1955. Pictured from left to right are (first row) Craig Turner, Lee Bitely, Diana Davison, Candis Knight, and Don Teesdale; (second row) Linda Powell, Wayne Wainright, Lorene Dakens, and Bob Kleyenberg; (third row) Brian Bitely, Bruce Bitely, Jane Meyers, and Jim Long; (fourth row) Connie Weeks, Christine Long, Sandy Teesdale, and unidentified; (fifth row) Paul Kleyenberg, Steve Powell, Mike Wainright, and Dick Kleyenberg; (sixth row) Jerry Manning, Pam Teesdale, Allen Norman, Ruth Holden, and teacher Mrs. Manier.

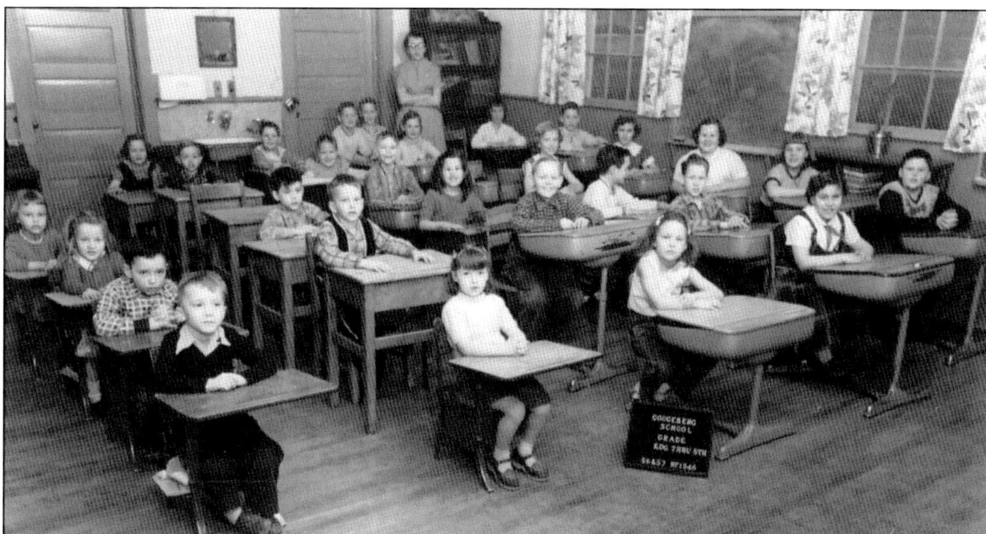

Another of Mrs. Manier's classes is seen the next year, in 1956–1957, at Gougeburg School. The students include, from left to right, (first row) Mitchel Pinckney, unidentified, Judy Ringleburg, Sandy Teesdale, and Al Norman; (second row) Ardi Lundin, Don Teesdale, Wayne Wainwright, Steve Powell, and Chris Long; (third row) Christine Powell, Paul Kaiserlian, Linda Lowell, Lee Bitely, and Pam Teesdale; (fourth row) Beverly Sjogren, Glen Wainwright, Craig Turner, Candy Knight, and Diane Davison; (fifth row) unidentified, Jane Meyers, Connie Weeks, and Paul Kleynenberg; (sixth row) Mike Wainwright, Bruce Bitely, and Kathy Pinckney; (seventh row) Brian Bitely.

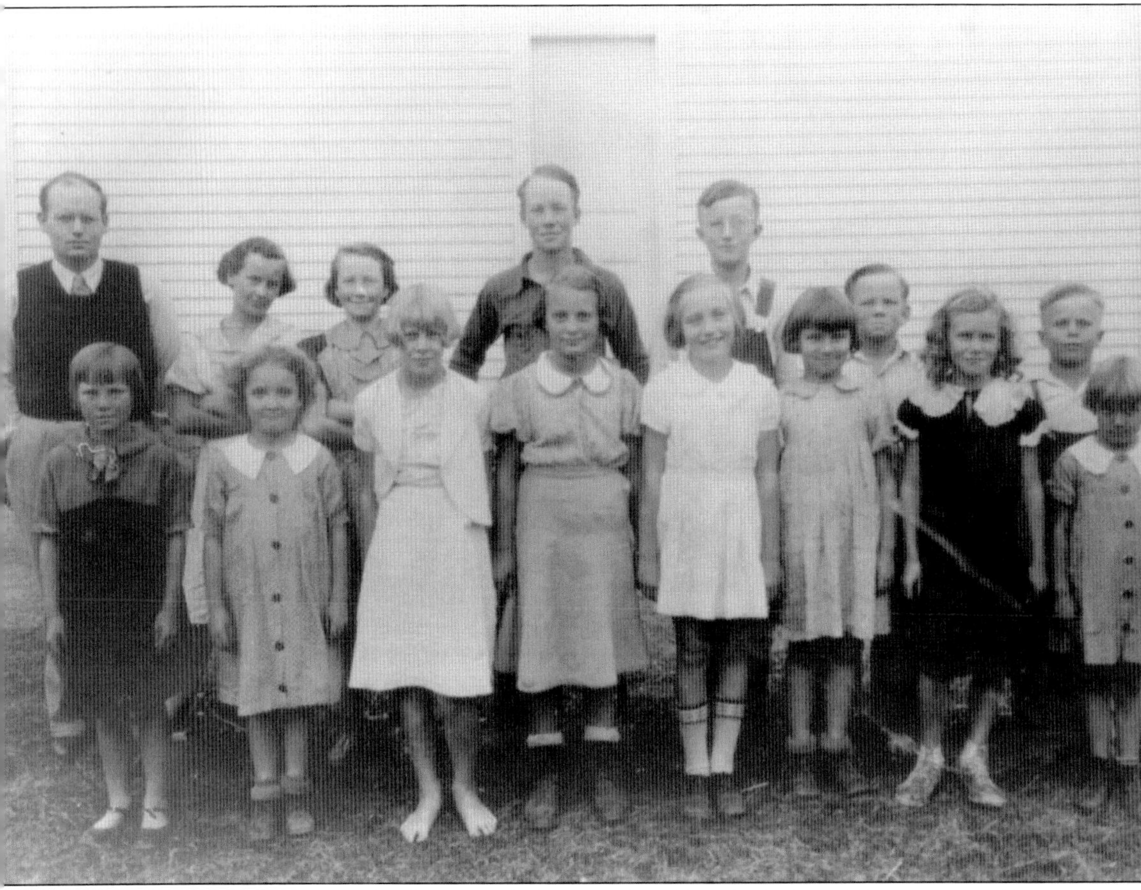

Students at Gougeburg School pose with their teacher, Mr. Clark. From left to right are (first row) Elaine Powell, Leona Wall, Geannette Pinckney, Ruth Helsel, Betty Jane Howard, Delores Wall, Lois Pinckney, and Ardith Wall; (second row) Clark, Janet Helsel, Pauline Powell, Russ Powell, Marvin Field Jr., Marvin Powell, and Lambert Friske.

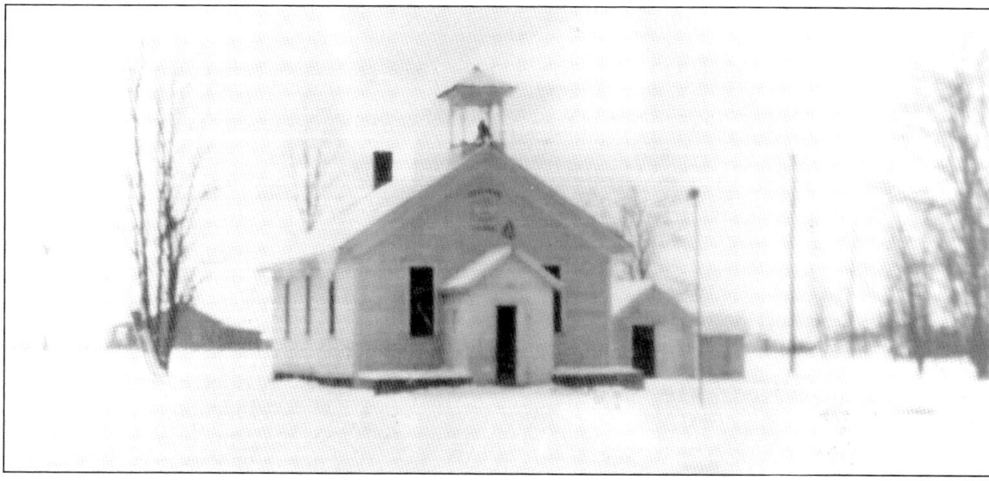

Chalmers School, District No. 4, was completed in 1854. The location was decided in a meeting on May 29, 1851. On September 29, the school board met and discussed costs and finishing the building. The decision was reached to heat the building for three months of winter schooling, and a half cord of firewood would be needed per student. The board also agreed to raise taxes to paint the school once $60 was reached.

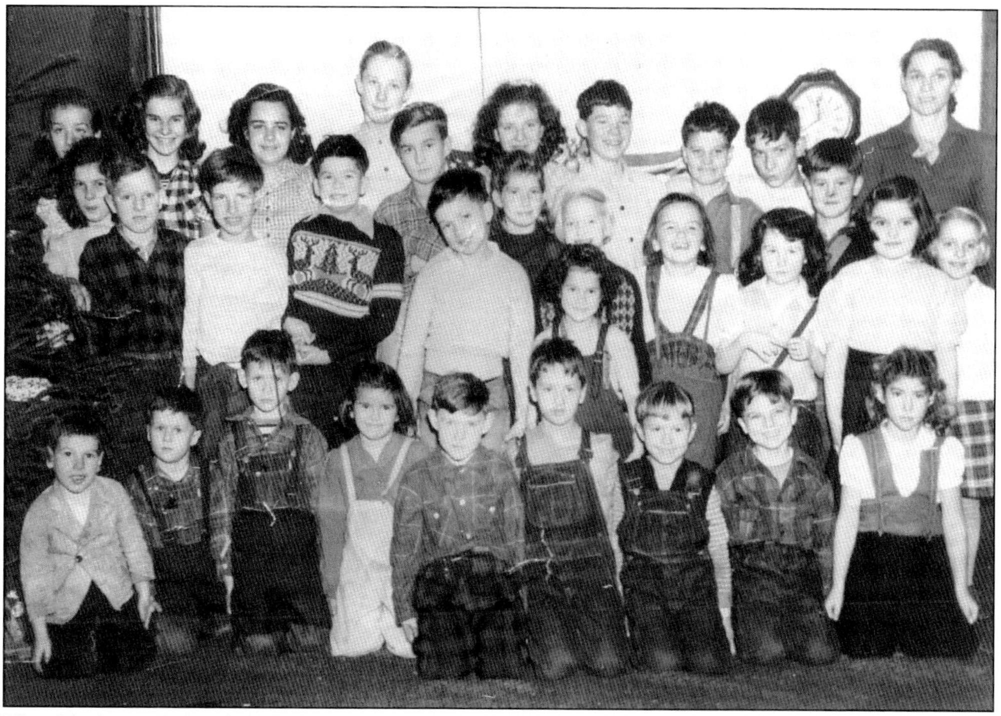

The Chalmers School class poses in 1946. Pictured are (first row) Albert Gunnell, Elmer Schultz, Frank Schultz, Kathy Colby, Jack O'Gorman, Leon Ingersoll, Edward Ingersoll, Kennis (Kent) Dixon, and Jean Cavanaugh; (second row) Shirley Denton, Gail Tayor, Ken Hoaglin, George Denton, unidentified, Donnie Cavanaugh, June Bristol, Sandy Denton, Judy Colby, Charlene Wiggins, Ruth Ann Kent, and Carol Bristol; (third row) Bertha Maciejewski, Evelyn Ring, Shirley Bradley, Duane Bradley, Dean Truac, Joyce Hoaglin, Ron Denton, Norman Nestor, Clarence "Bud" Hoadlin, John Nestor, the teacher, and Mildred Ring.

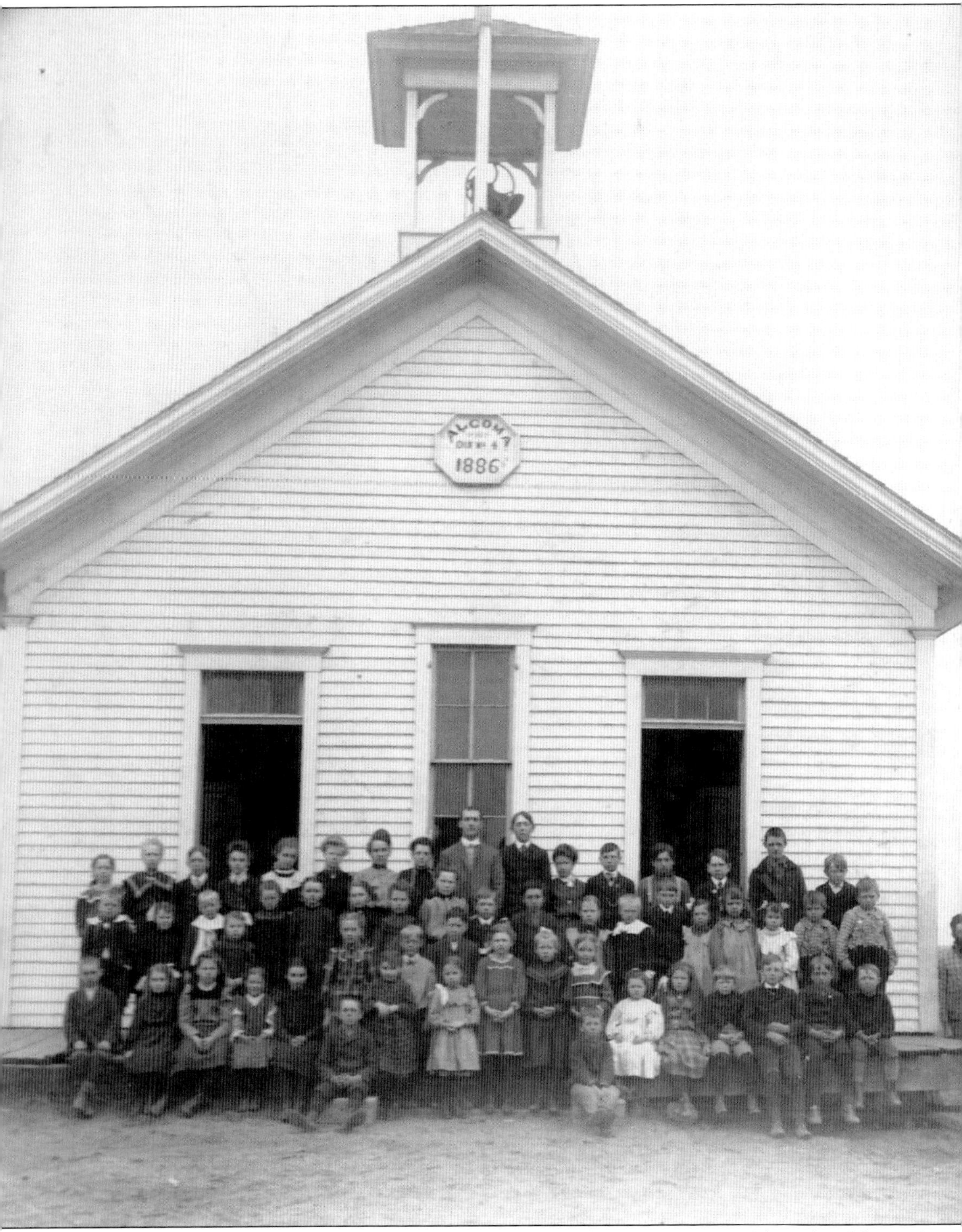

Students and teachers stand outside Chalmers School, District No. 4. The school housed kindergarten through the eighth grade. Eighth-grade graduations in the 1930s were held for all of the township one-room schools in Kent County.

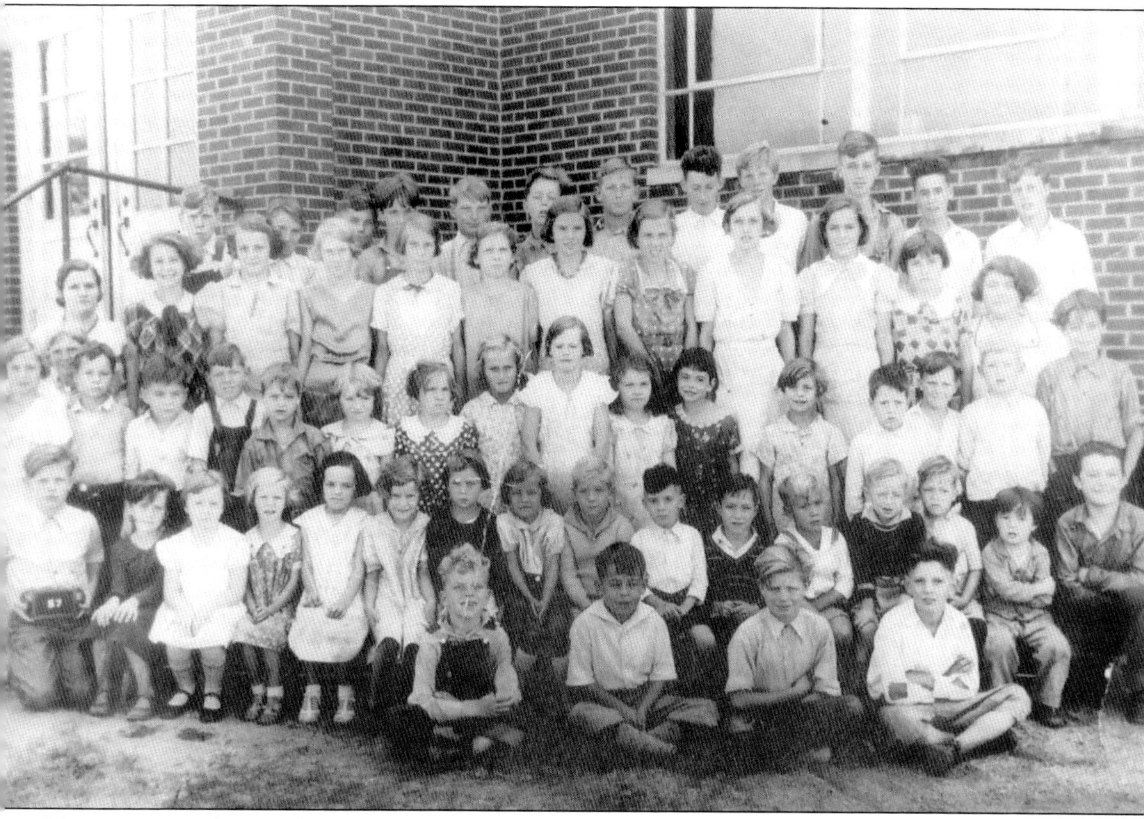

Mrs. Cooper and Mrs. Elberts Edgerton's class of 1934 poses for a photograph. Pictured are (first row) Roger Dunn, Charles Rhean, Paul Cramer, and Bud Fisk; (second row) Ed Cramer, Ann Burrows, Jean Wheeler, Lila Ruge, Joan Gross, Edna Ball, Rovella Tompkin, Nancy Rhean, Bruce Jewell, Gordon Fisk, Arthur Porter, Dewey Jewell, Junior Morris, Aaron Porter, Alfred Ball, and Lewis Ball; (third row) Ella Eberts Crossin (teacher), Jennie Cramer, Eleanor Jones, Jim Tompkins, two unidentified students, June Ives, Isabella Burrows, Dorreen Burrows, Nola Smith, Betty Hamilton, Luella Ball, unidentified, Lyle Ruge, Max Fisk, and Ellis Ball; (fourth row) Rose Cooper (teacher), Noreen Fisk, Charlene Gross, Mildred Loveless, Leona Loveless, Doris Bunn, Esther Gross, Betty Rose, Janet Tompkin, Helen Holcomb, and Ruth Jackson; (fifth row) Hollis Dunn, Howard Holden, Gordon Smith, Arden Ives, Harry Jones, James Burrows, Bill Jones, Gordon Fisk, William Burrows, Herbert Fisk, Earl Grant, and Harold (Bud) ?.

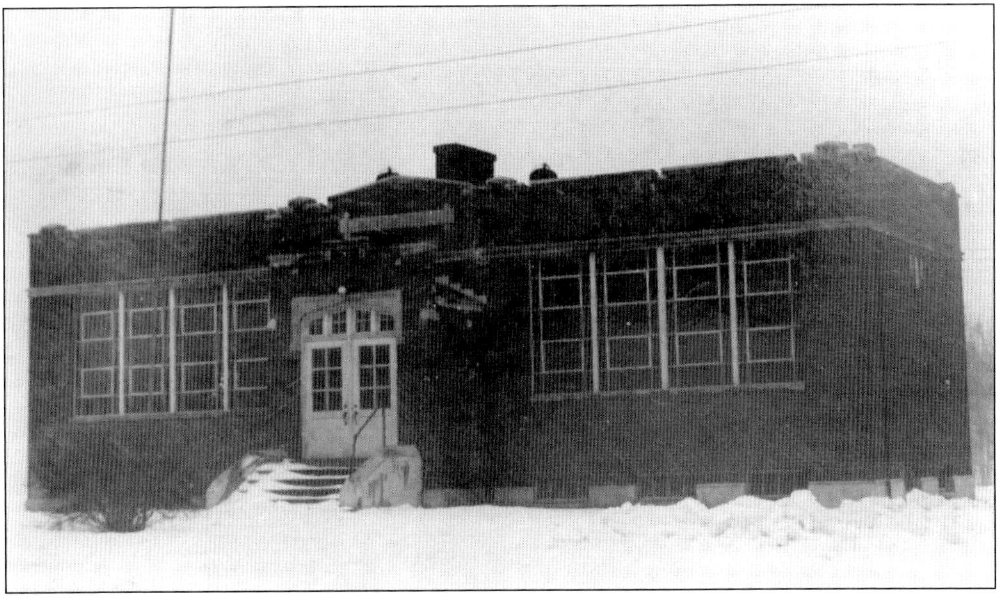

The brick Edgerton School building was on 13 Mile Road, approximately a half mile west of Northland Drive. This two-room school had a cornerstone dated 1926. The building was demolished after being badly damaged in the 1965 tornado. (Donated to the ATHS by W. Gordon Smith.)

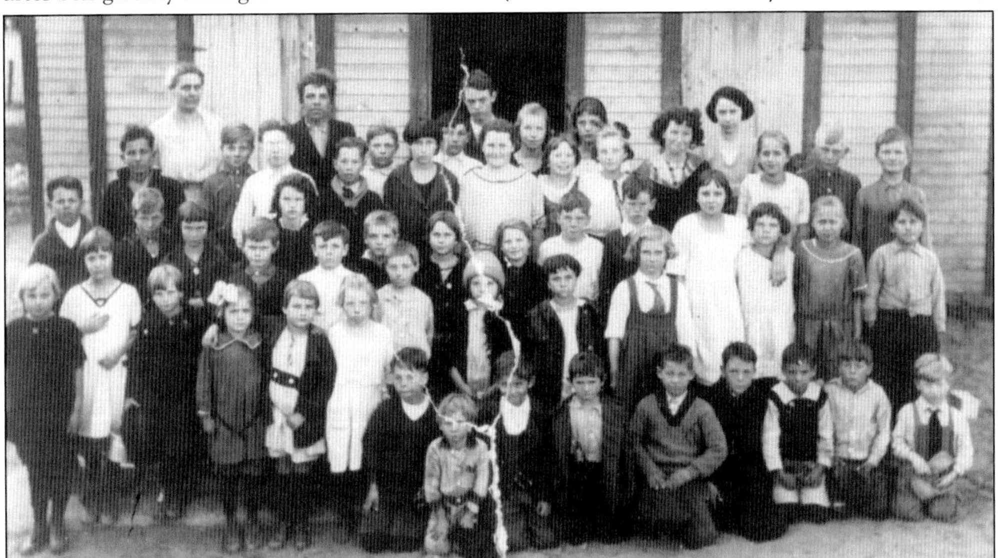

Here are Edgerton School students in 1922. From left to right are (first row) Dorothy Chaffee, Beatrice Evans, Vivian Lewis, Evelyn Gross, Lucille Stevenson, Mary Holden, George Fisk, Clare Horton, Jack Keristlers, Bernice Uplinger, Jim Finch, Robert Nickloson, Wilford Marshal, Clifford Holcomb, and Russell Dunn; (second row) Ervin Holcomb, Alton Porter, Ila Porter, Wayne Burrows, Ilene Porter, Amos Evans, Willie Spicer, Myrtle Bradley, Earl Holden, Ruth Armstrong, Dorothy McNitt, Edith Bradley, Orin Porter, Pearl Thomas, Alfritta Bradley, Helen Keristlers, and Vernon Phieffer; (third row) Harold Gross, Earl Burrows, Ellsworth McNitt, Lyle Finch, Wayne Cramer, Reva Porter, Tobias Spicer, Inez McNitt, Crystal Porter, Gertrude Fisk, France Evans, Arvilla Chaffee, Mildred Porter, Ruby Gross, Forrest Dakens, and Charles Burrows; (fourth row) Mrs. Stevenson, Dale Gross, Aubury Gross Poerwe, and Miss Carry.

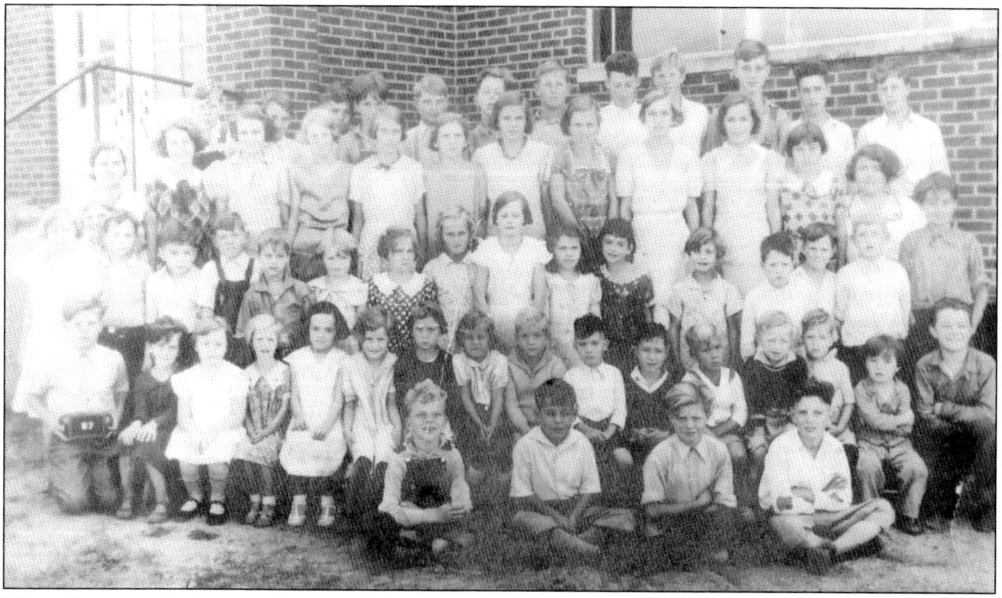

This photograph shows Edgerton School students around 1934. The first person on the left in the second row is one of the teachers, Ella Ebert Crossin. The first person on the left in the third row is the other teacher, Rose Cooper. Longtime families of Algoma represented here include Jewell, Gross, and Fisk.

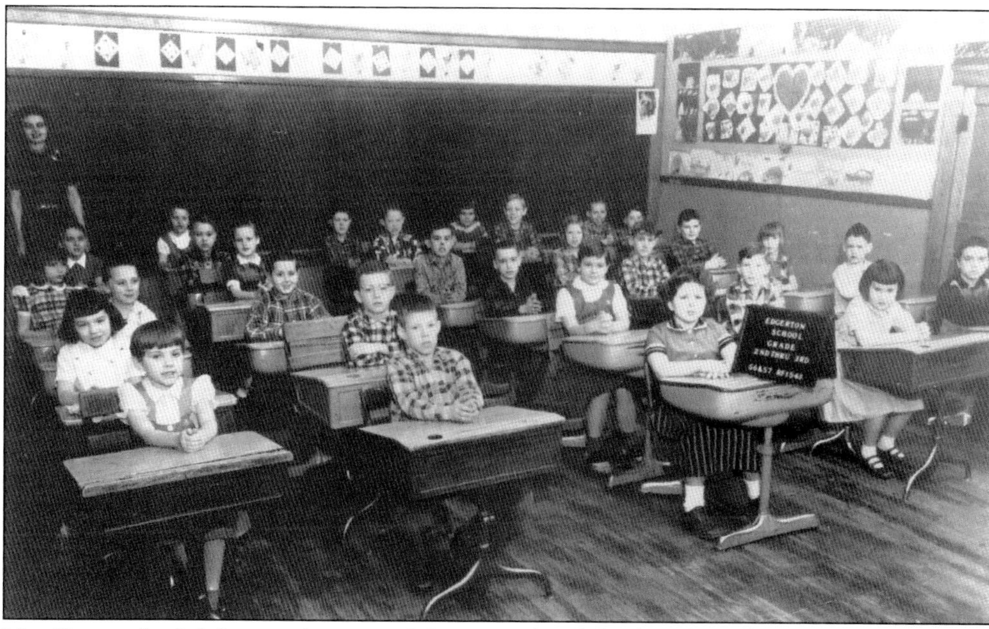

Mrs. Harvey (back left corner) poses with her second and third grade students at Edgerton School in 1956–1957. Pictured are (first row) Cathy Anway, Nancy Smith, Norman Pees, and Chris Vogel, Judy Bean; (second row) Bill Borden, Ronny Moorman, Leonard Fisk, Carol Sue Teesdale, Ronny Johnson, and Mary Tyrell; (third row) Connie Hunting, Sandra Brownyard, Jerry Vogel, Tom Waid, Wayne Peterson, and Richard Nielson; (fourth row) Sharon Richardson, Tom Hoskins, Frank Verdine, Joan Borden, Larry Hoskins, and Susan Burfee; (fifth row) Arnold Magoon, Dick Bouwkamp, Linda Brown, Mike Becker, Ronald Nielson, and Kenneth Smith.

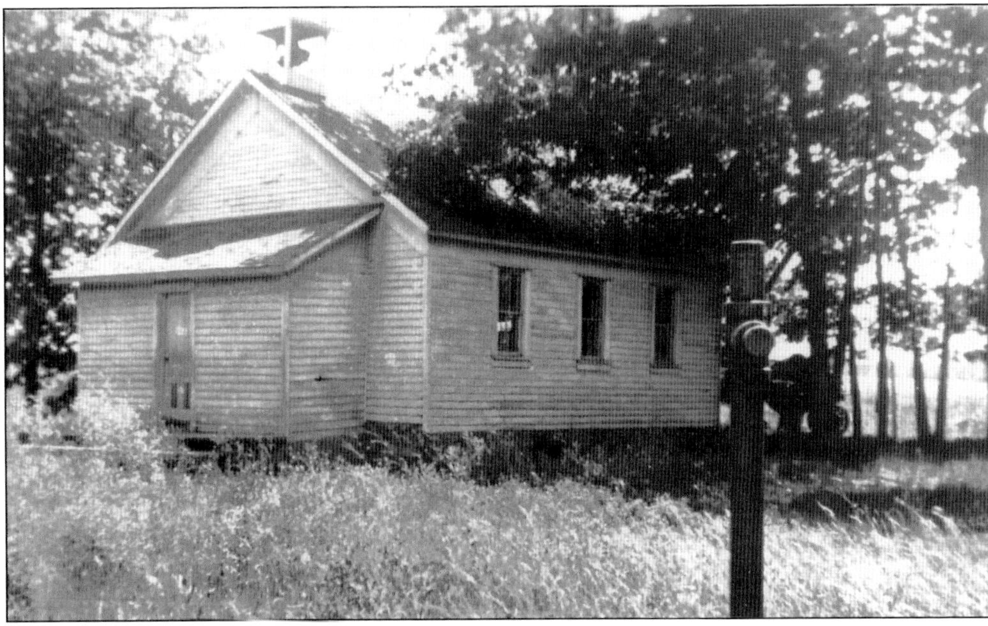

Block School was constructed between 1870 and 1876. Originally located at the corner of 12 Mile Road and Wolven Avenue, it was moved to the southeast corner of 11 Mile Road and Elstner Avenue in the 1920s. In this mid-1940s image, one can see a well pipe, possibly up to a quarter mile into the ground, that never struck water. The school closed in 1942 and was demolished around 1958.

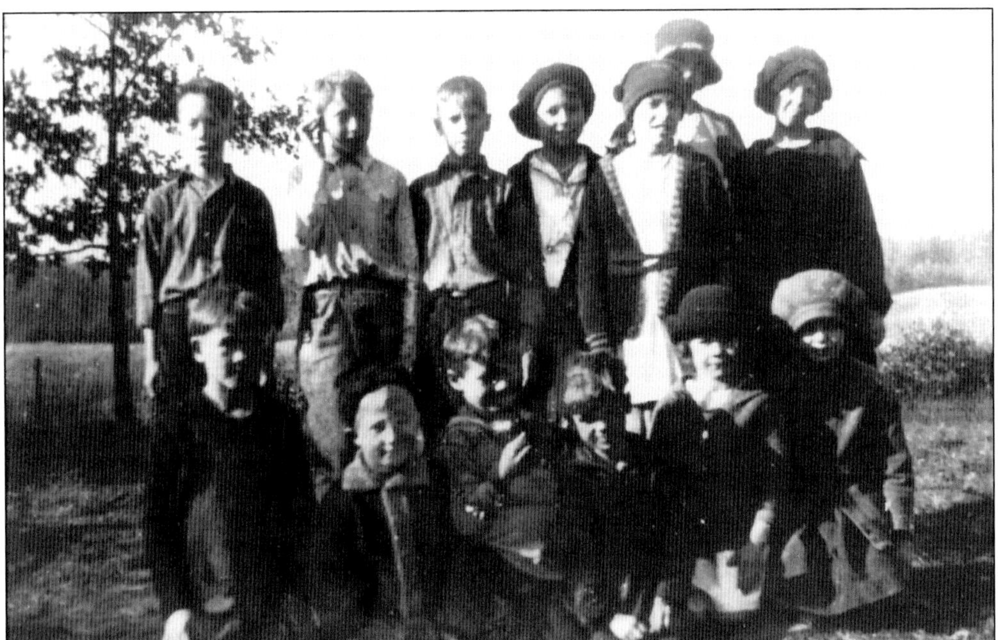

Block School students pose for a group photograph in 1925. From left to right are (first row) Roy Williams, Alfred Elstner, Merlyn Holden, ? Williams, Edith Manbeck, and Bertha Hockeborn; (second row) Howard Wolven, Donaven Turner, Harold Wolven, Martha Cooper, Maxine Post, Anne Hagbom, and Evelyn Elfstrom. (Photograph donated by Bertha Hockeborn Norman.)

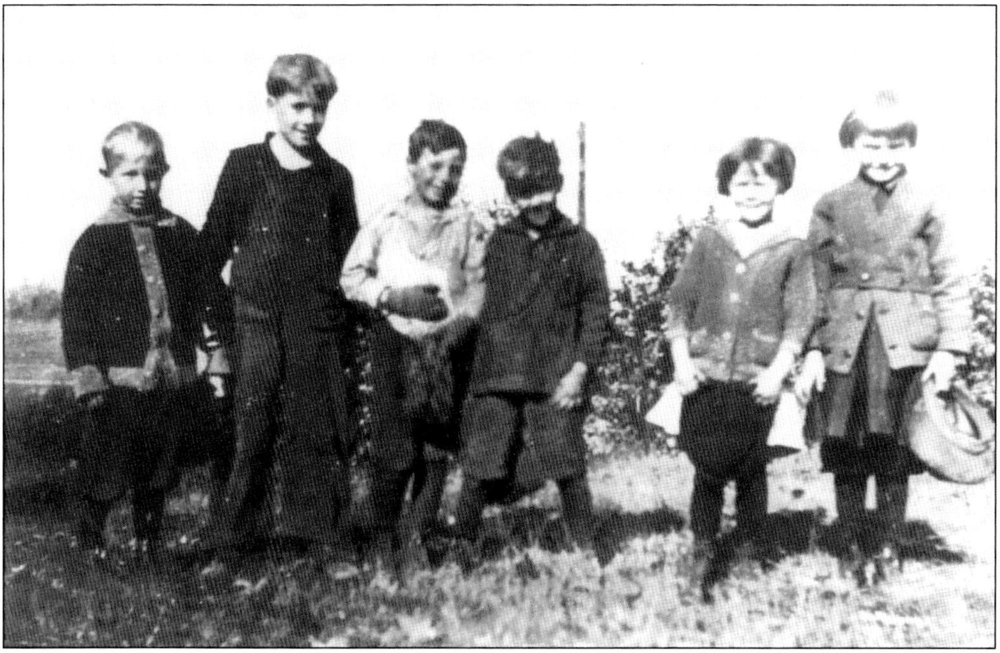

Block School students in 1925 are pictured here. From left to right are Alfred Elstner, Roy Williams, Merlyn Holden, ? Williams, Edith Manbeck, and Bertha Hockeborn.

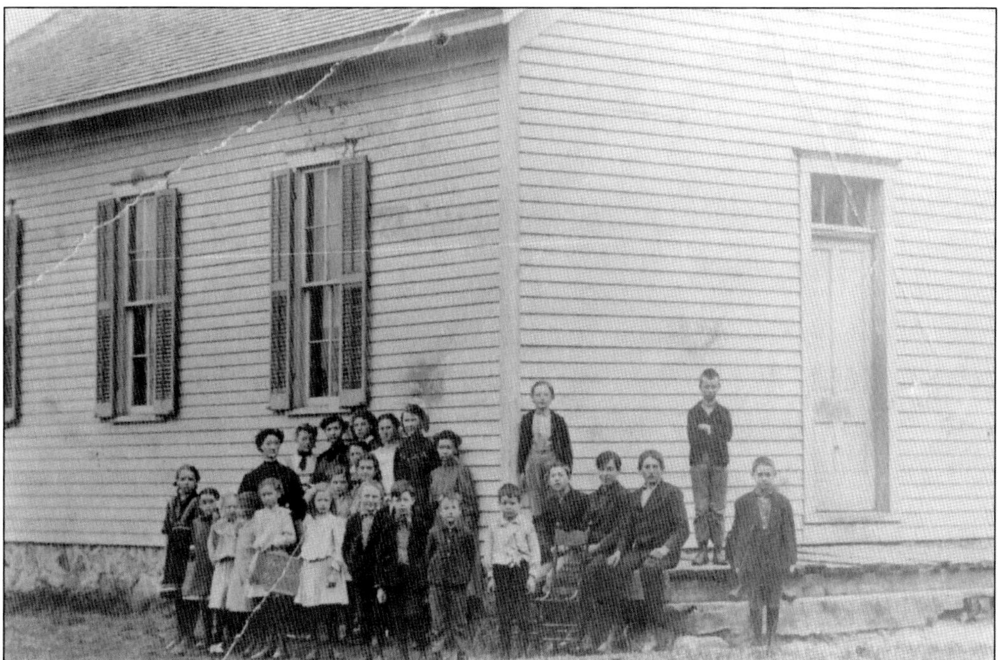

Hull School students stand in front of the building in 1907. The student holding the slate is Lorena Lambert Johnson. Some of the other students include Selma Nyland, Marie Colby and her sister Katherine Stockdale, Glen and Lyle Reyburn, Tressie Putnam, and Loretta Lambert Johnson.

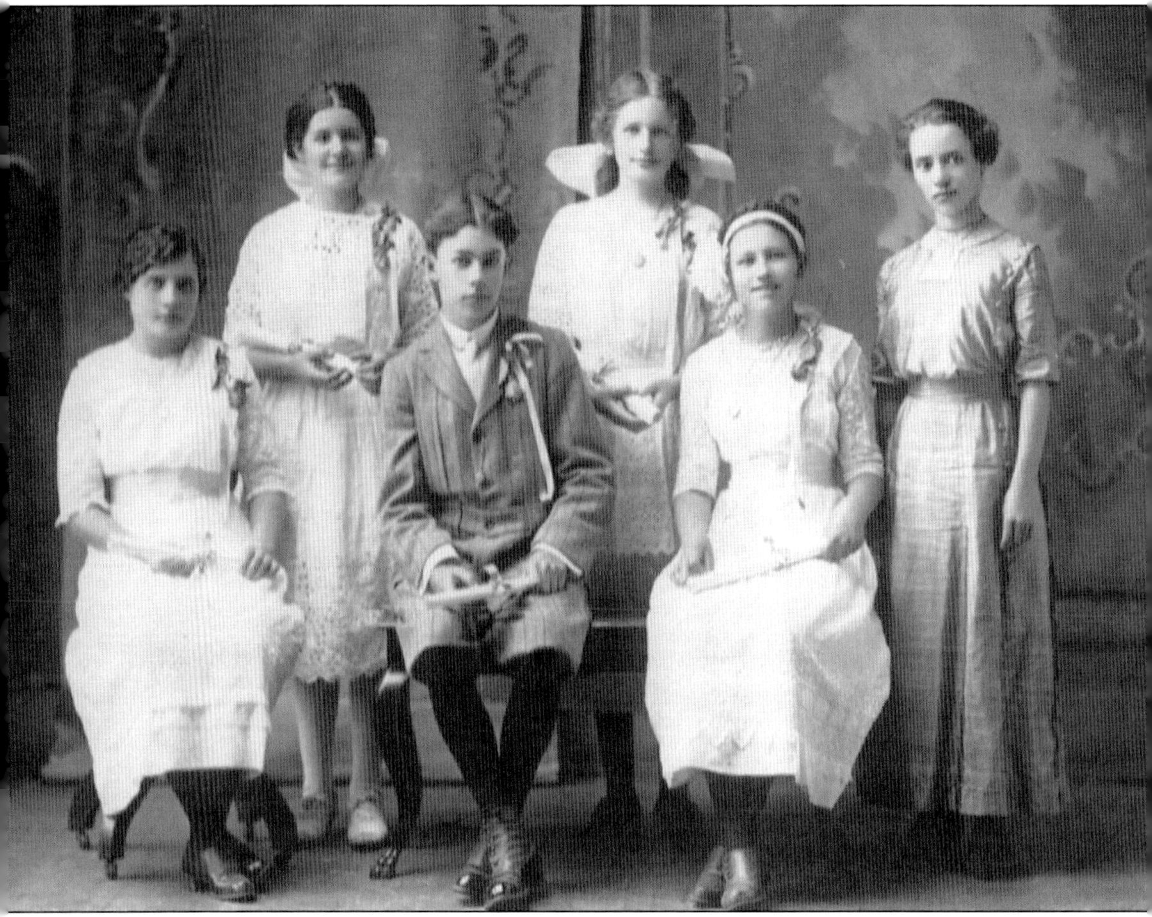

This is an eighth-grade graduating class from Hull School in 1913. Pictured from left to right are Lareta Lambert, Rena Stockdale, Lonna Lambert, Guy Reyburn, Mildred Colby, and teacher Edith Ferguson. (Donated to the ATHS by Ireta Johnson Kraft.)

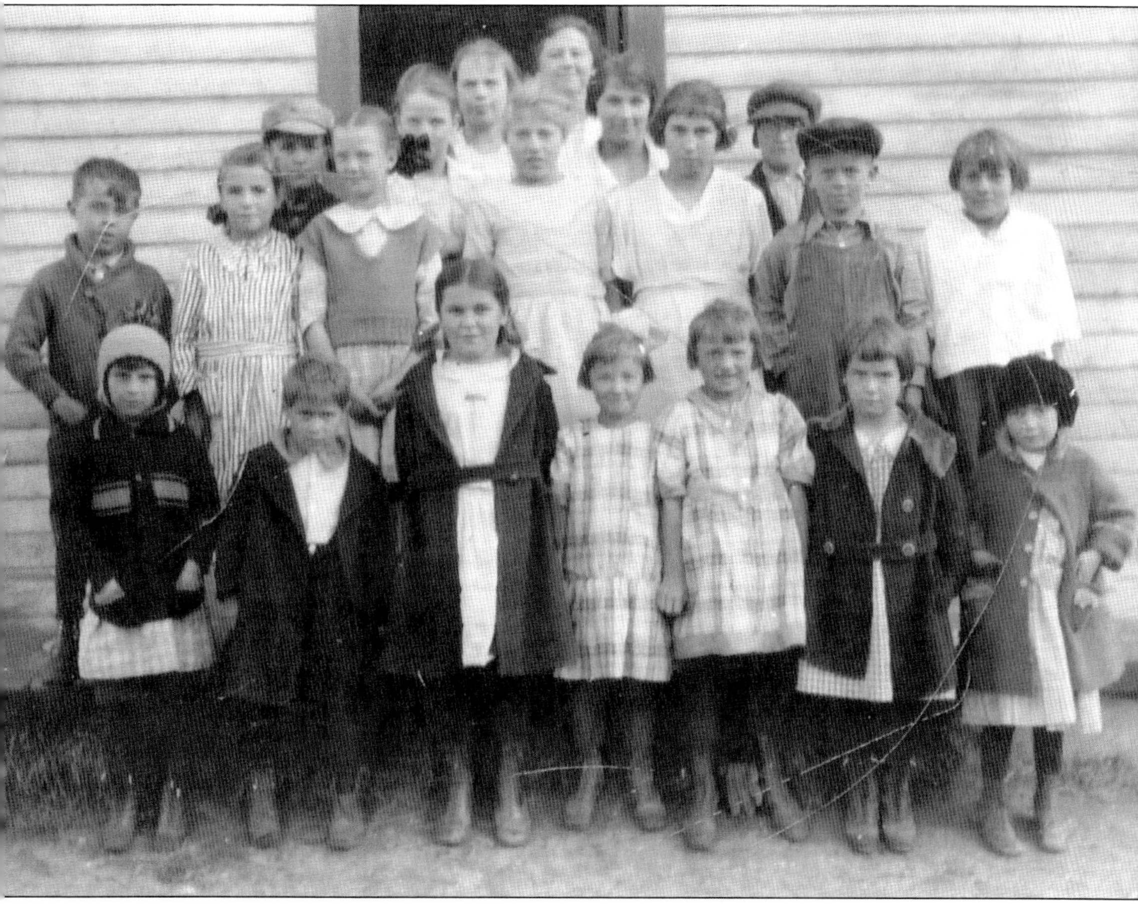

Teacher Mildred Colby's Hull School students pose for the camera in October 1922. Pictured from left to right are (first row) Orida Hull, Howard Hull, Edna Pennington, Garret Bower, Lisa Bower, Loanetah Hull, and Martha Fry; (second row) Wayne Helsel, Wanda Hull, Beth Hull, ? Traxler, Margaret Hull, Royd Suley, and Margerite Traxler; (third row) Victor Pennington, Levia Suley, Lila Suley, Clara Traxler, and Freddie Fry.

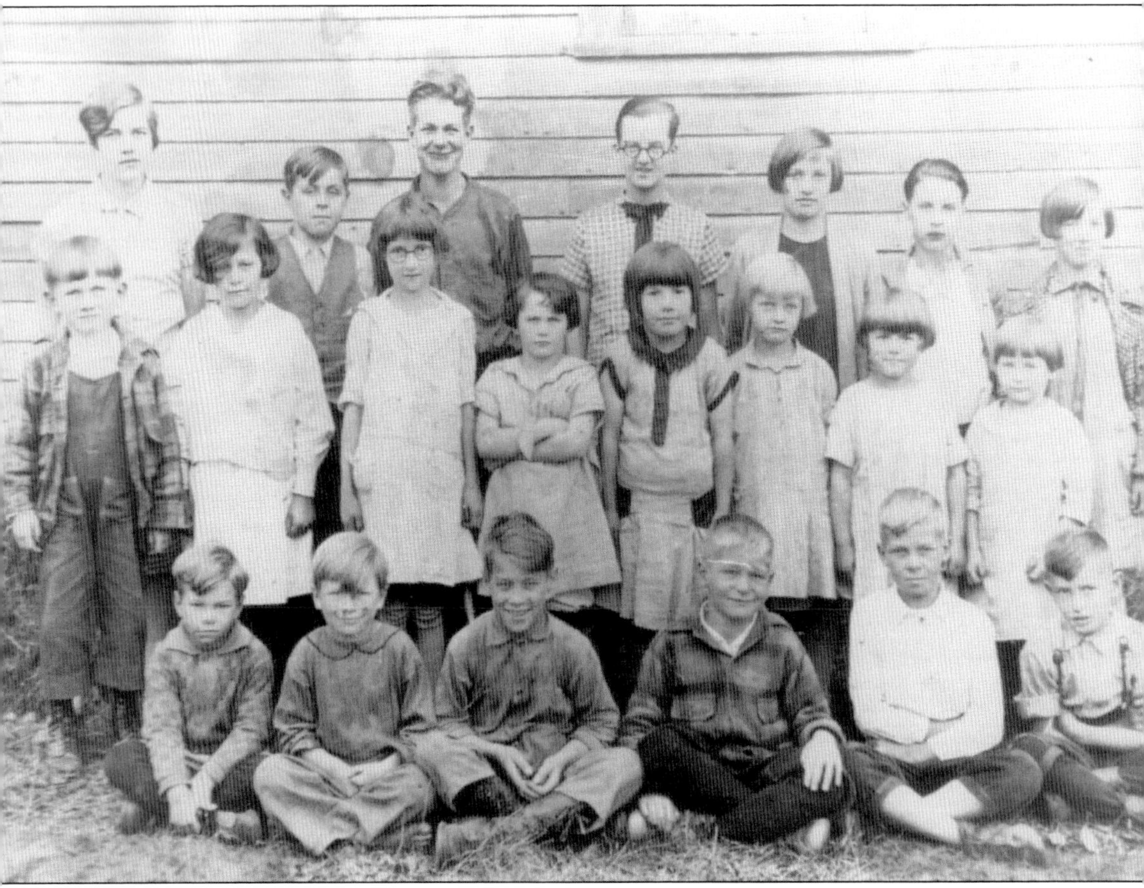

Marion DeJong taught at Hull School and is seen here with her students in 1927. From left to right are (first row) Dale Towns, Carl Reyburn, Howard Hull, Glen Dennis, Claude Dennis, and Beon Bowers; (second row) Howard Reyburn, Florence Owen, Martha Fry, Josephine Owen, Rose Reyburn, Gladys Bowers, Ruth Pennington, and Kittie Reyburn; (third row) DeJong, Wayne Helsel, Ralph Dennis, Beth Hull, Sila Bowers, Orida Hull, and Garnet Bowers.

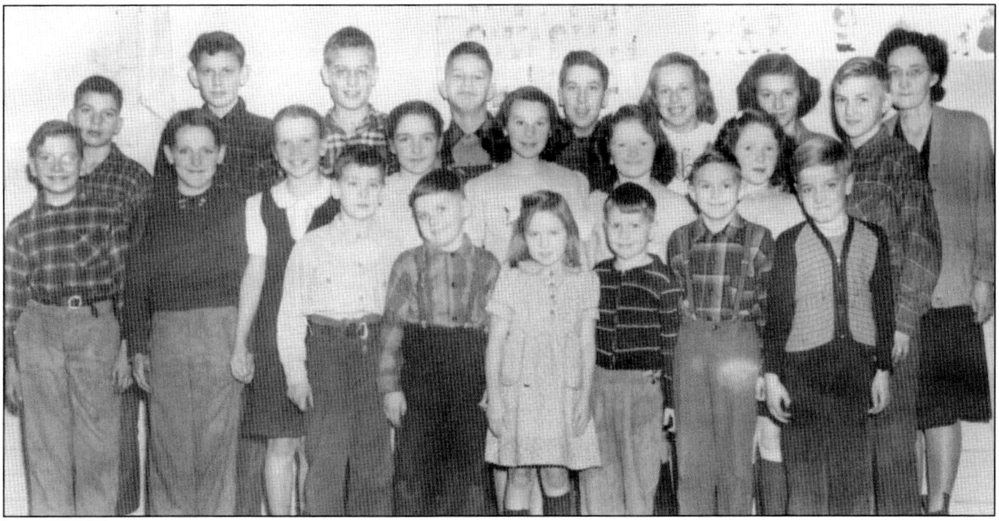

The Hull School class of 1949 poses for a photograph. From left to right are (first row) Earl Mourer, two unidentified students, Gordon Courturier, ? Carlson, and William Westover; (second row) Gordon Johnson, Gale VanDen Broeck, Helen Courturier, Carol Jean VanDen Broeck, Joyce Totten, Judy Van Dyke, and Joyce Van Dyke; (third row) Loren Johnson, Donald Lymburner, Ward Johnson, William Reyburn, Eugene Mourer, Arleen Tuesley, Marcia DeVries, Robert Carlson, and teacher Mrs. Westover.

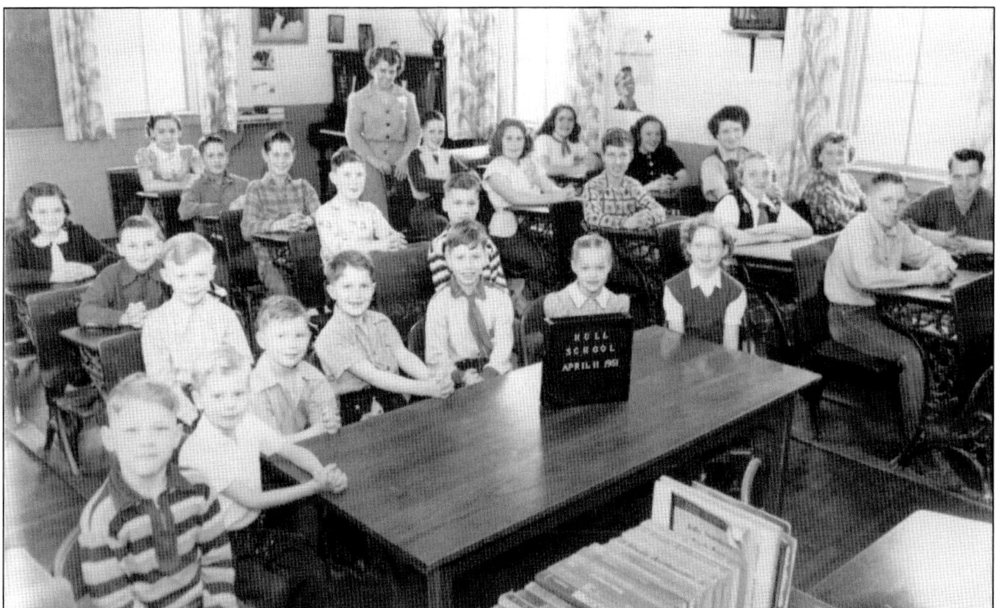

Hull School students pause in 1951 for a classroom photograph with teacher Mrs. Coster. Pictured are (at the table from left to right) Judd Ring, Billy Courson, Joe Seibold, Dick Seibold, Gordon Courtier, Gayle Ring, and unidentified; (first row, front to back) John Elve, unidentified, and Jeanne Coursen; (second row, front to back) Rush Ring, Jack O'Gorman, John Nester, Leon Ingersoll, and Genevieve Gryzen; (third row, front to back) Gale Taylor, June Bristol, Ken Hoaglin, Alicia ?, Gale VanDenBrock, and Coster; (fourth row, front to back) Norman Nester, Dorothy Safford, Joyce Hoaglin, Nellie Barr, and ? VanDenBrock.

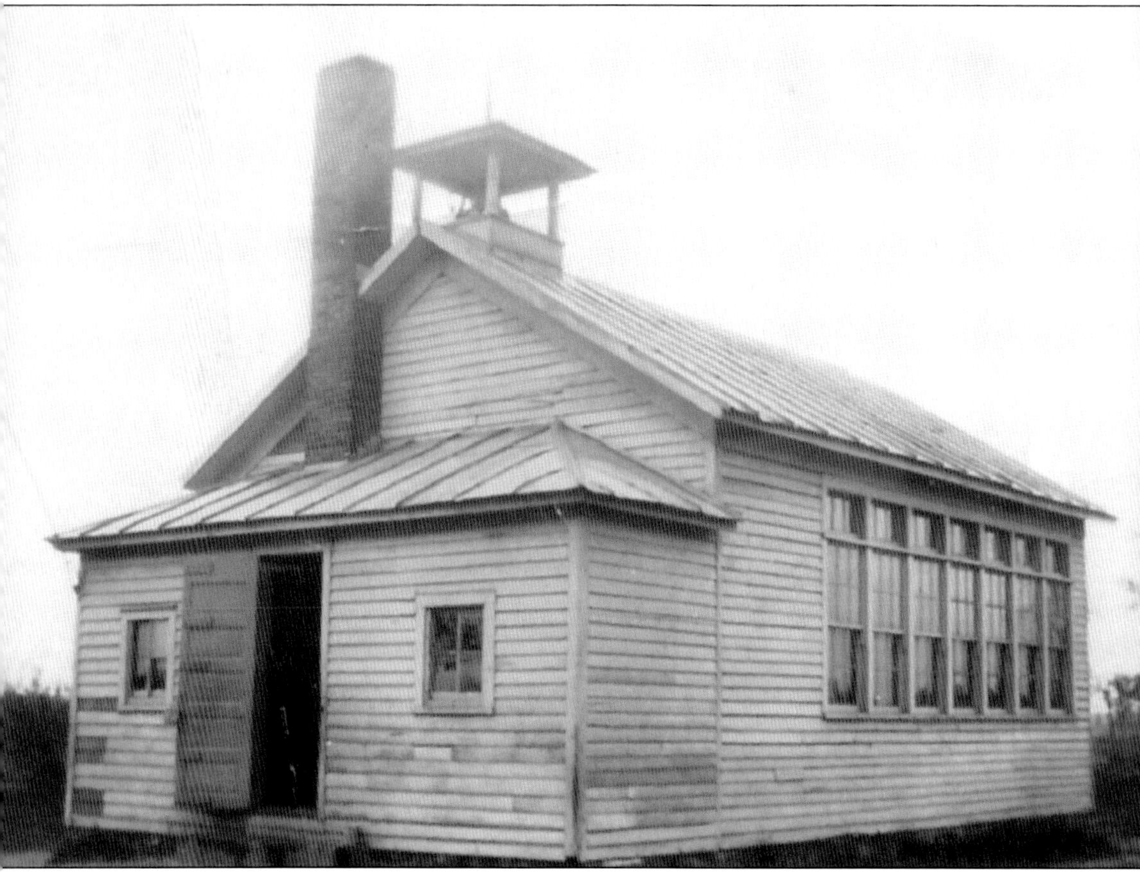

This photograph of Foxville School was taken in 1928. The school was likely named after Amon Fox, who owned the property on which the initial school was built. It was later moved across the road and renovated; windows were added to the north side to fix lighting issues.

Established in the 1860s, Burchtown School was located on Indian Lakes Road Northeast. It was near a town or settlement known as either Burchtown, Burchville, or simply Burch's Depot (there are railroad tracks nearby, to the east). The school closed in 1961.

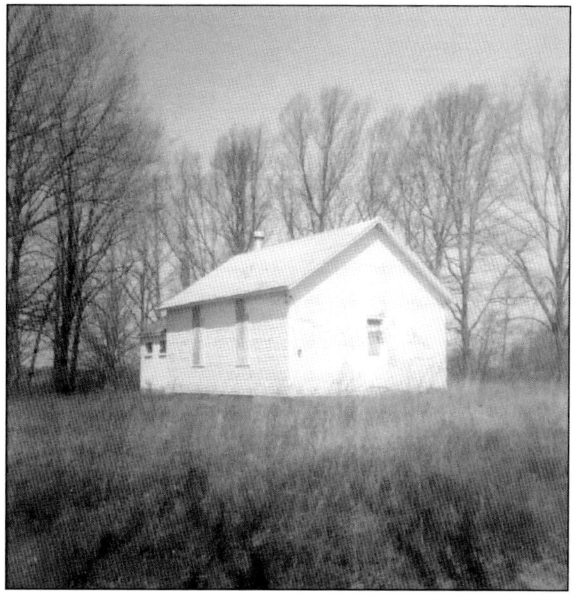

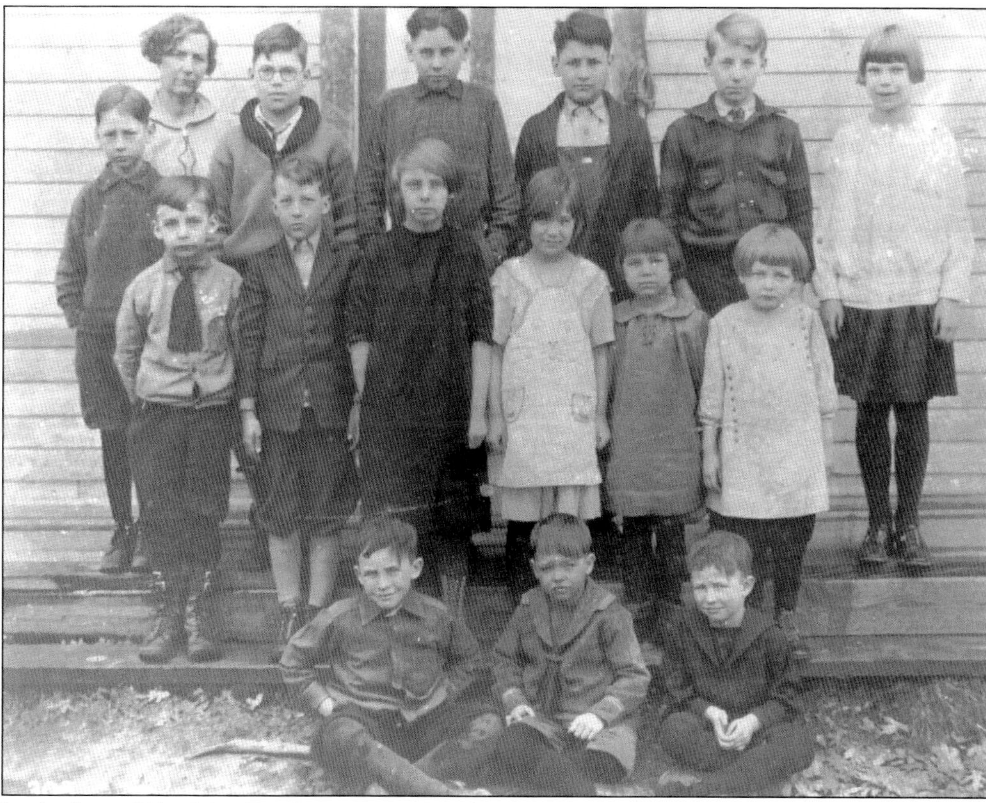

In the late 1920s, Mrs. Frank Peterson's Burchtown School students pose for the camera. From left to right are (first row) Jack Kelly, Charles "Bud" Nason, and Junior Kelly; (second row) Henry Hoskins, Ivan Gates, Dorothy Hoskins Smith, Hazel Nason Gilbert, Mary Nason Noe, and Jean Hudson Keeft; (third row) Niel West, Rober Nason, Edward West, Max Humphrey, Howard Tompsett, and Barbara Nason.

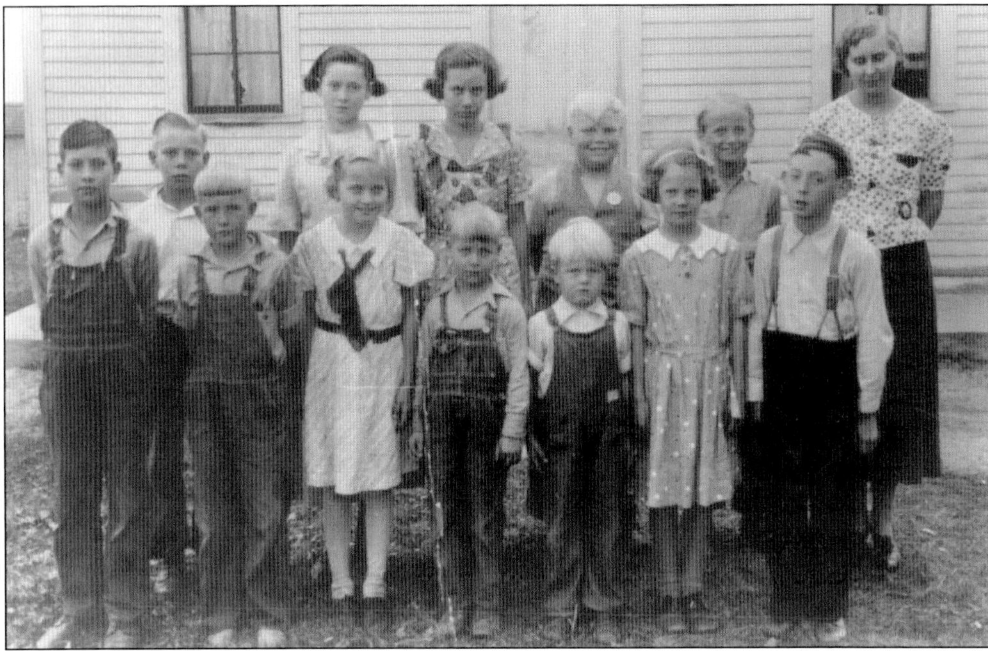

Morningstar School students, under the tutelage of teacher Mrs. Weaver, are seen here. From left to right are (first row) Charles ?, Bill O., Ruth Hammerlind, Robert H, Robert E., Helen Peck (Miller), and two unidentified; (second row) Albert Hammerlind, Jane ?, Dorothy ?, George Frazer, Lyle Proctor, and Weaver.

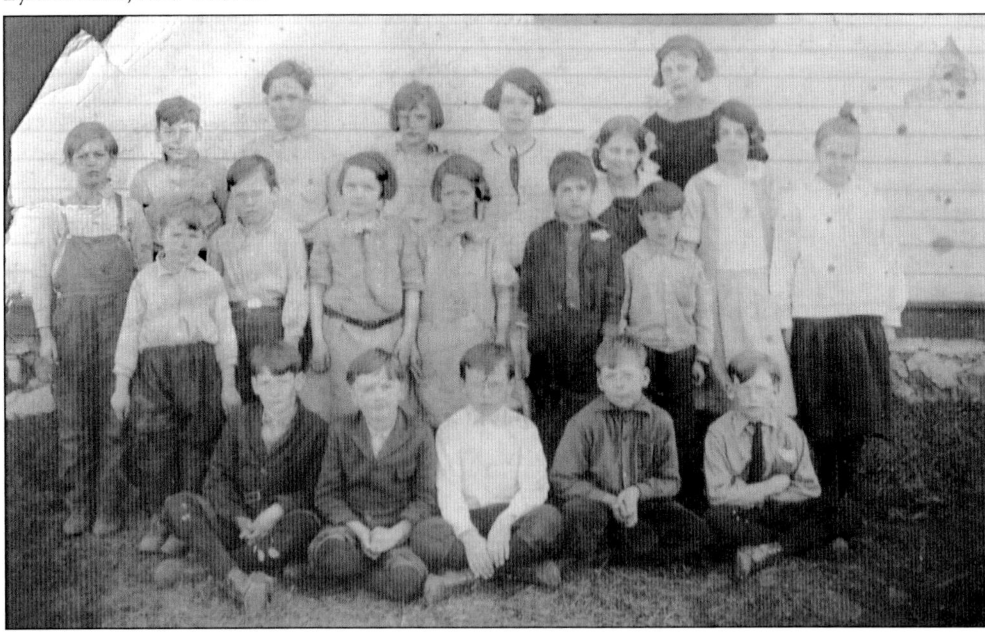

Under the guidance of teacher Orsie Benham, this is a Morningstar School class. From left to right are (first row) Martin Ingersoll, Raymond Burkhorst, Norman Parks, Robert Norman, and Lowell Ingersoll; (second row) Forrest Norman, Arthur Parks, Doris Rawson, Irene Ingersoll, Donald Davis, and Robert Ingersoll; (third row) Harry Bottruff, Clinton Ingersoll, Clare Caine, Ruth Jean Filkins, Florence Ingersoll, Ruth King, Orsie Benham, Bessie Ingersoll, and Bernice King.

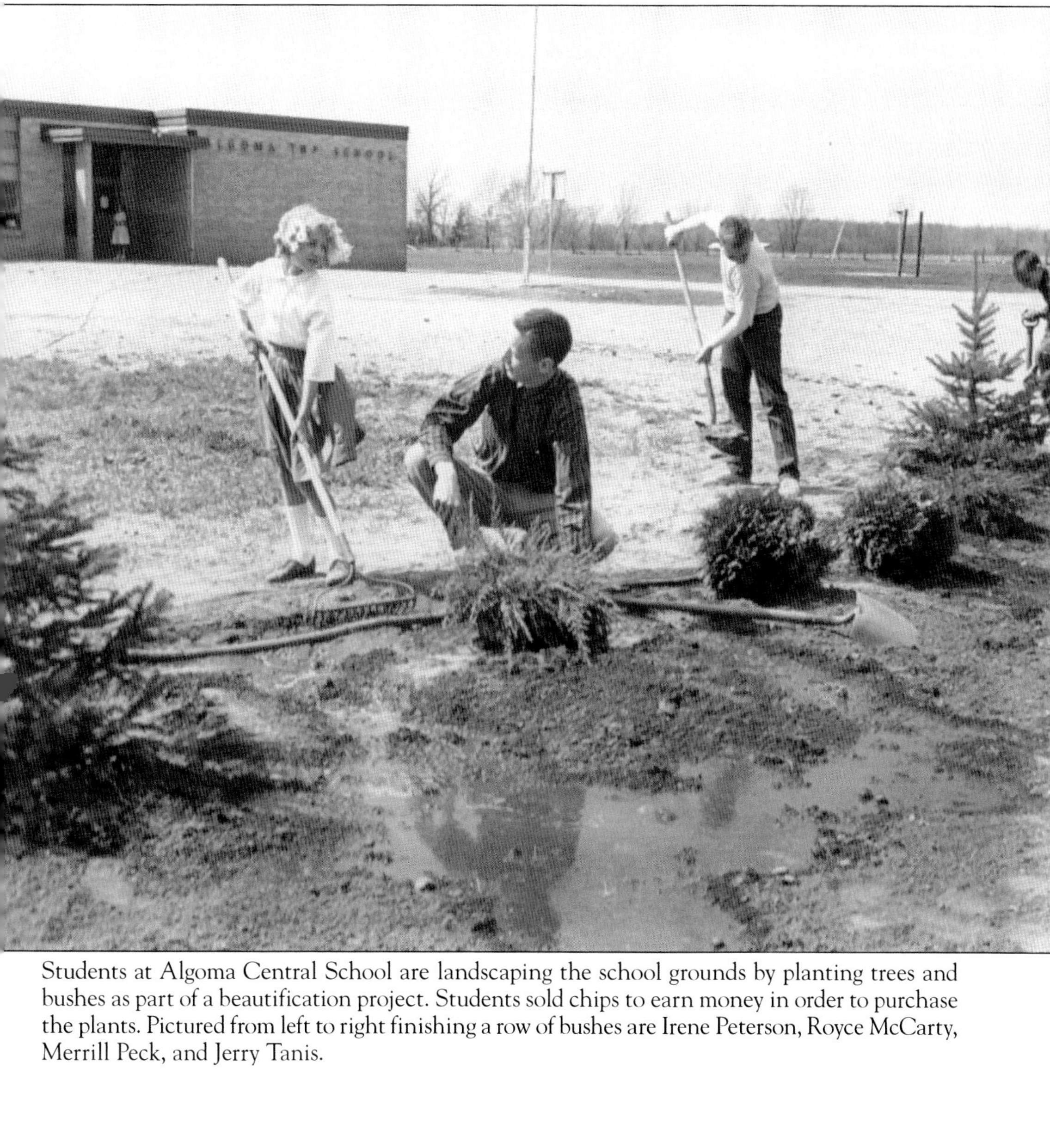

Students at Algoma Central School are landscaping the school grounds by planting trees and bushes as part of a beautification project. Students sold chips to earn money in order to purchase the plants. Pictured from left to right finishing a row of bushes are Irene Peterson, Royce McCarty, Merrill Peck, and Jerry Tanis.

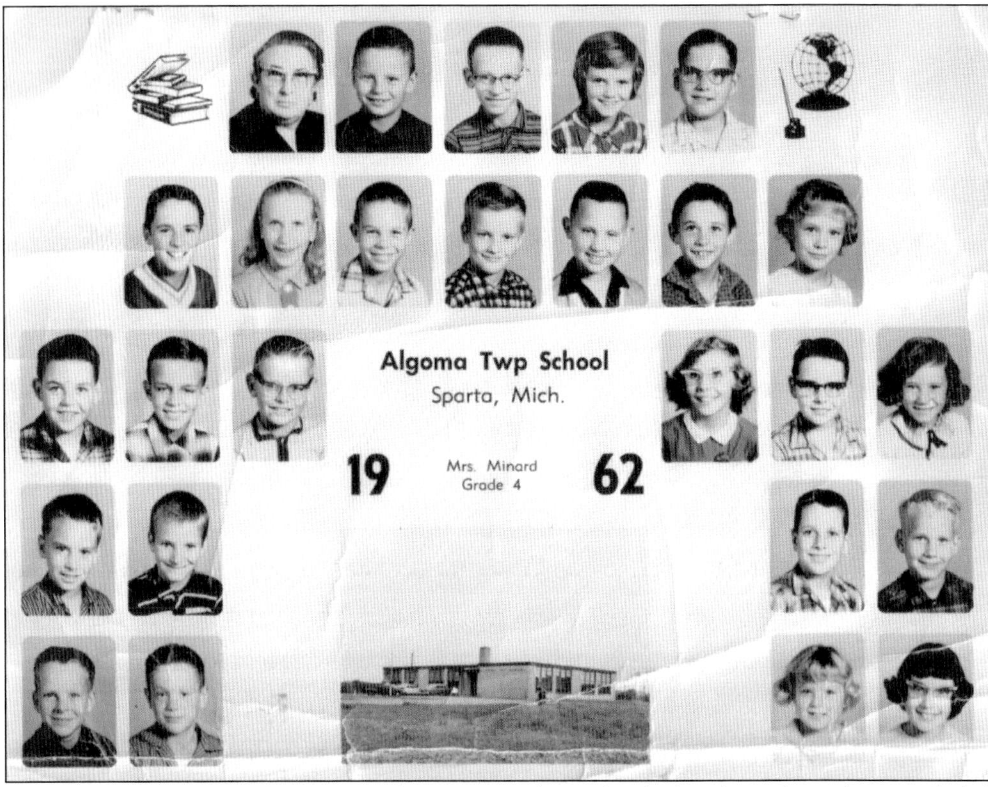

During the 1962–1963 school year, Algoma Township School's fourth grade students included, from left to right, (first row) Keith Teesdale, Tom Knight, Donna Buczynski, and Cindy Marvin; (second row) Archie Ingersoll, Greg Mosher, John Szubinski, and Terry Lacy; (third row) John Mosher, Wayne Wheeler, Scott Merryman, Linda Fries, Bob Teesdale, and Linda Behm; (fourth row) Allen Ingersol, Mae Ingersoll, Larry Scholten, David Mapes, Steve Mieras, Rohn Crystal, and Martha Lamphear; (fifth row) teacher Mrs. Minard, Fred Schmid, Dan Batchelder, Sue Wiggins, and Max Derks.

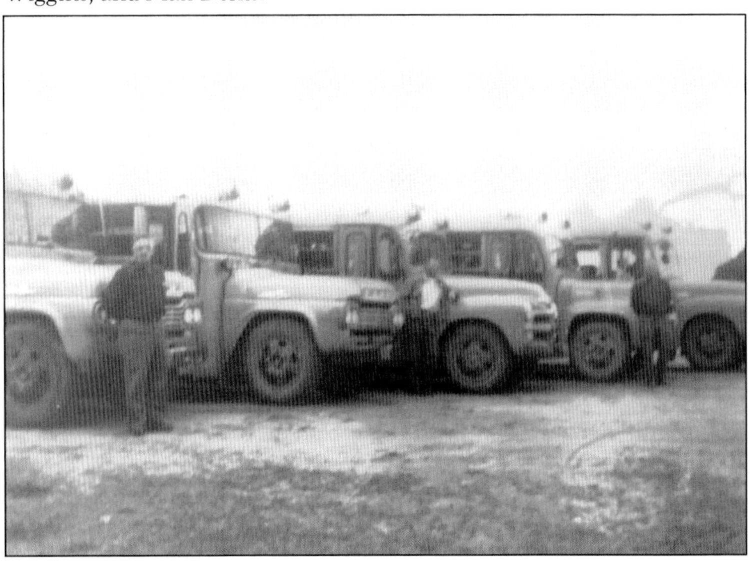

Algoma Township school buses and drivers are seen here in May 1967. From left to right are "Doc" Luckey, Dick Koert, Don Grey, and Bob Dufort; one driver not pictured is Irvin Flanagan. This was the last year Algoma bused its students before they started attending Cedar Springs, Rockford, and Sparta schools.

Pictured in 1912 is United Brethren Church. Early community settlers in Algoma founded the church before Swedish settlers bought and renamed it Algoma Baptist Church. A more modern church building has since been constructed here, across from the Algoma Cemetery on Grange Avenue.

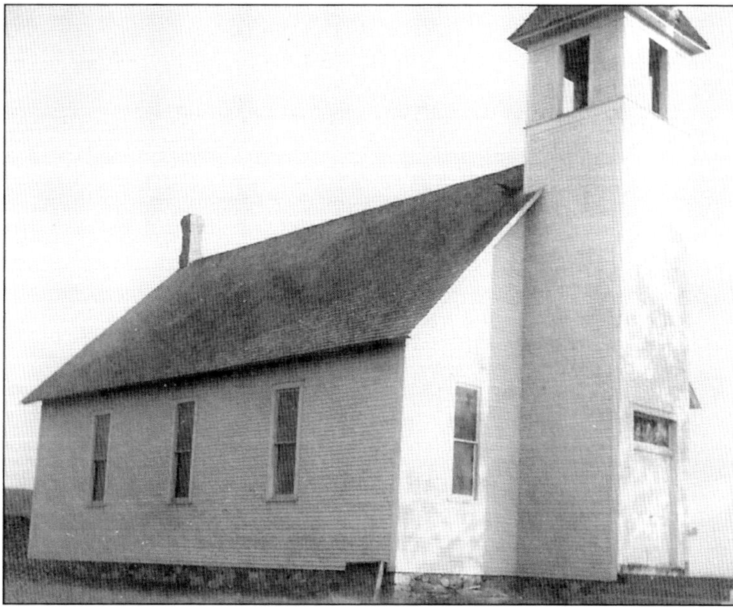

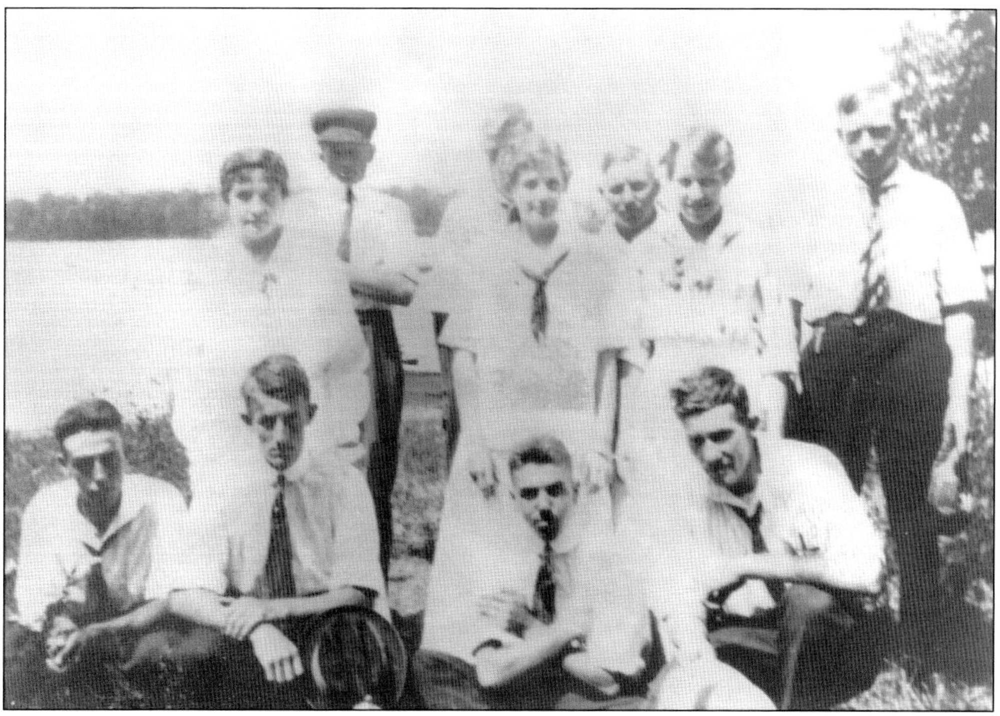

Here is a United Brethren Sunday school class picnic. Pictured from left to right are (first row) Harry Minion, Marvin Field Jr., Clifford Johnson, and Rowland Dillie; (second row) Lareta (Johnson) Lambert, Marcus Bloom, unidentified, Larena (Johnson) Lambert, Harry Anderson, Zelda Dillie, and Victor Johnson.

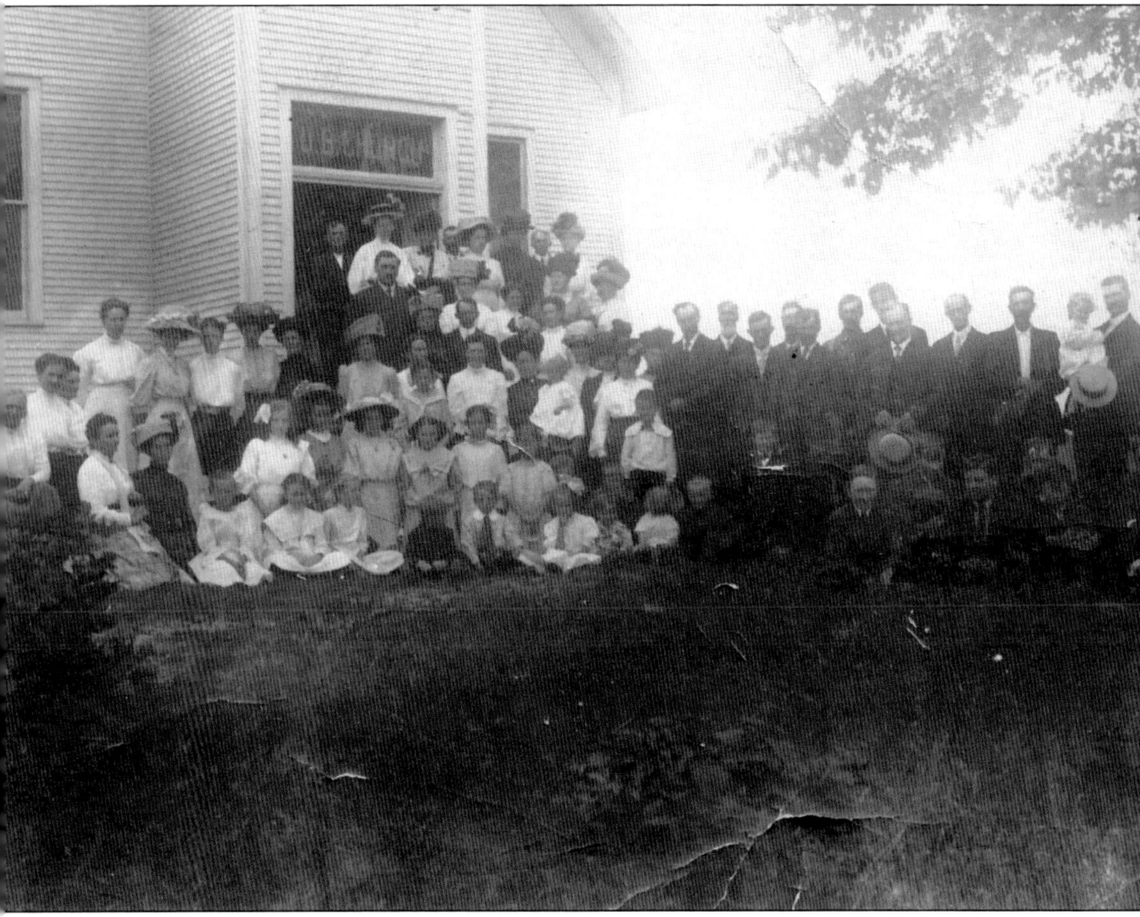

Algoma Baptist Church initially rented and shared a building with United Brethren Church before purchasing it outright in 1921. The church bought an additional 20 acres across the street and constructed a new building there. Vacant since 1969, the congregation conveyed their interest in the structure to Algoma Township in 1998, and the township demolished it in October 2004 because it was cost prohibitive to preserve the historic building.

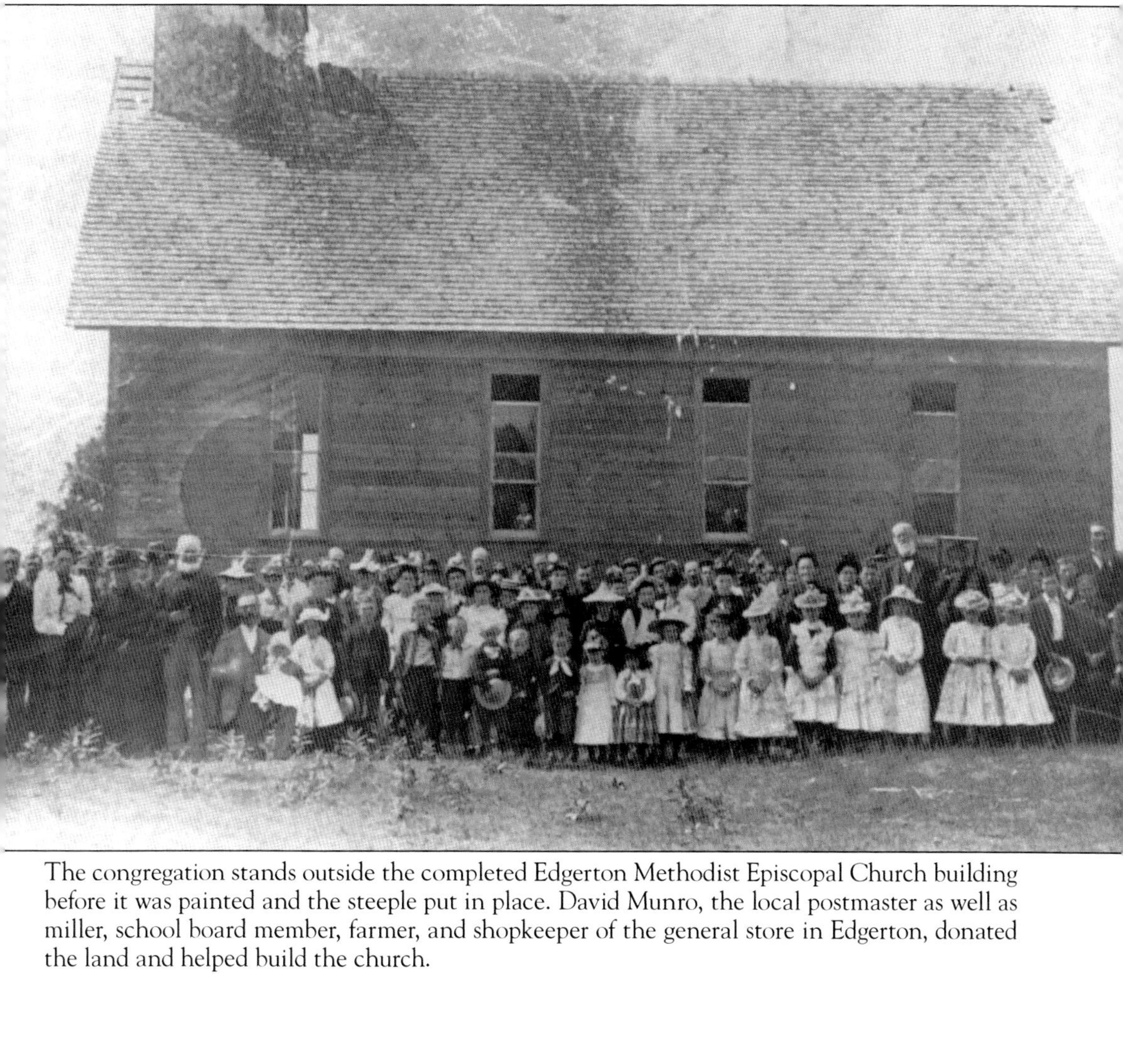

The congregation stands outside the completed Edgerton Methodist Episcopal Church building before it was painted and the steeple put in place. David Munro, the local postmaster as well as miller, school board member, farmer, and shopkeeper of the general store in Edgerton, donated the land and helped build the church.

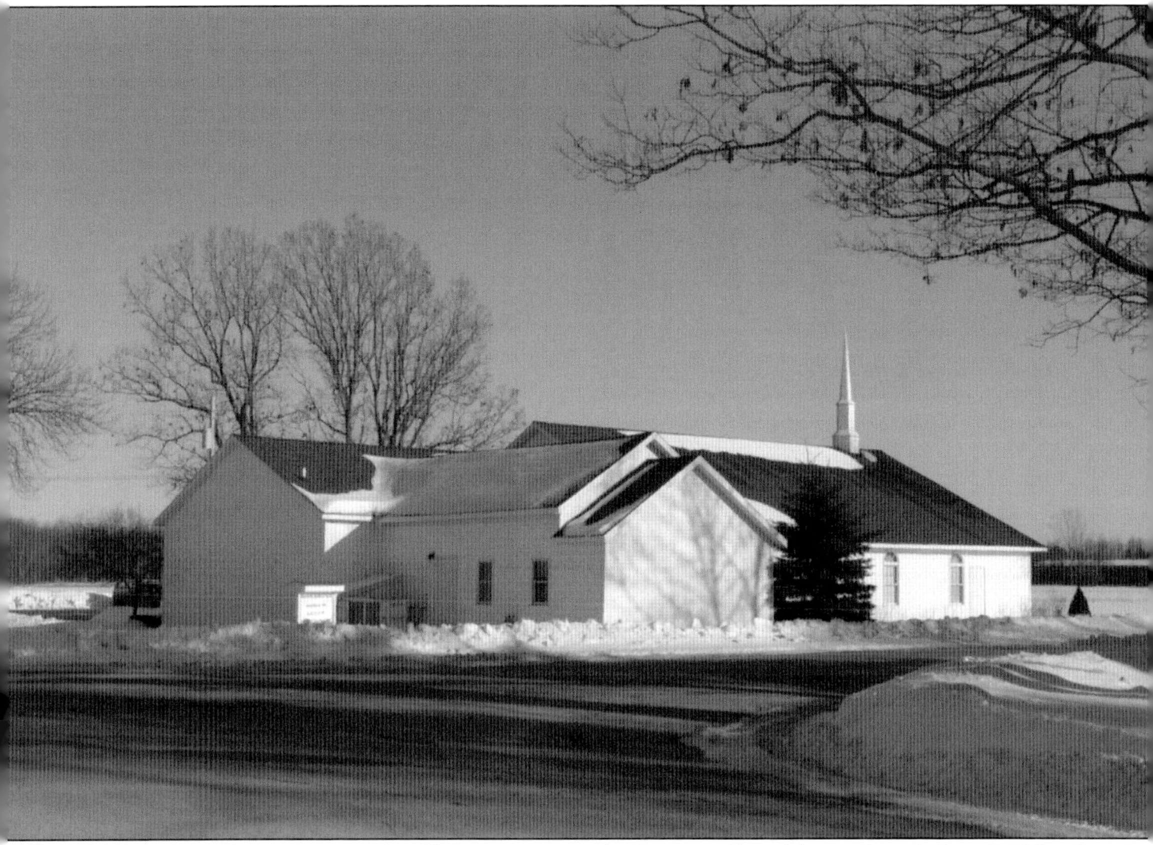

Maranatha Community Church (now Maranatha Baptist Church) was founded in 1980 by the Calkins, Hoskins, Lundin, and Sargent families. The church began under the leadership of Pastor Jim Calkins in Edgerton but moved to the old Foxville School on the corner of Indian Lakes Road and Algoma Avenue due to congregation growth. Multiple additions were made to the original building.

Three

Farms and Homes

Farming helped support and grow the community of Algoma Township when logging slowed down. The various farms in the area produced all types of dairy, livestock, and produce. Without that vast variety, the township would have faded away. The richness of the soil drew settlers to an area that established itself because of agriculture.

The homes Algoma residents live in are filled with memories, and though many of them no longer exist, photographs and relics paint a picture of life in the past in the township. These homes were built by hand, and they reflect the hard work residents put into creating a community of family, worship, and commerce.

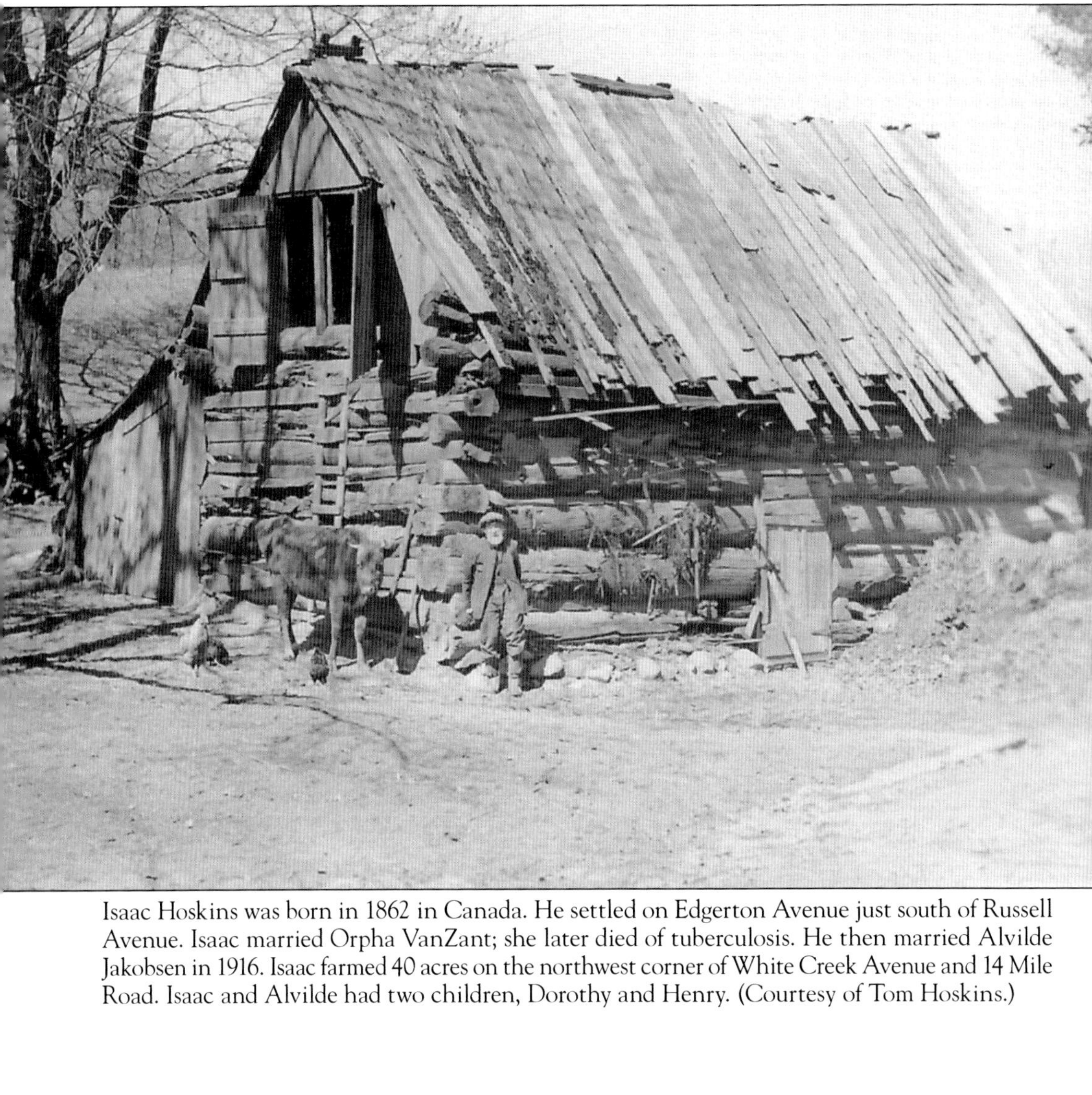

Isaac Hoskins was born in 1862 in Canada. He settled on Edgerton Avenue just south of Russell Avenue. Isaac married Orpha VanZant; she later died of tuberculosis. He then married Alvilde Jakobsen in 1916. Isaac farmed 40 acres on the northwest corner of White Creek Avenue and 14 Mile Road. Isaac and Alvilde had two children, Dorothy and Henry. (Courtesy of Tom Hoskins.)

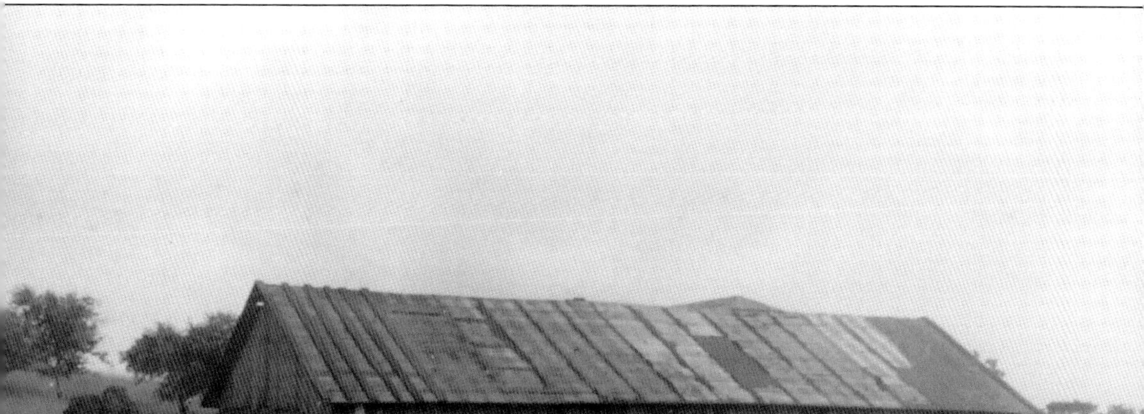

Norman Ackley erected Caine's Sawmill, also known as Morningstar Mill, in 1852. James Caine emigrated from the Isle of Man, and when he arrived in America he purchased part of the mill in 1866 and rebuilt it. He married Mrs. M. Rappleyea Fearson. Following James's death by lightning strike in the mid-1870s, Mrs. Caine called upon J. Thayer Gould to run the mill.

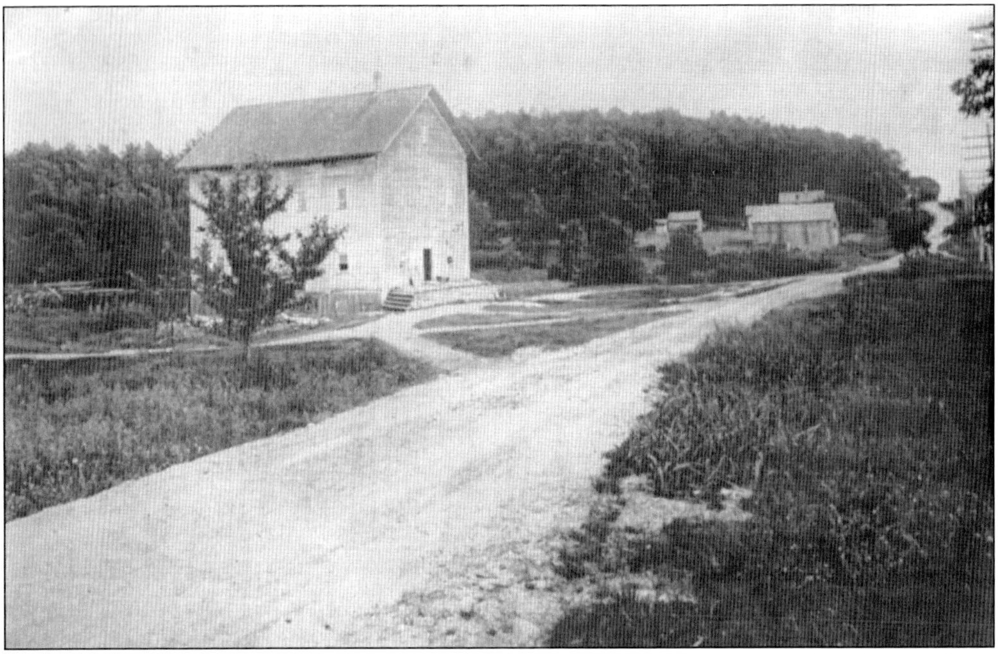

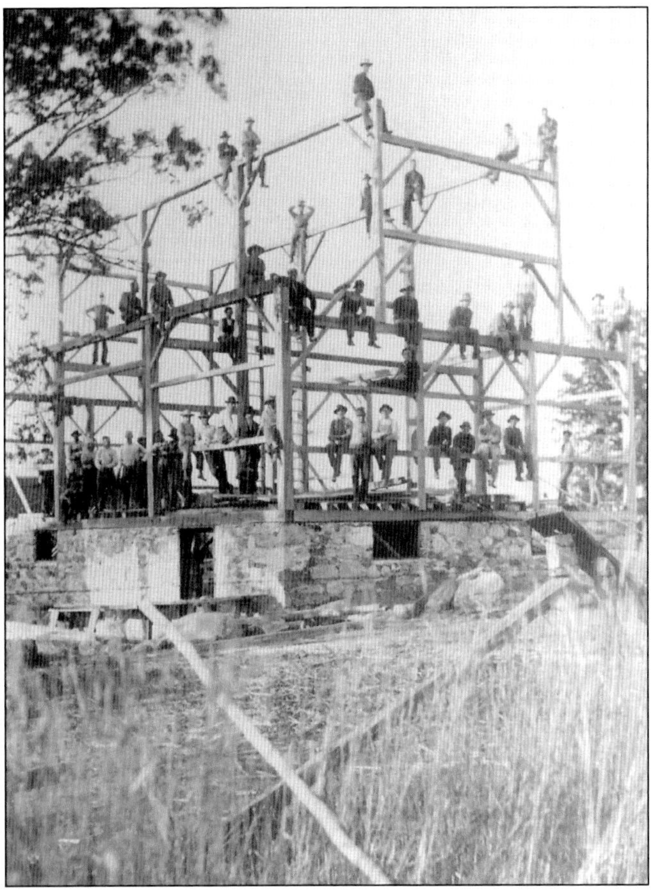

The gristmill, or flour mill, in Algoma Township was run by David Munro, starting 1875. The three-and-a-half story building was an addition to a sawmill constructed 20 years prior. The mill ran for more than 61 years, succumbing to fire on April 7, 1936.

Morris and Ollie Bowler, who came from Ireland, settled the Bowler farm in 1877. It is located on 140 acres on 15 Mile Road, where they raised livestock and grew feed crops potatoes. This photograph is of a barn raising in 1885. The farm was designated a Michigan Centennial Farm in 1996.

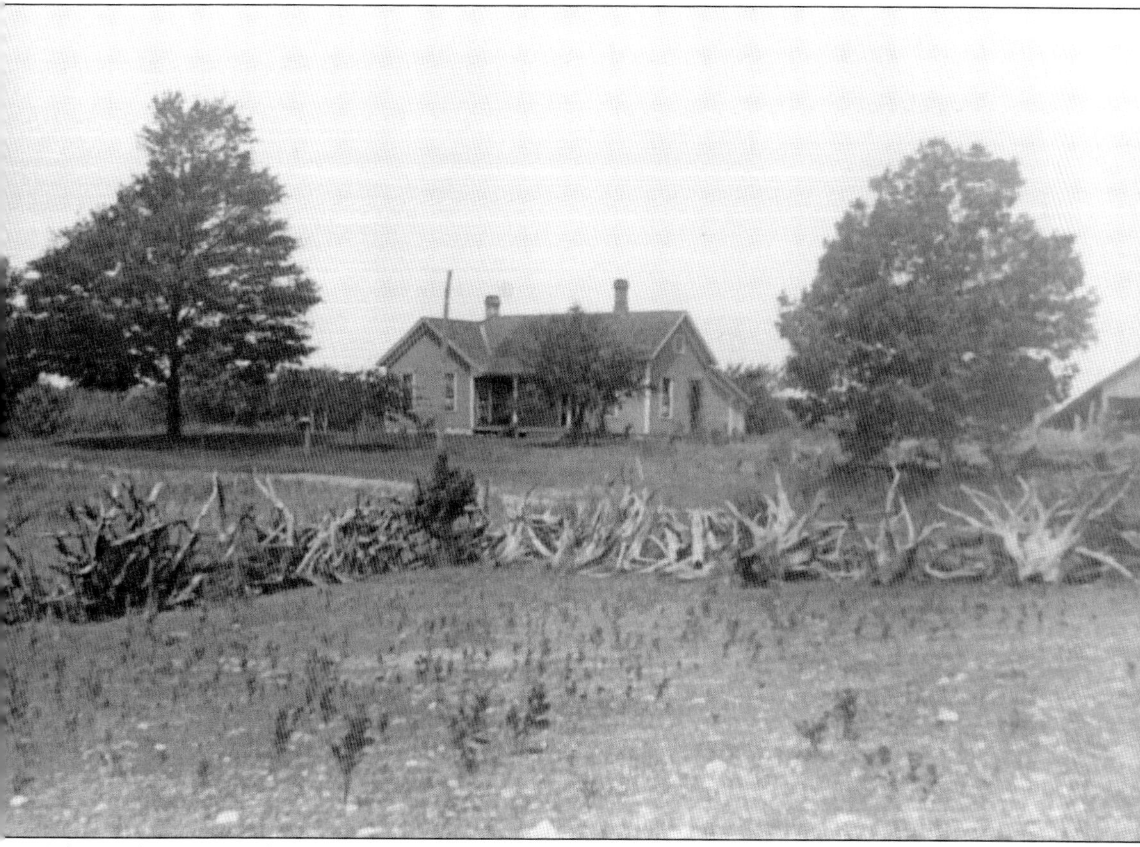

John and Emma Erickson were married in Sweden in 1873 and moved their family to America in 1881. After living in Chicago and Bangor, Maine, the Ericksons moved to Algoma Township. They built a home at 1591 Rector Road, pictured here. Their children Albin, Eric, Anna (Sjogren), Selma (Peterson), Edward, and Edith (Friske) were born before John and Emma moved the family to Algoma.

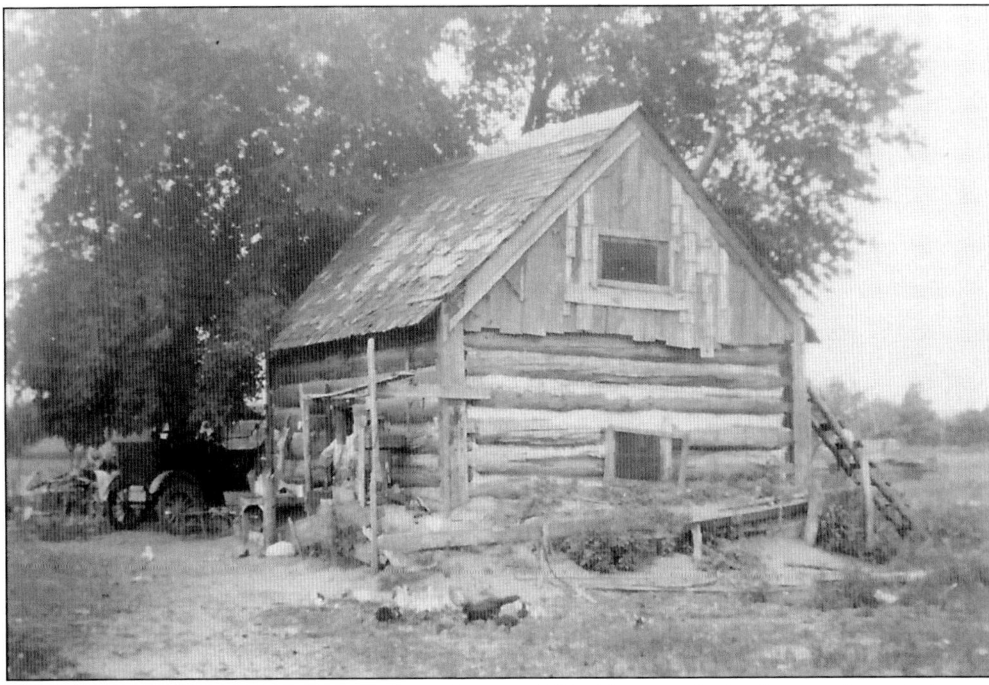

John Wesley Hoskins married Fannie Jane Yates in 1903. Above is the log home where their nine children were raised, on Hoskins Avenue near Cedar Creek. The cedar shingles sometimes would catch fire via sparks from the chimney. The boys took turns climbing up to put them out. Below is the new frame home under construction in 1929. Their sons were unable to complete it before Fannie died in 1931. (Above, courtesy of Janet Lynn Hoskins; below, courtesy of Tom Hoskins.)

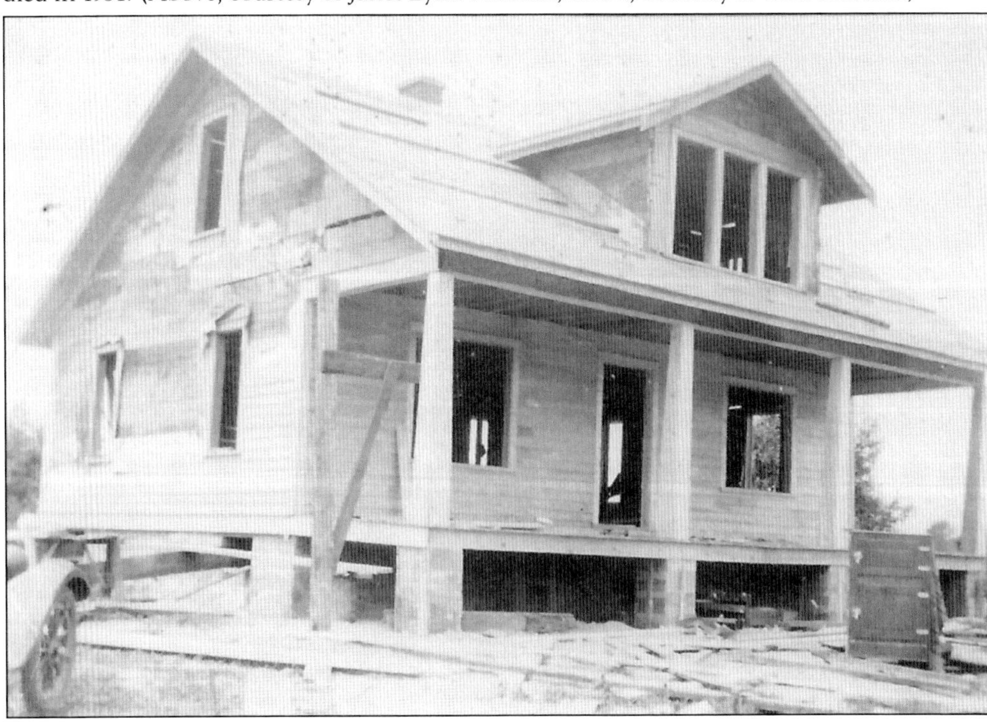

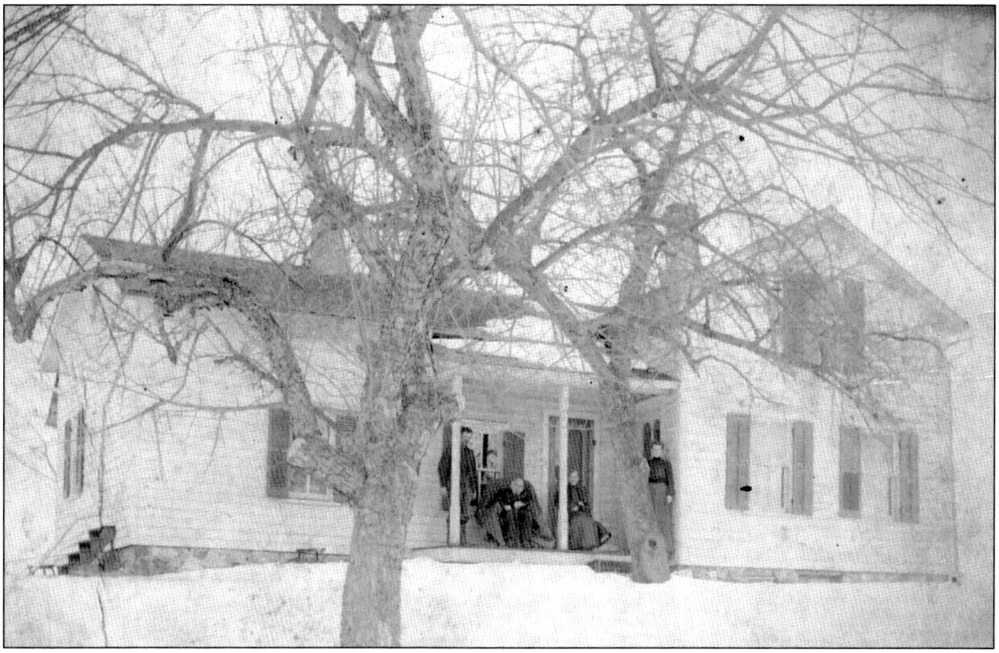

This is the Rawson home around 1900. Pictured from left to right are John, Harley, Hannah, and Anna Rawson. The house was on Grange Avenue north of 13 Mile Road. John's wife, Edith, taught school in Algoma for close to 50 years, including at Morningstar, Gougeberg (in the late 1940s), and Chalmers.

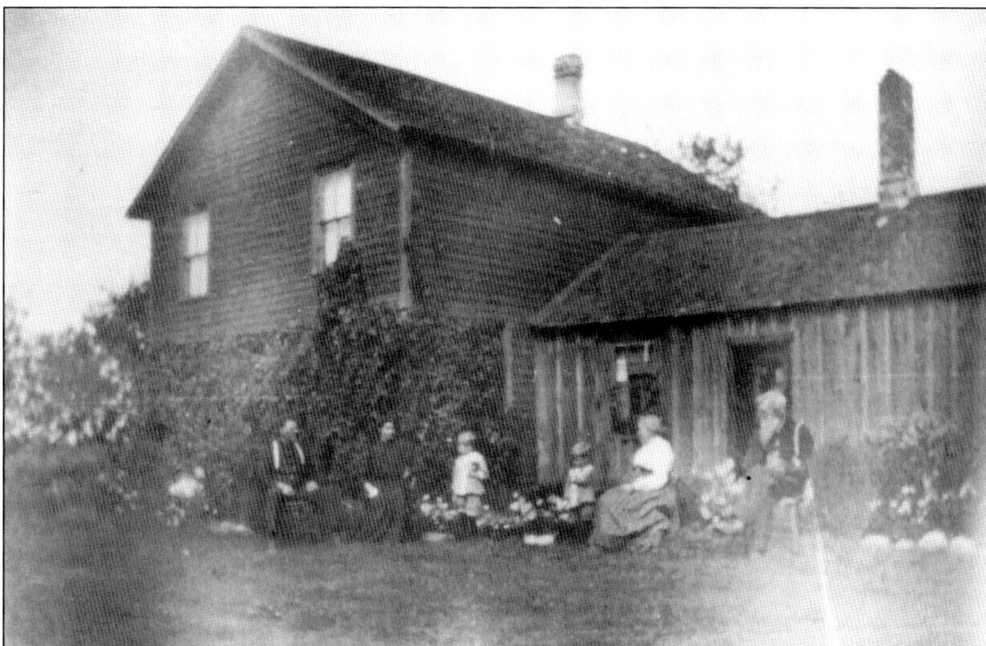

This farm home, located on Grange Avenue, belonged to the Botruff family. The house burned down sometime in the 1900s. Pictured from left to right are Orson, his wife Iva, their children Roy and Ray, and Grandma and Grandpa Botruff.

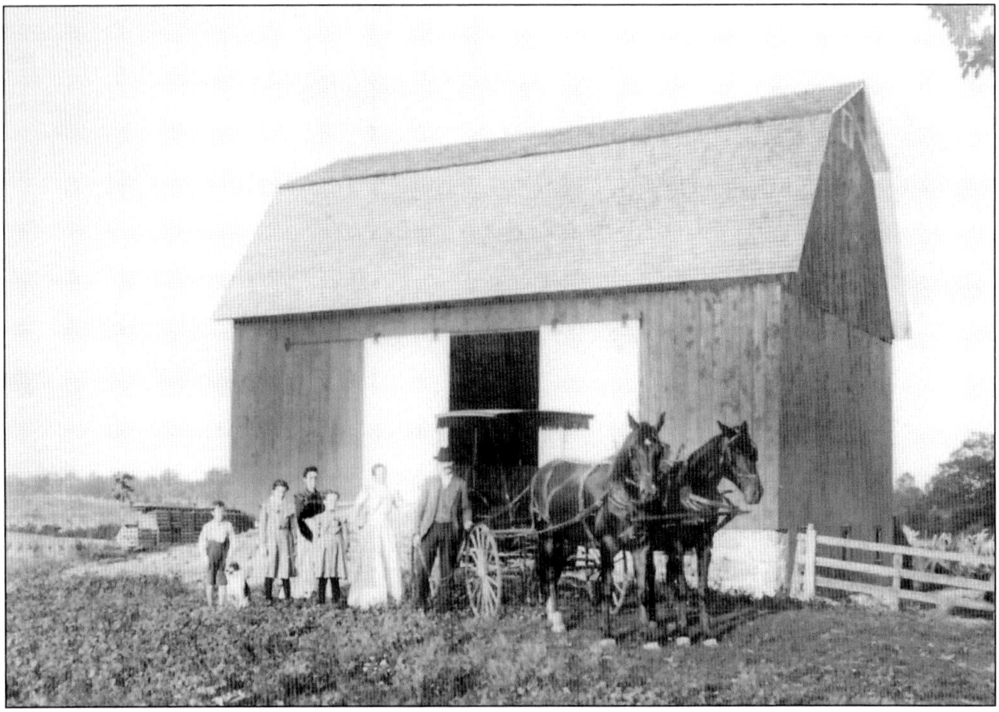

This barn on the Jewell estate was built shortly before 1905. Seen here from left to right are Harry Minion, Maime Jewell, Lottie Minion, Ruth Jewell, Sarah Jewell, and John Jewell. Buggies with fringed tops, like the one pictured, sold for $65.95 in the 1905 Sears, Roebuck catalog.

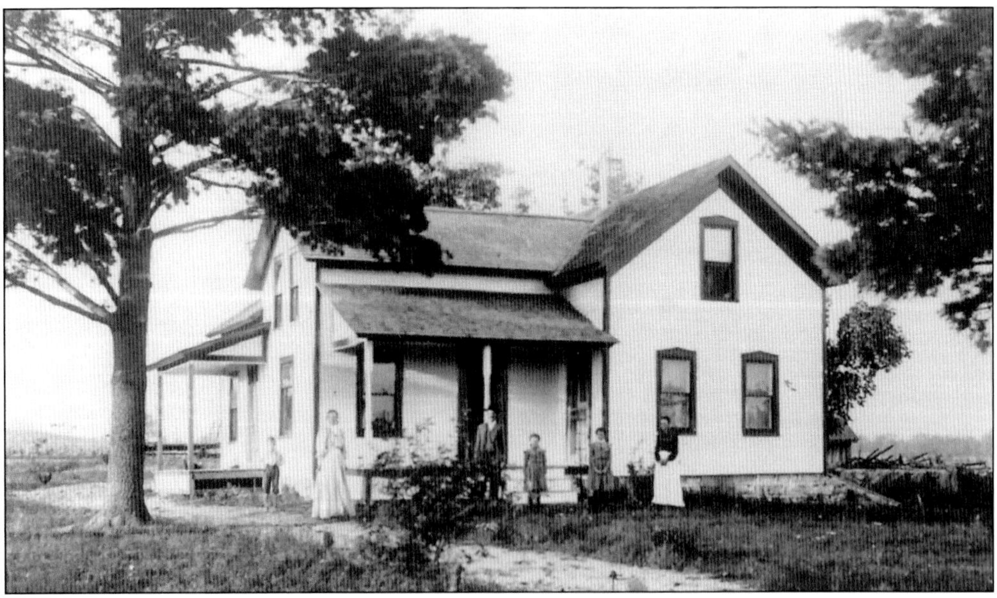

John Jewell's home at 2645 12 Mile Road is pictured in either 1905 or 1906. Pictured from left to right are Harry Minion (son of Lottie Minion), Sarah Jewell (John's wife), John Jewell, Ruth and Maime Jewell (John's daughters), and Lottie Minion (the housekeeper). This property was sold to the Michigan Department of Natural Resources in 1986 by John's son Richard Jewell. (Donated to the ATHS by Richard Jewell.)

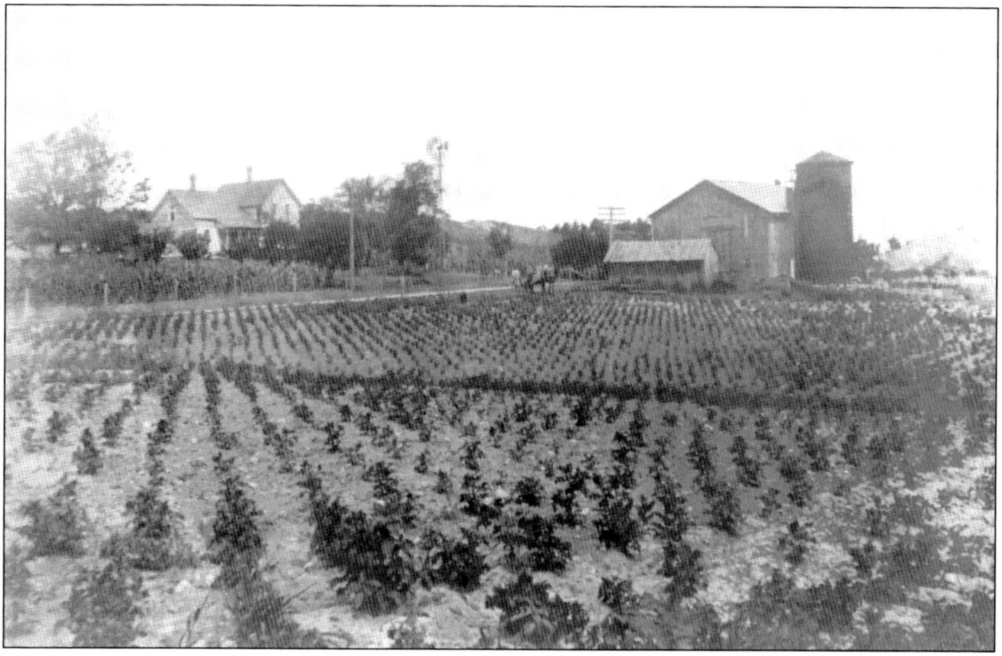

The Ray Loveless farm, seen here around 1910, was 80 acres, with 40 acres on each side of Summit Avenue, south of 11 Mile Road. Corn and potatoes were farmed on the property. Ray was born on September 6, 1876, and died January 15, 1948. He married Ida Mae Austin on March 15, 1904. She died at age 92 on November 11, 1969.

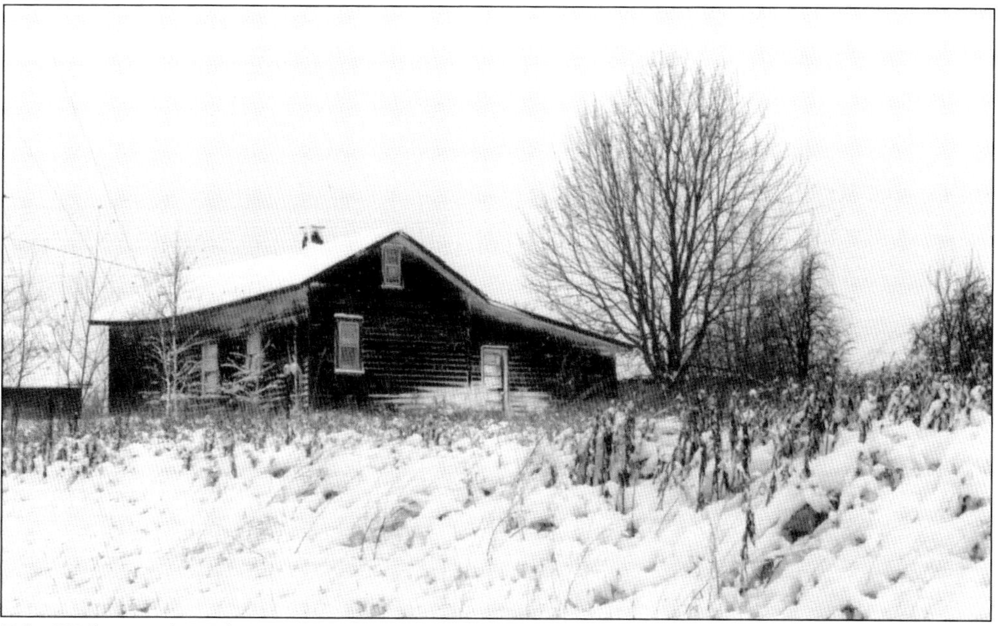

Felix Walincus, the "Blue Man," was born in Lithuania in 1893. A genetic condition or work-related incident caused his skin to have a blue coloration. He immigrated to Algoma Township around 1920, settling on a small 20-acre farm on Indian Lakes Road, just west of Pennington Avenue, around 1925. He then bought an 80-acre farm on the northwest corner of 14 Mile and Edgerton Drive. There he farmed until his death in 1975. (Courtesy of Tom Hoskins.)

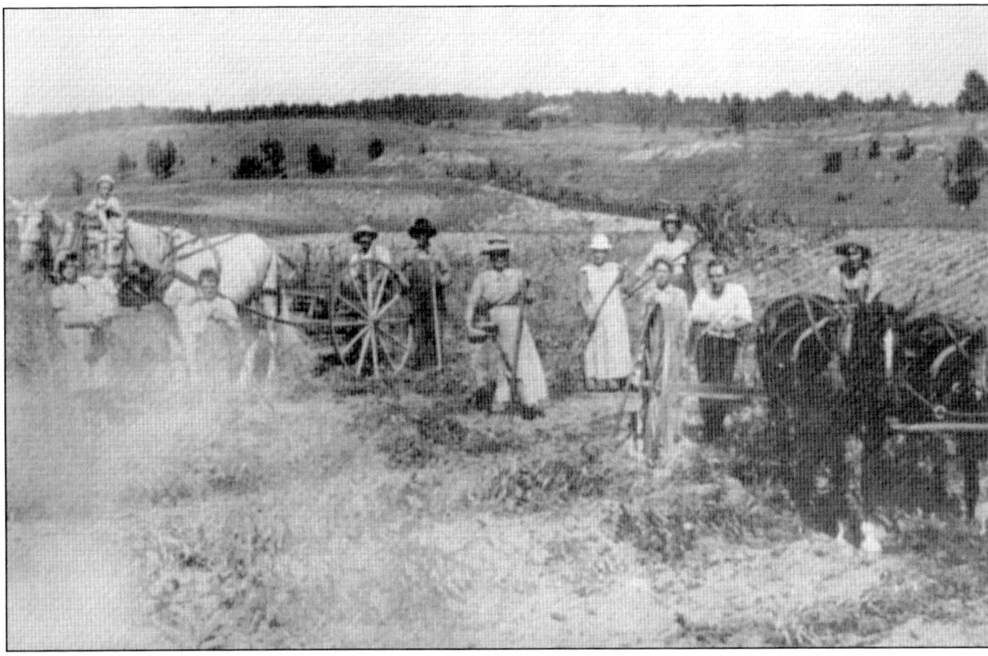

People have come together in 1913 to harvest the bean field on the Erick Lundin farm. Pictured are Evelyn Lundin (holding Edna), Clifford (on the horse), Roy and Erick (on bean puller), George Pardee (neighbor), Anna Erickson, son Bobby, Hilda Lundin, Cash Dillie (beans on fork), a hired man named Harry, Walter Erickson, and Rollo Dillie (on rake).

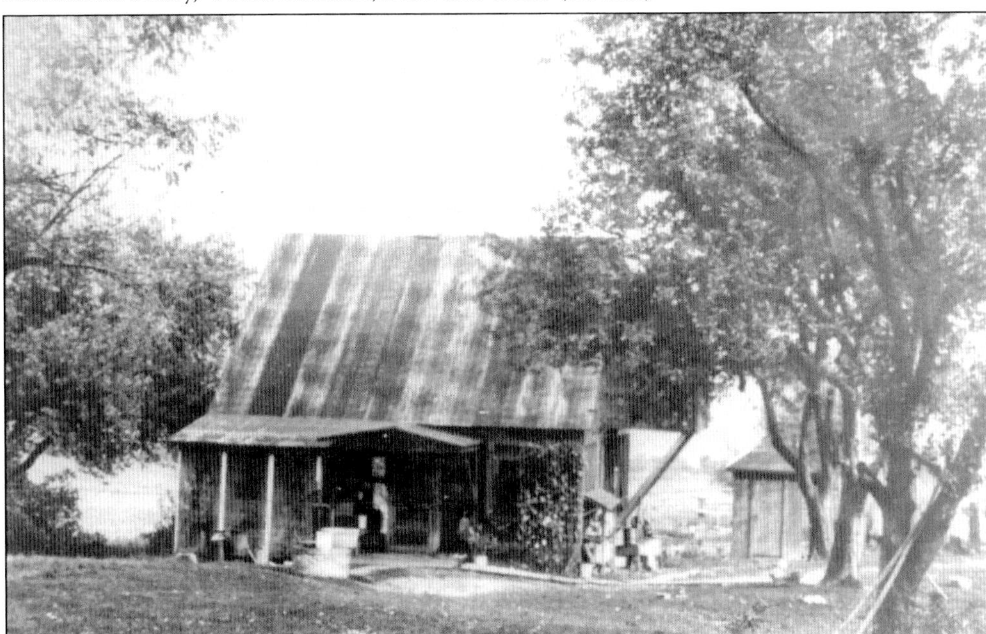

This c. 1922 photograph of the Lundin home was taken from 13 Mile Road. Erik J.H. Lundin purchased 120 acres from Charlie Turner in 1910 and built this house in less than two weeks. The home had a single door leading into the kitchen. The upstairs could be closed off in the winter with two doors at the top of the stairs.

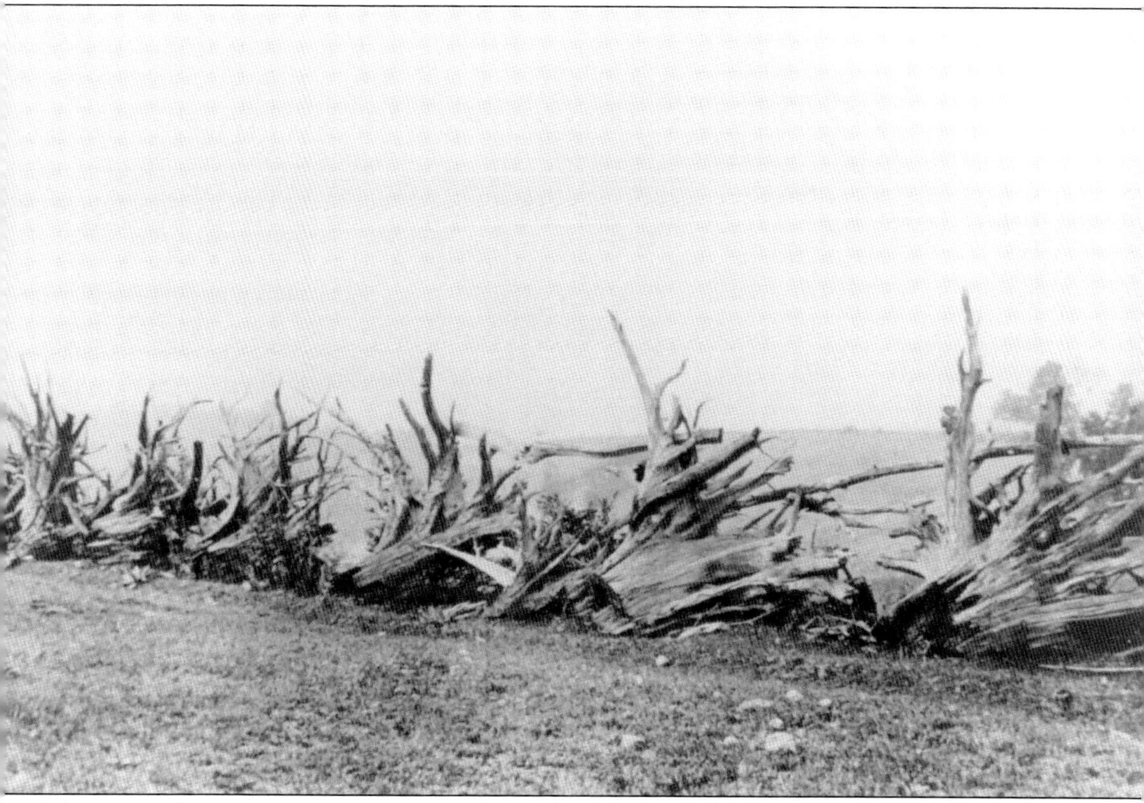

This stump fence, seen here in 1922, was located on the Lundin farm. Erik and Hilda Johnson changed their name to Lundin in the 1890s after moving from Sweden to Chicago. Erik purchased 120 acres in Algoma Township from Charlie Turner in 1910 and built the house where his youngest three children were born.

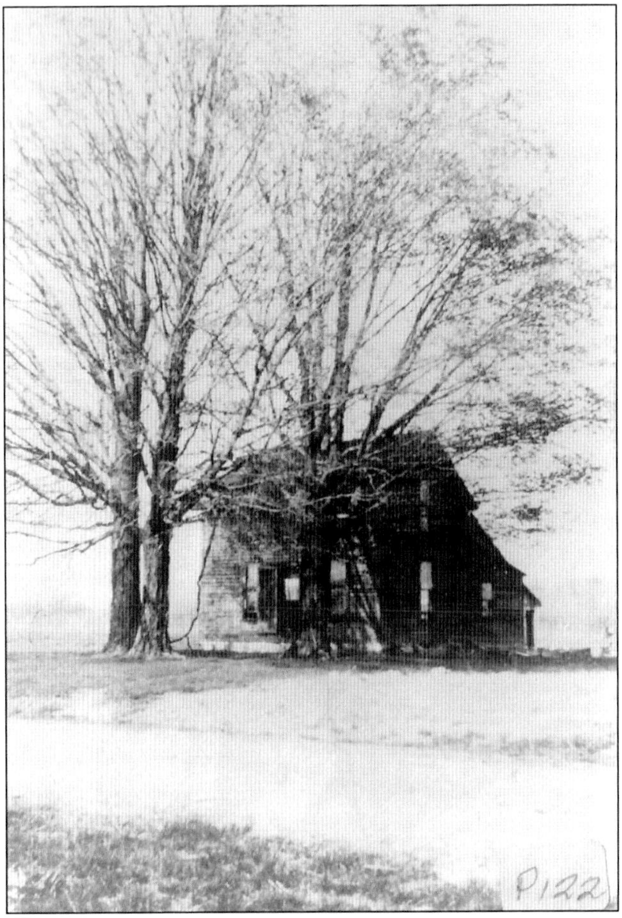

Malcolm and Caroline (Dieckmann) Rosell settled in Algoma Township in 1920. They purchased the 35-acre farm seen at left from Ralph and Olive Gold. The home was located at 9852 Pine Island Drive. The farm was very sandy and was often suffered from drought. Malcolm had an egg route in Grand Rapids, and he also sold produce from the garden. In addition to chickens, the family usually had cows and sometimes a pig. Caroline grew up in Chicago but adjusted to farm living well. Forty additional acres were purchased in the late 1920s and 40 more in the late 1930s in order to pasture 15 cows and stock. Malcolm and Caroline had three daughters: Barbara, Imogene, and Irene.

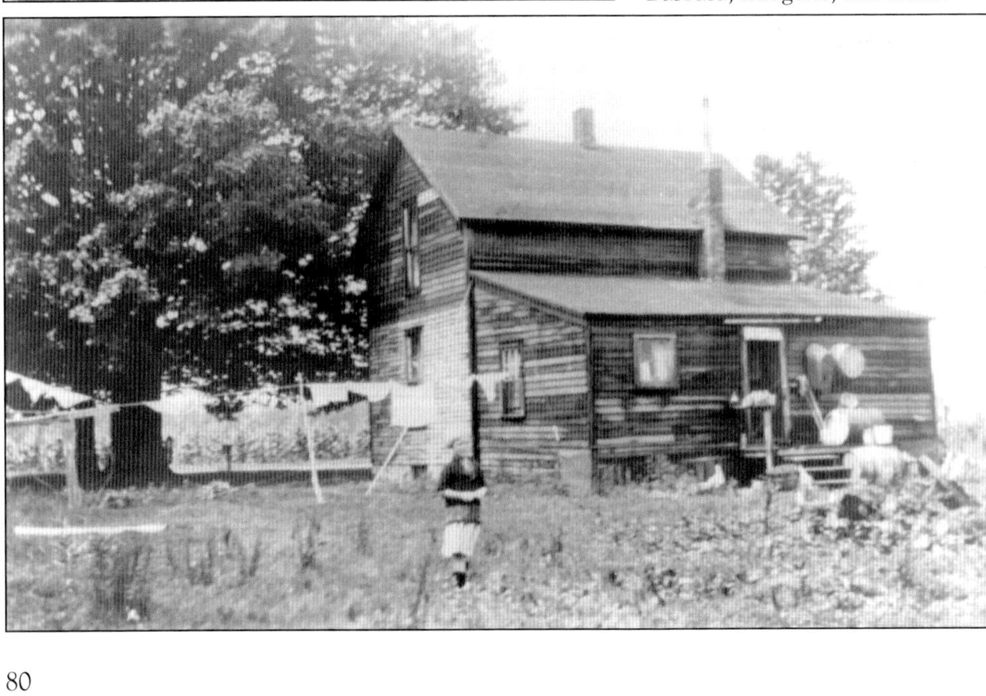

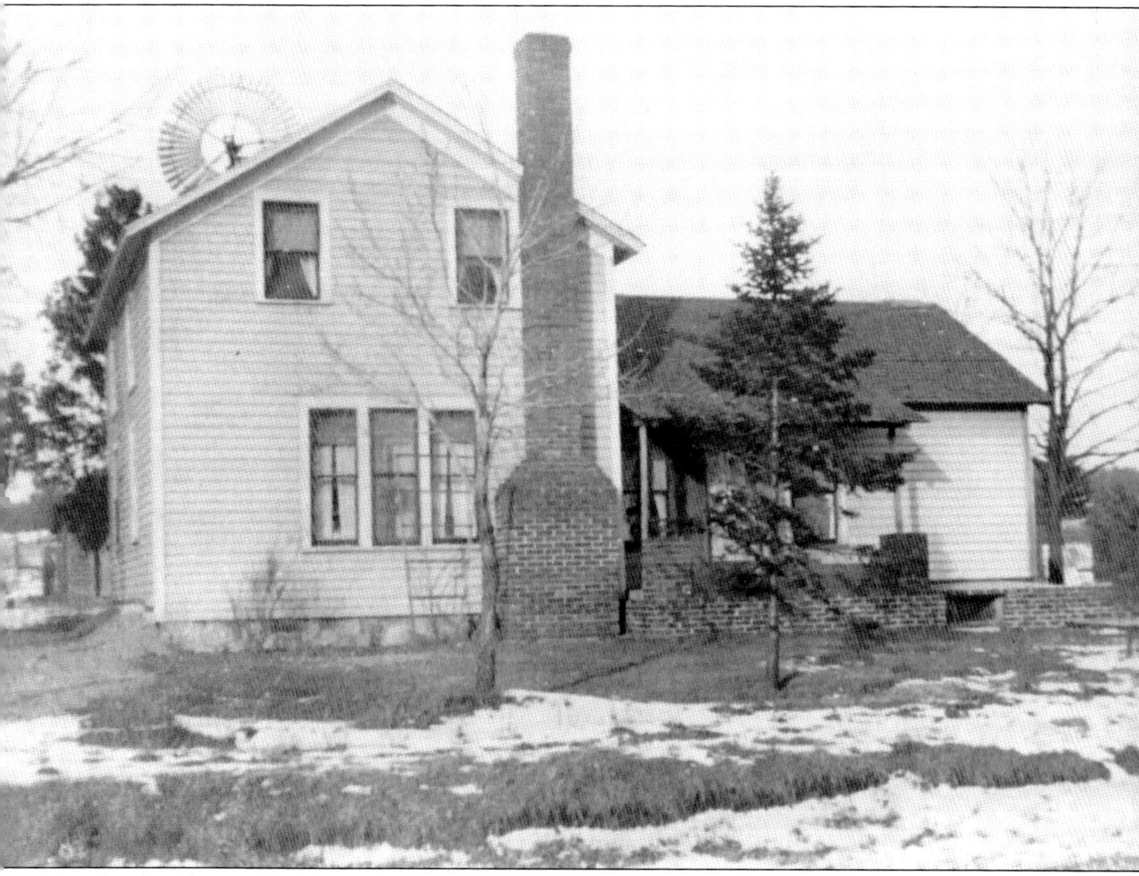

Ward and Helen Smith purchased the 30-acre farm at 4351 13 Mile Road from Truman Burch in 1923. This was the first home in the area with electricity produced from a Delco-Light system. The house burned to the ground in July 1942. Prior to the fire, the front porch had been enclosed.

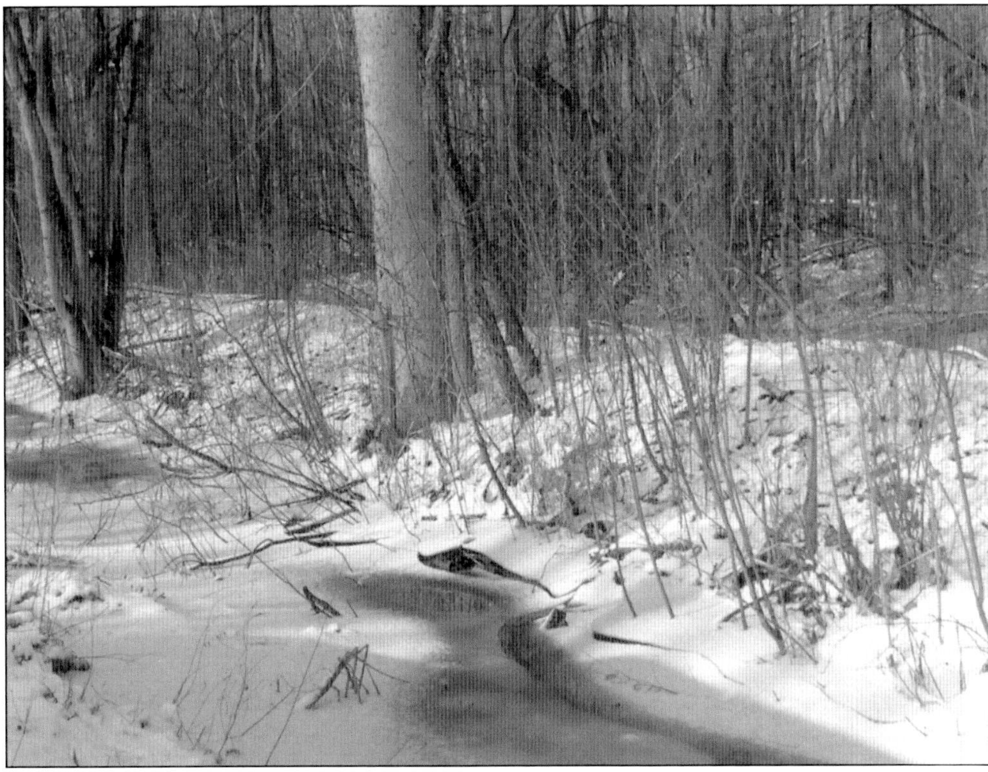

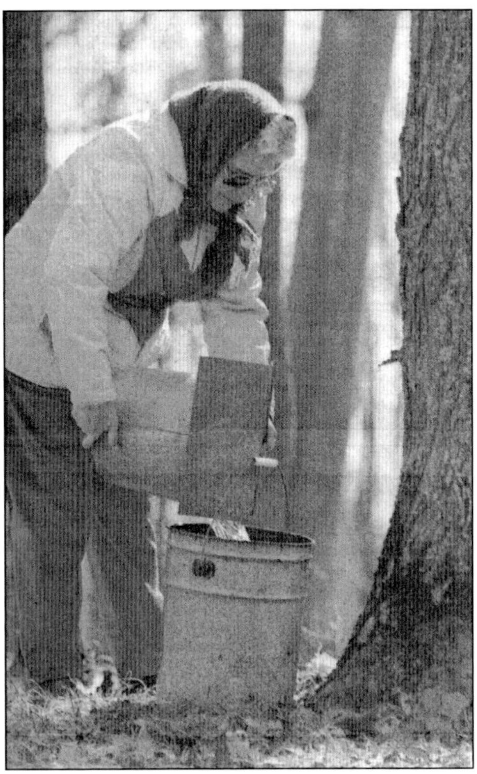

The Cok family has preserved 126 acres of property along the Rogue River in a conservation easement through the Land Conservancy of West Michigan. Stu Cok purchased the property in 1953 and built his home there in 1964. Pictured is a tributary stream on the property. (Courtesy of Linda Willetts.)

Gwen Dufort collects sap from maple trees on the Dufort farm in this 1992 photograph. The Dufort family has been making maple syrup since the end of World War II. Approximately 400 trees are tapped each year, and the sap is boiled down with an evaporator in a sugar shack, used since the 1950s, to produce about 100 gallons of syrup.

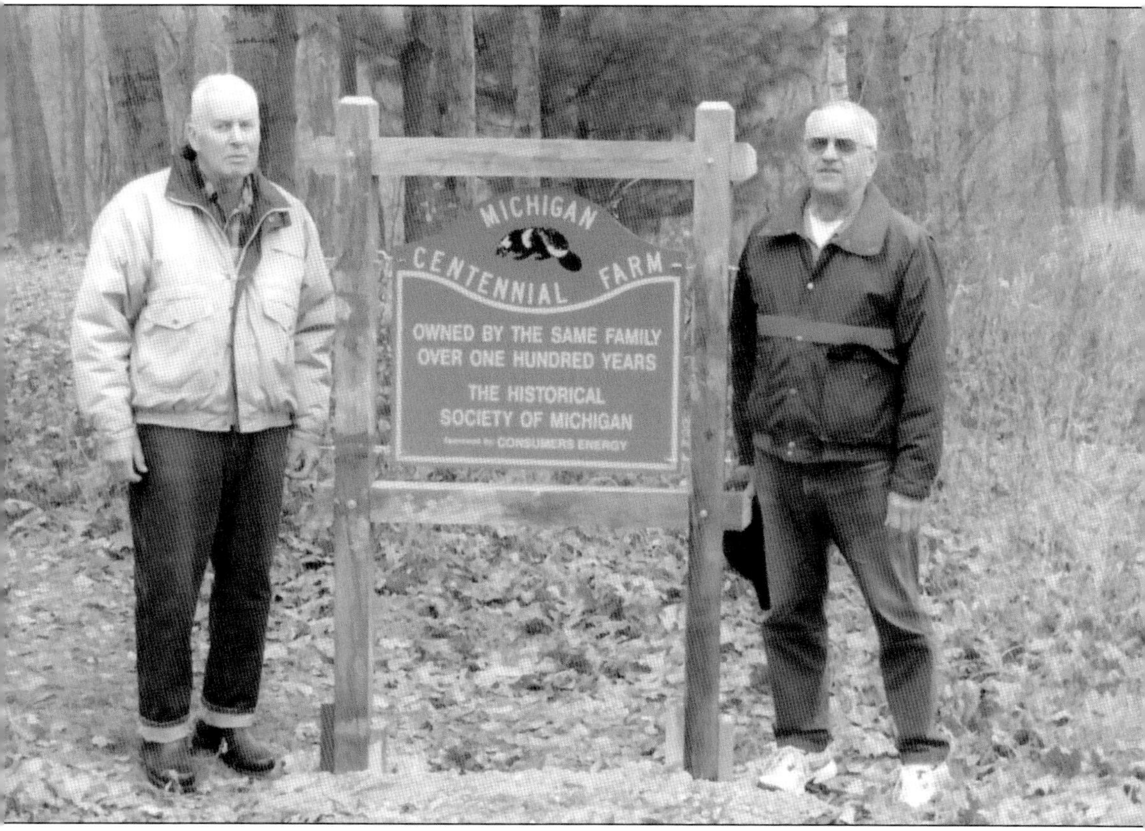

The Woodhull farm was designated a Michigan Centennial Farm in 2013. The 40-acre property started in the family of George and Emma Goller. Emma had two children by a previous marriage. Her son Arthur acquired the property, passing it down to his son Kenneth, who passed it down to his sons Larry Woodhull (left) and Gary Woodhull (right). Larry owns the property at the time of this writing.

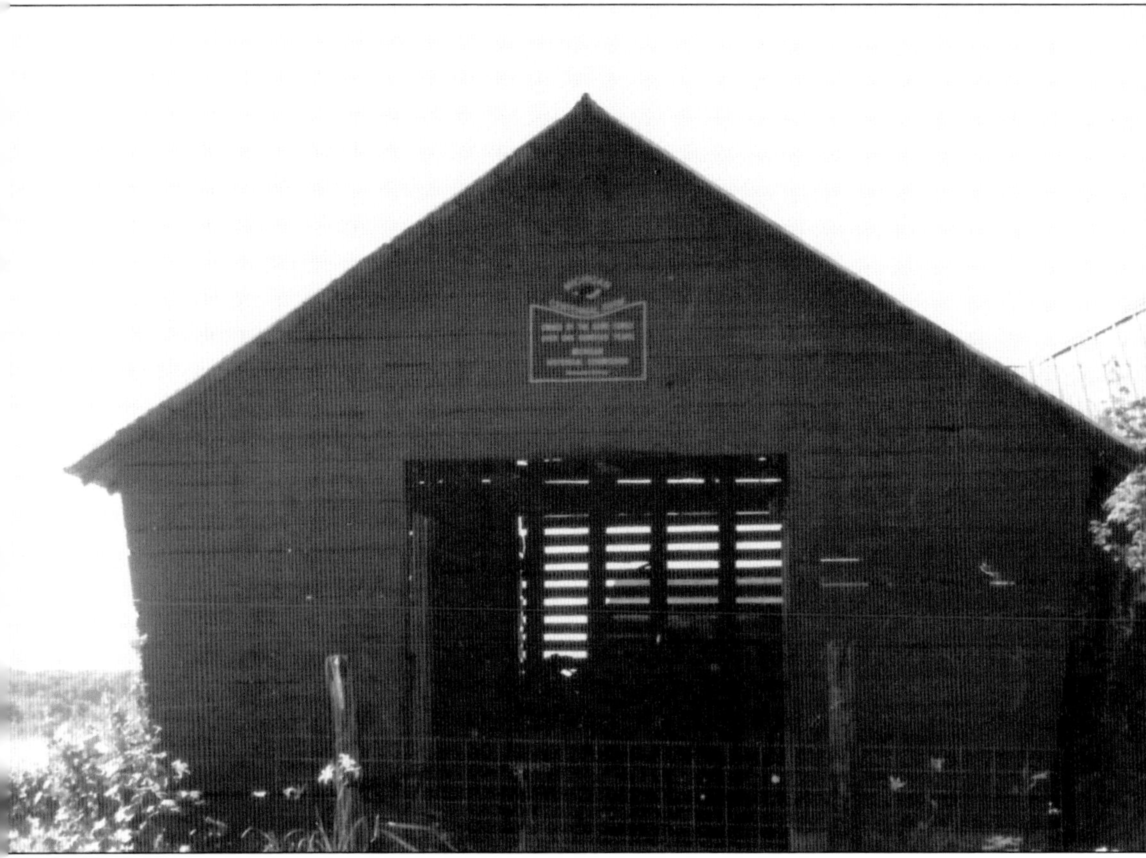

The farmstead known as the Helsel-Rector, or Rector-Norman, farm was originally purchased from the government by John Ball for $1.25 per acre. H.D. Rector purchased that land from his in-laws, the Helsel family, in 1892. The farm was certified as a Michigan Centennial Farm by Dan Norman, great-grandson of Leota Rector, who was H.D. Rector's daughter-in-law.

Four

Local Government, Fire Department, and Landmarks

Algoma has always been full of industrious, willing people able to step up and take on roles to help the township. The local government has been responsible for guiding and growing the community. Logging, which drew settlers to the area, was an important pillar in establishing the township. Once a government was in place, it controlled the construction of roads upon which people drive and built the bridges and railroads residents cross over.

Today, the township has a fire department of volunteers that keep residents safe. There are also several historical markers that represent unique landmarks in Algoma: the stone culvert in Trestle Park and the concrete through arch bridge, "Rainbow Arch Bridge," on Pine Island Drive.

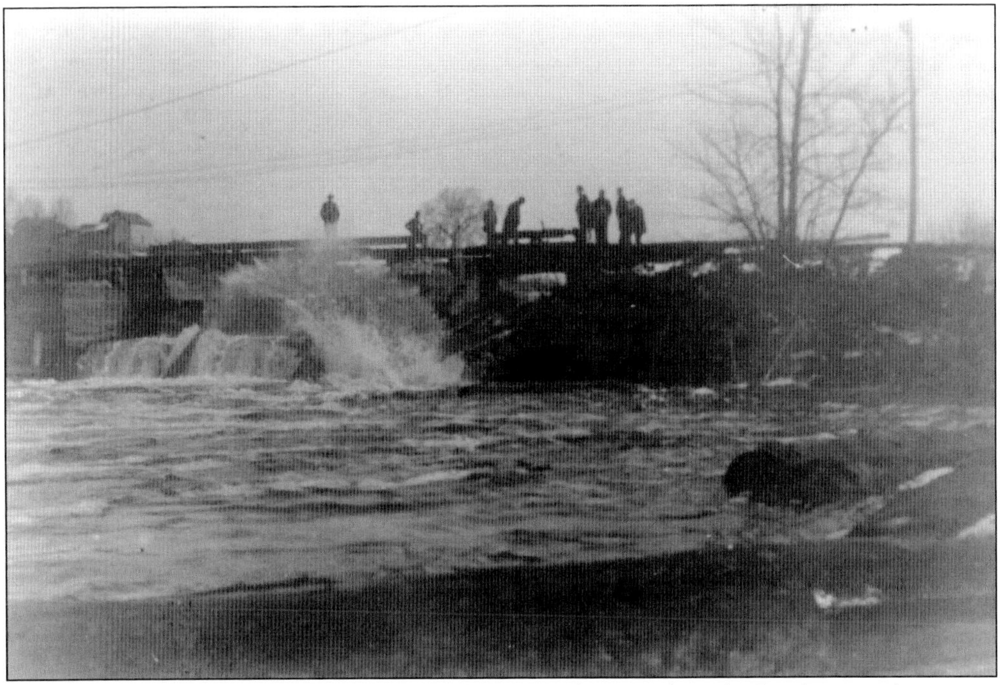

Lumbering was big business in the Rockford area until 1910, when the last logging drive went down the Rogue River. This 1900 photograph shows the Rockford Dam. Here, "bubble cuffers" (a logger who walked on logs in the water), also known as boom men, are running logs down the log chute on their way downstream to the Jericho sawmill.

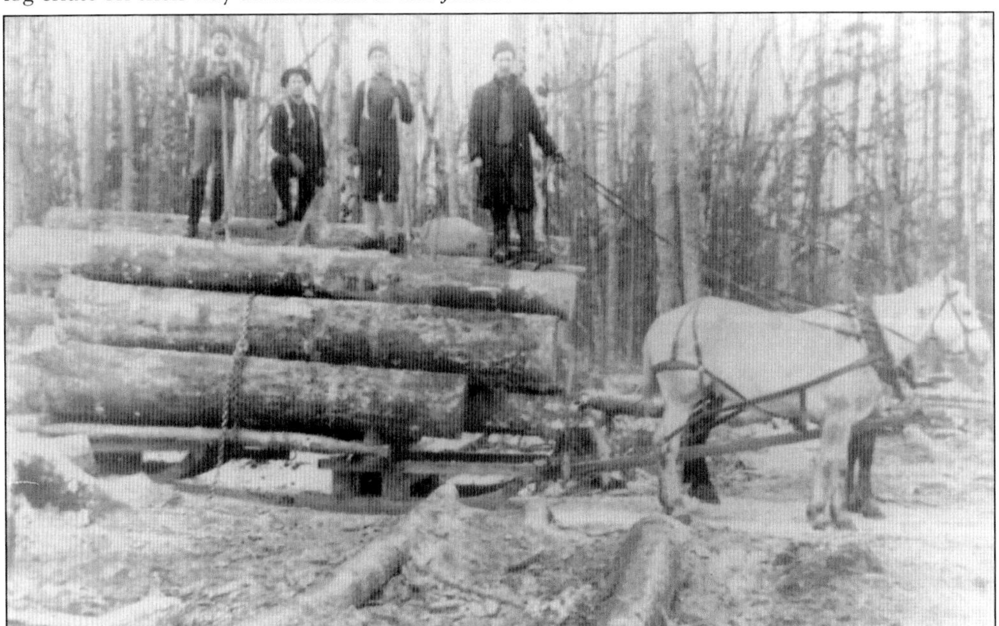

Hauling sleighs were used in the transport of lumber in Algoma and the nearby townships of Solon, Tyrone, and Sparta. The runners were four inches wide and seven inches deep. These sleighs could handle being piled 8 to 12 feet high. (Donated to the ATHS by Barbara Erhart.)

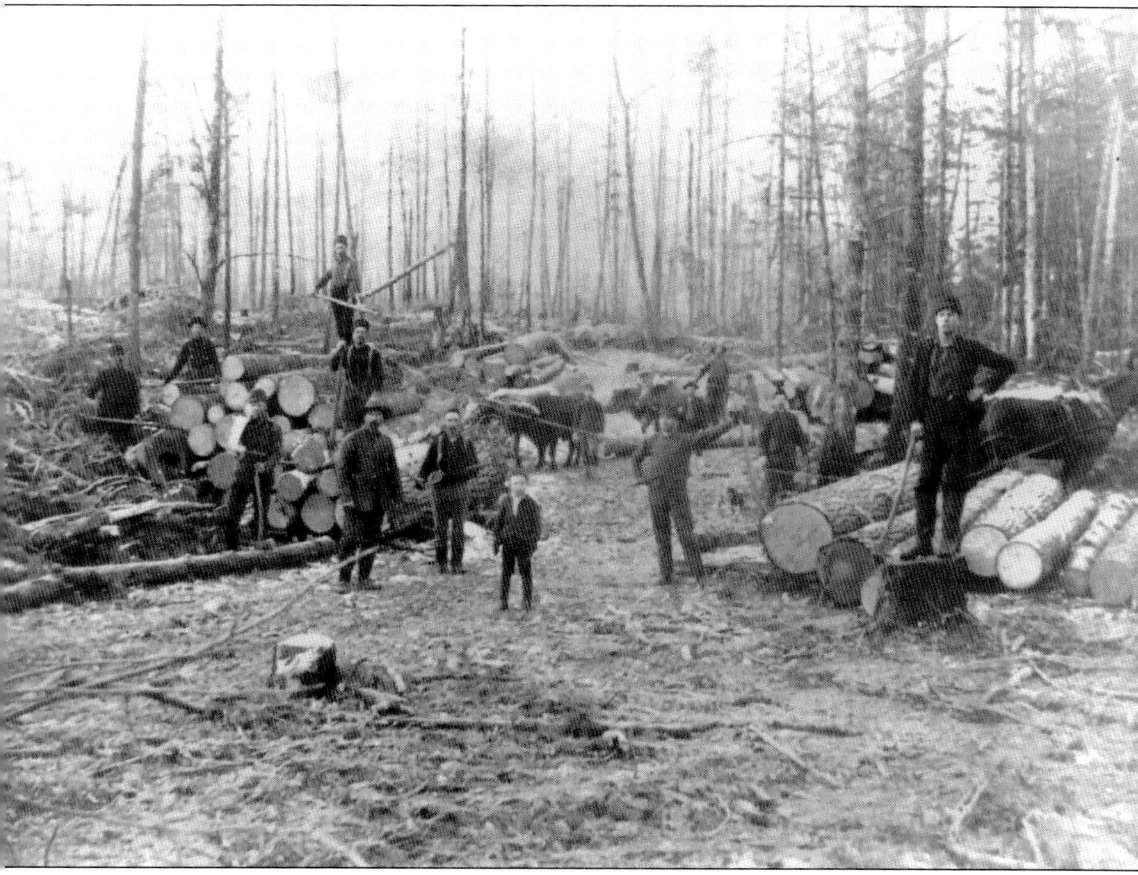

The forests north of 13 Mile Road were typically all pine, which was the wood of choice in making shingles. This logging operation in 1890 was located near the corner of 13 Mile Road and Division Avenue. Pictured among the group are Romney Eaton of Erie, Pennsylvania, Jim Wallace, Dan Myers, Eugene Meyers, and Don Meyers (the boy).

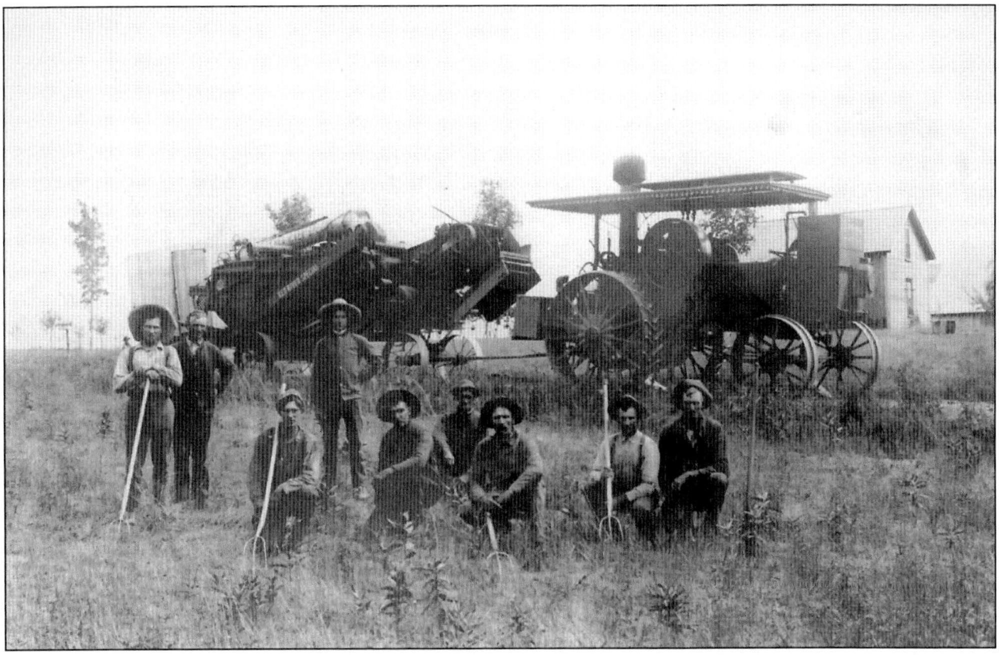

Ray Thompson is seen here with his threshing crew. In the background is a steam-powered tractor. A threshing crew separated the edible parts of grain from chaff, or inedible straw. This operation occurred after harvesting and before winnowing, or removing pests like weevils, stored grain. (Donated by Myrtle Norman Powell.)

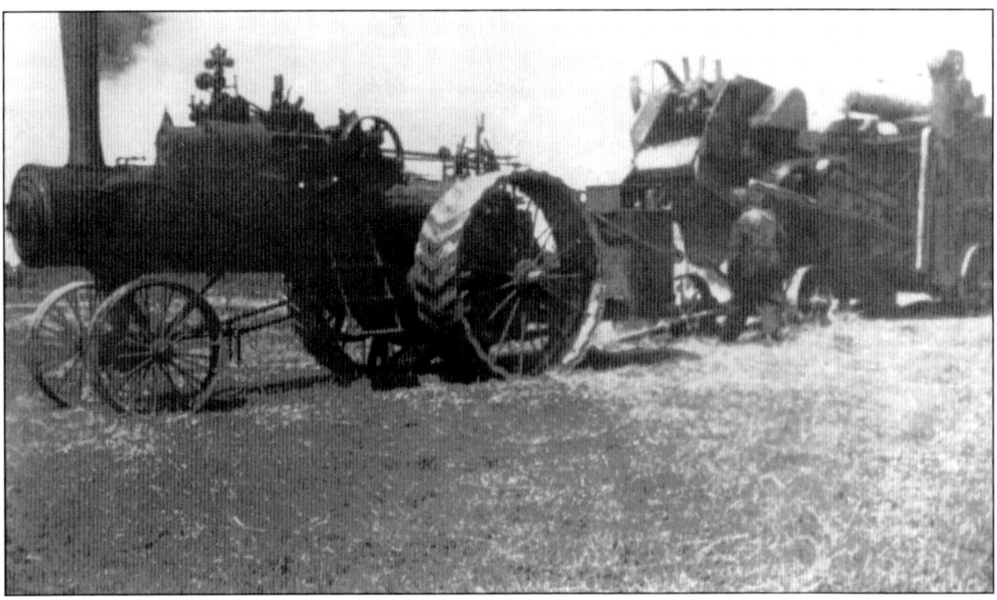

Pictured is John Mosher's steam-powered threshing machine. The contraption was taken right into the field and made threshing work easier and more efficient for farmers, allowing them to harvest larger volumes of grain.

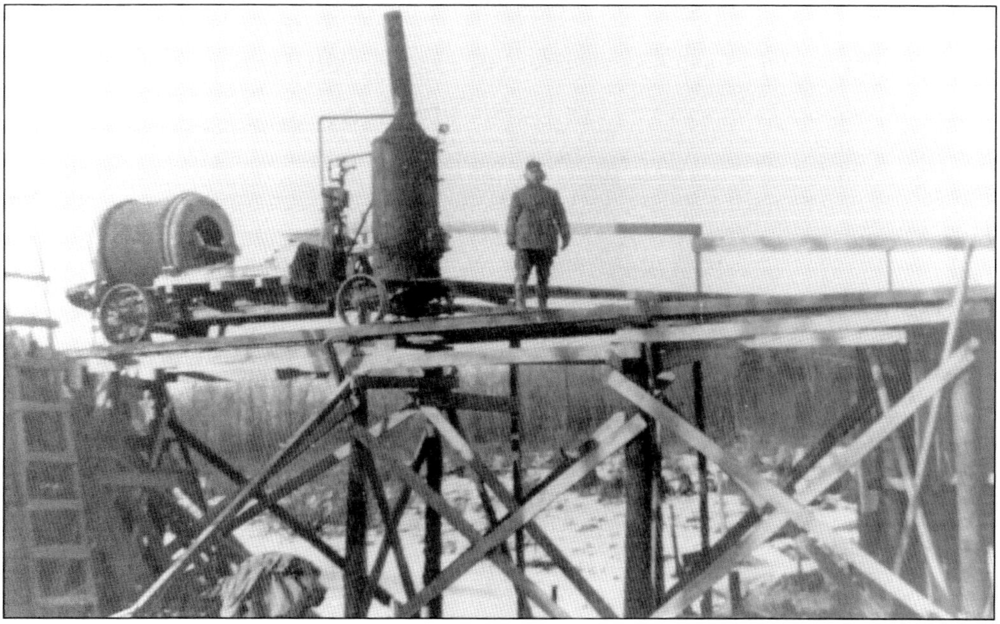

This steam donkey, attached to a modern cement mixer, was used for the construction of the new 13 Mile Road bridge in the winter of 1920 and 1921.

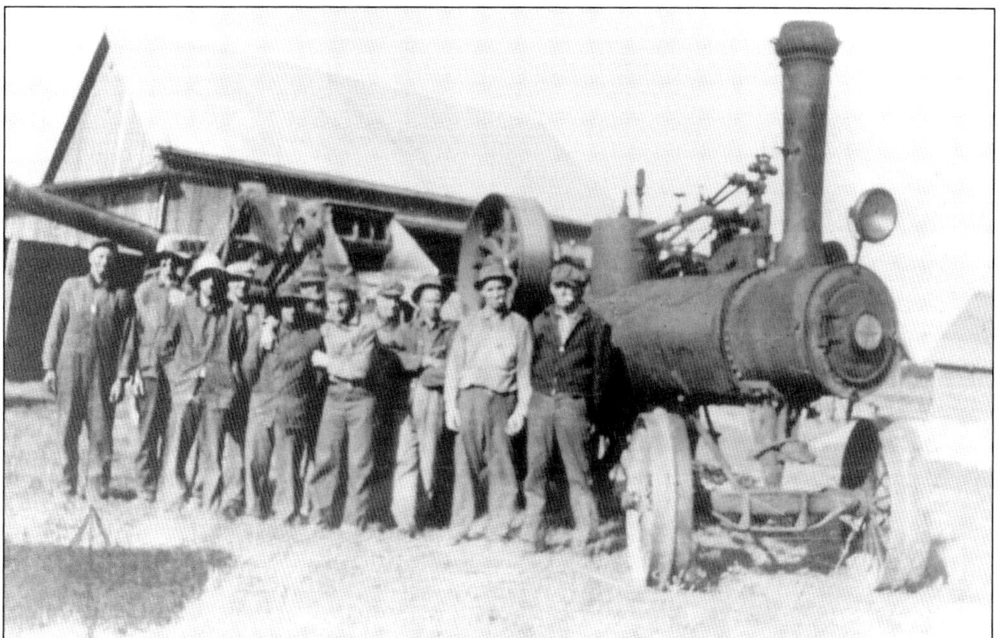

Burton Bradley (far left) gathers his threshing crew on his Algoma Avenue farm. Burton married Via Fessell in the early 1900s, and together they had three children: Loretta, Ray, and Ruth. Burton also owned and rented farms and property in the Foxville area. Before Ruth was born, they owned a restaurant in Cedar Springs.

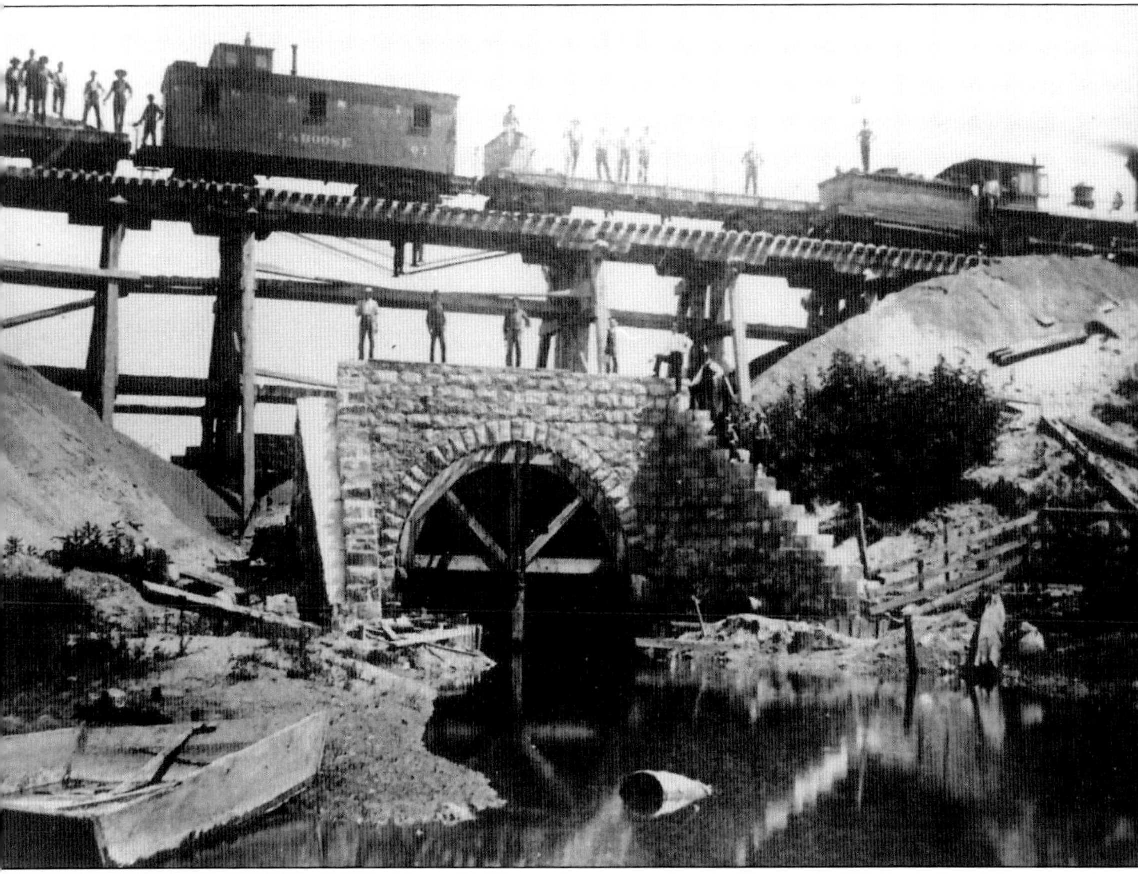

This stone culvert was built in 1885 over Stegman Creek (formerly Wicked Creek), west of David Munro's mill, for the Grand Rapids and Indiana Railroad. A flood in 1883 washed out the previous trestle. James Ward House built the culvert using stone from his farm. The culvert received a Michigan Historic Site designation in 1996 from the Michigan Historical Commission and is now a Michigan Historic Civil Engineering Landmark in Trestle Park located on Summit Avenue north of 13 Mile Road.

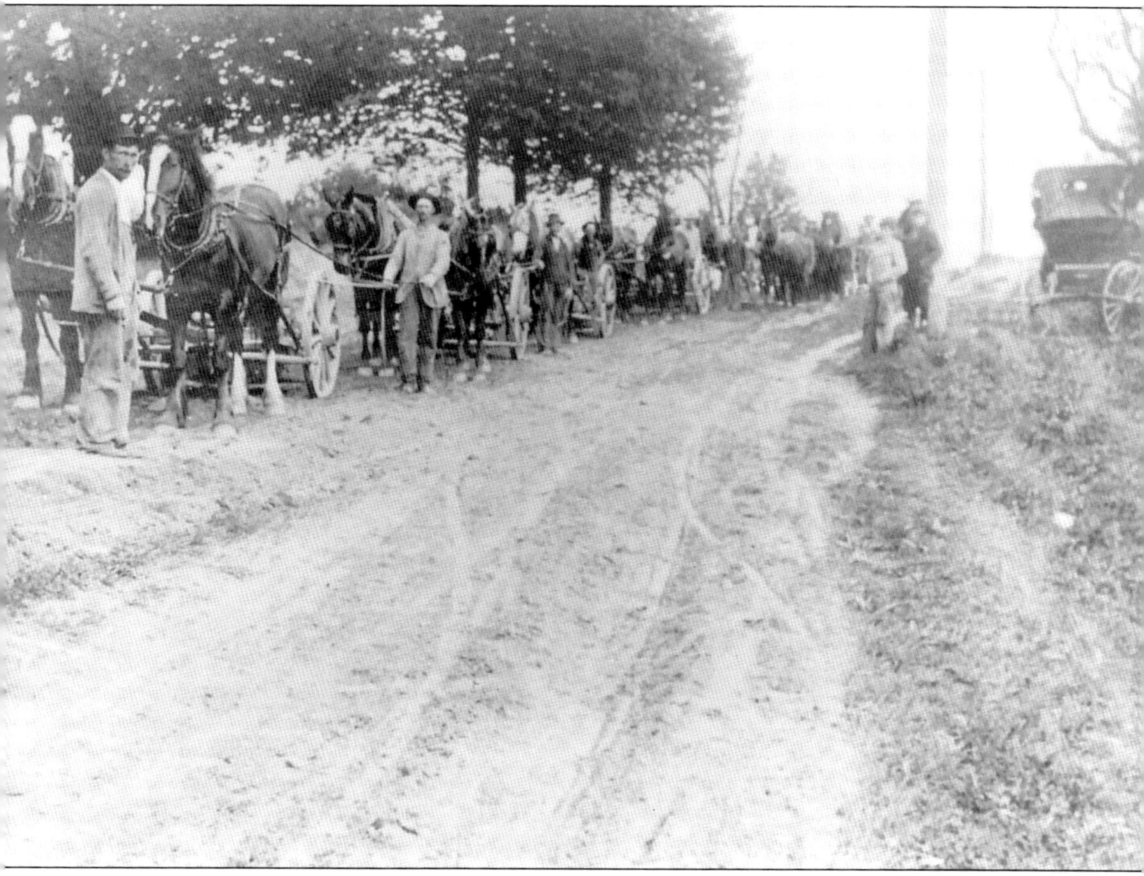

Forrest Montgomery ran one of the road building crews (pictured) in Kent County between 1918 and 1920. Many of the crewmen were working off unpaid taxes putting down gravel, and some even lent their names to the roads that were constructed: Rector, Friske, and Elstner are a few examples. (Donated to the ATHS by Barbara Erhart.)

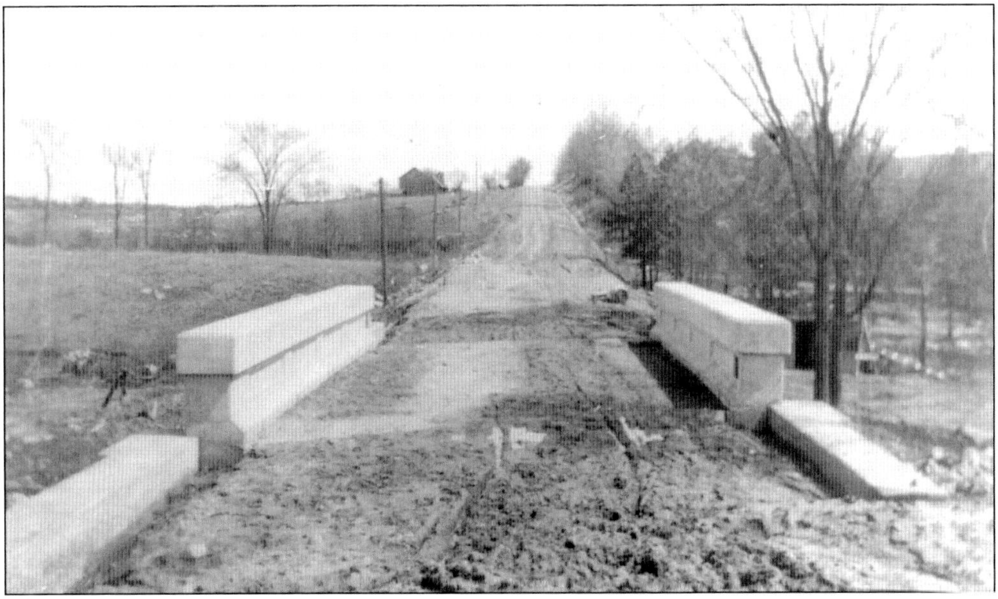

This 1922 look at the bridge over Cedar Creek shows the wider grade just added on the uphill slope. This photograph is the eastward view of the newly completed bridge on 13 Mile Road as it passed the Lundin farm.

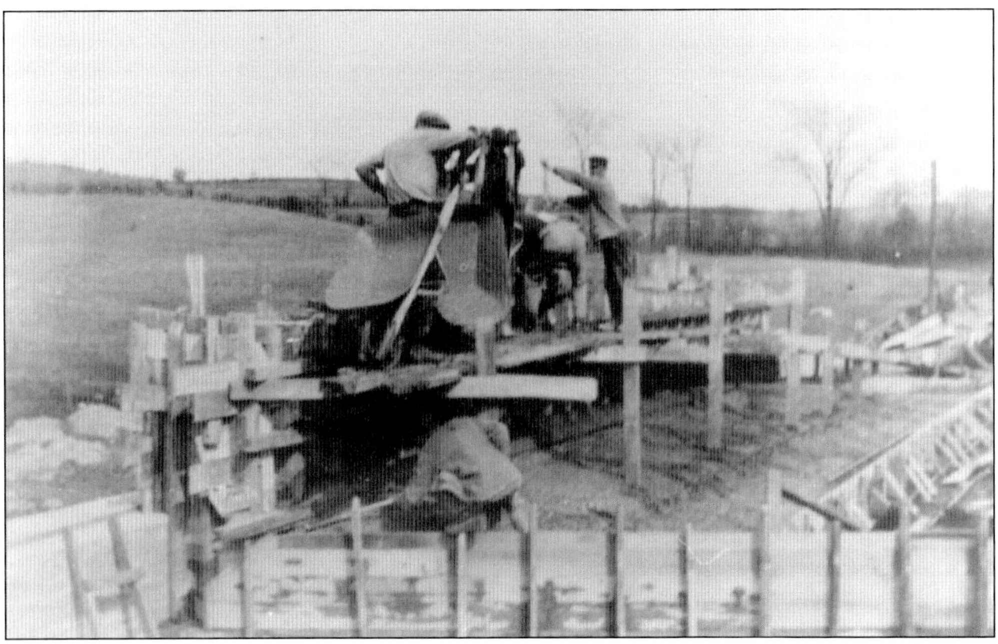

Workmen pour concrete into rail footings on a sunny spring day in 1921. The weather and time of year were ascertained by the clothing the men are wearing: only long-sleeve shirts. The footings are on the north side of the 13 Mile Road over the east side of Cedar Creek.

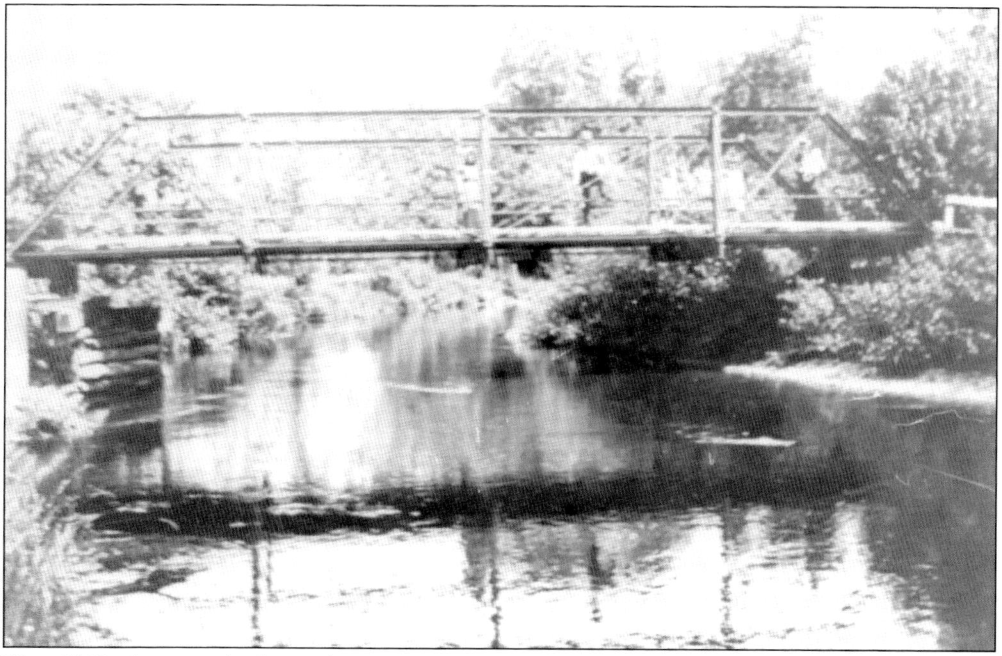

This 1901 photograph shows the queen post truss steel bridge built over the Rogue River on Pine Island Drive after the 1886 flood. This bridge was replaced in 1924. Abigail Bristol (in the bonnet), Guy Bristol (Abigail's son), and Alma Bristol (holding a baby) stand on the bridge with little girls Mabel and Edith.

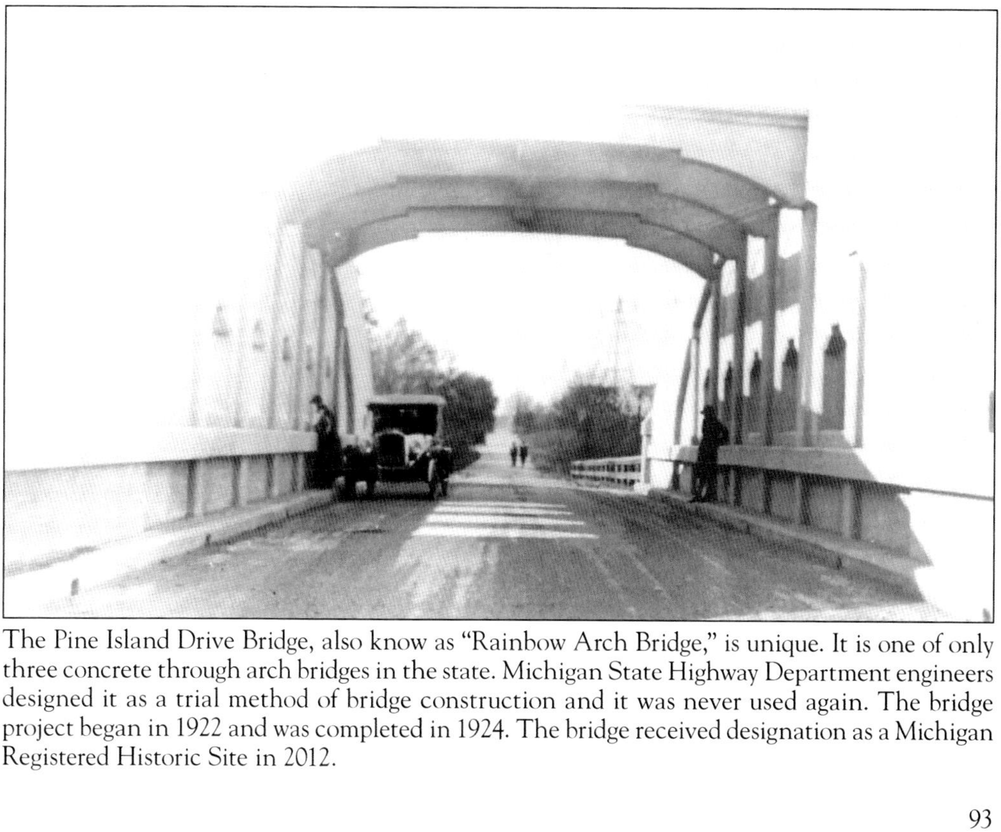

The Pine Island Drive Bridge, also know as "Rainbow Arch Bridge," is unique. It is one of only three concrete through arch bridges in the state. Michigan State Highway Department engineers designed it as a trial method of bridge construction and it was never used again. The bridge project began in 1922 and was completed in 1924. The bridge received designation as a Michigan Registered Historic Site in 2012.

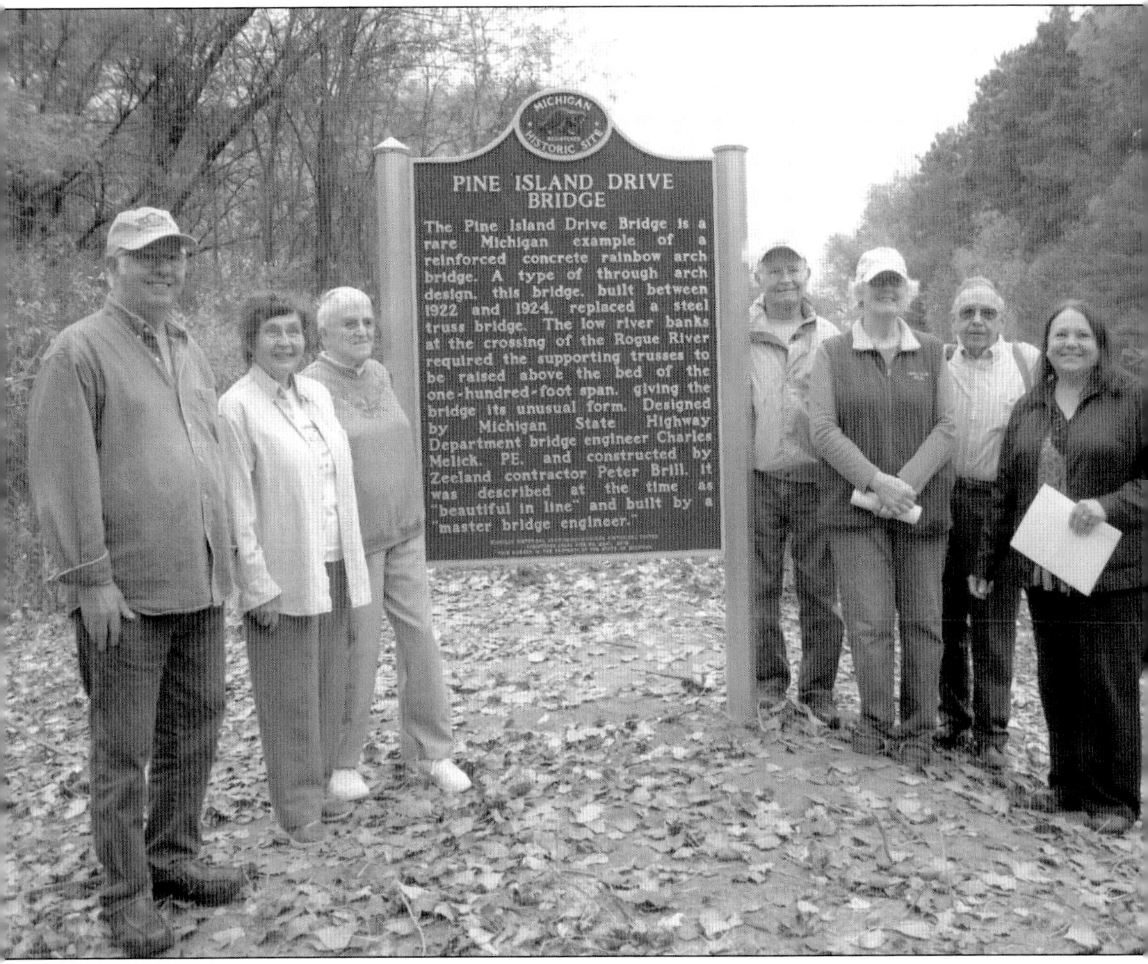

On the day of the dedication on October 17, 2014, members of the Algoma Township Historical Society pose with the newly erected Michigan Registered Historic Site sign designating the Rainbow Arch Bridge on Pine Island Drive. Repairs on the bridge had recently finished up. Pictured from left to right are trustee Ed Ingersoll, Ruth Wieda-Empie, Irene Lamphear, vice president Dale Darling, treasurer Laural Walkons, trustee Paul Smith, and president Julie Sjogren.

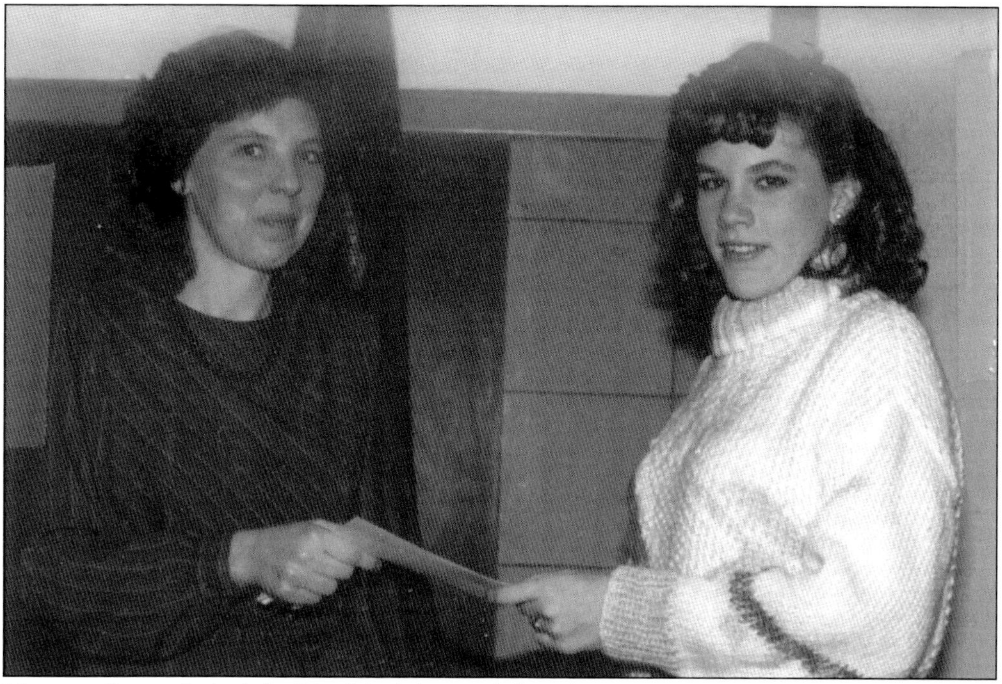

Maureen Carmody (right) of Rockford designed the Algoma Township arrowhead logo in 1986. Township officials had asked students from Sparta, Rockford, and Cedar Springs High Schools to compete to create a design that used no more than two colors and included the date of charter establishment of the township, 1849.

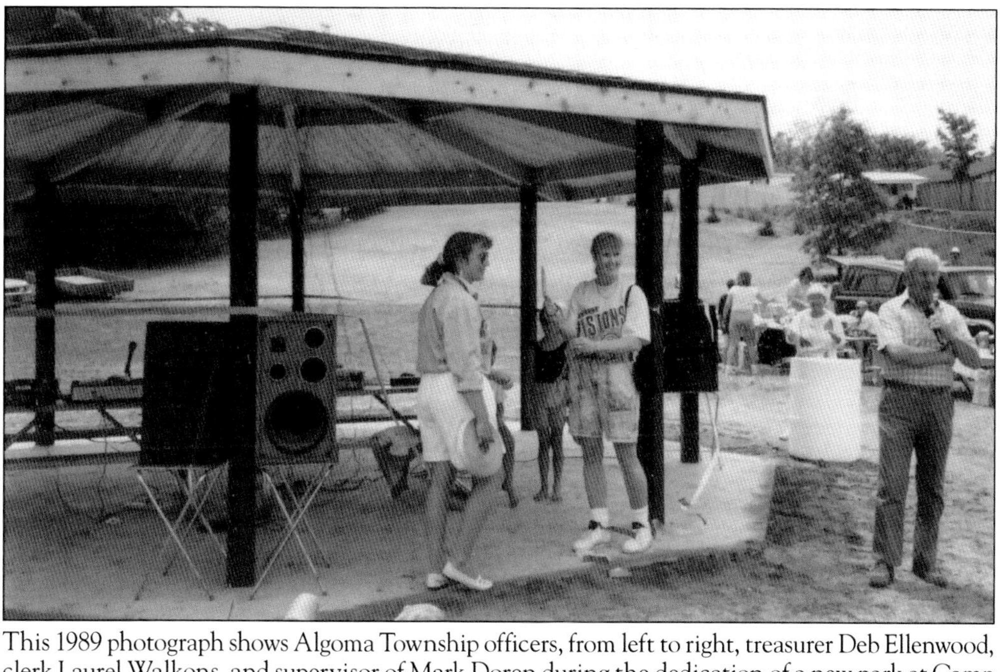

This 1989 photograph shows Algoma Township officers, from left to right, treasurer Deb Ellenwood, clerk Laurel Walkons, and supervisor of Mark Doren during the dedication of a new park at Camp Lake. Initial plans included a basketball court, tot playground, picnic area, playground equipment, and open shelter. The area was developed using grants and community development funds.

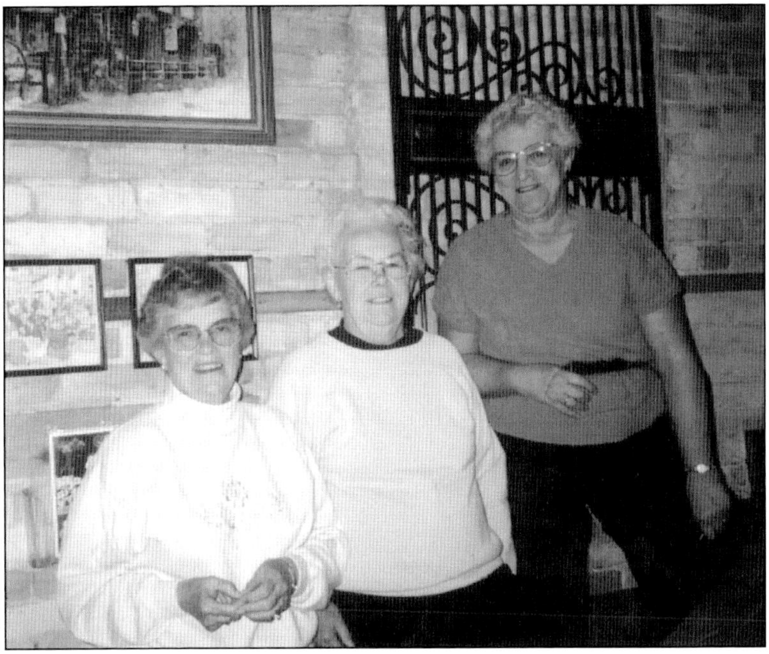

Pictured from left to right, Betty Mieras, Luella Bitely, and Irene Lamphear worked many elections for Algoma Township, including the one seen in this 1996 photograph. As election workers, they checked voters to ensure they were registered, made sure the voting machines were working properly, and helped the lines of voters to move quickly and smoothly.

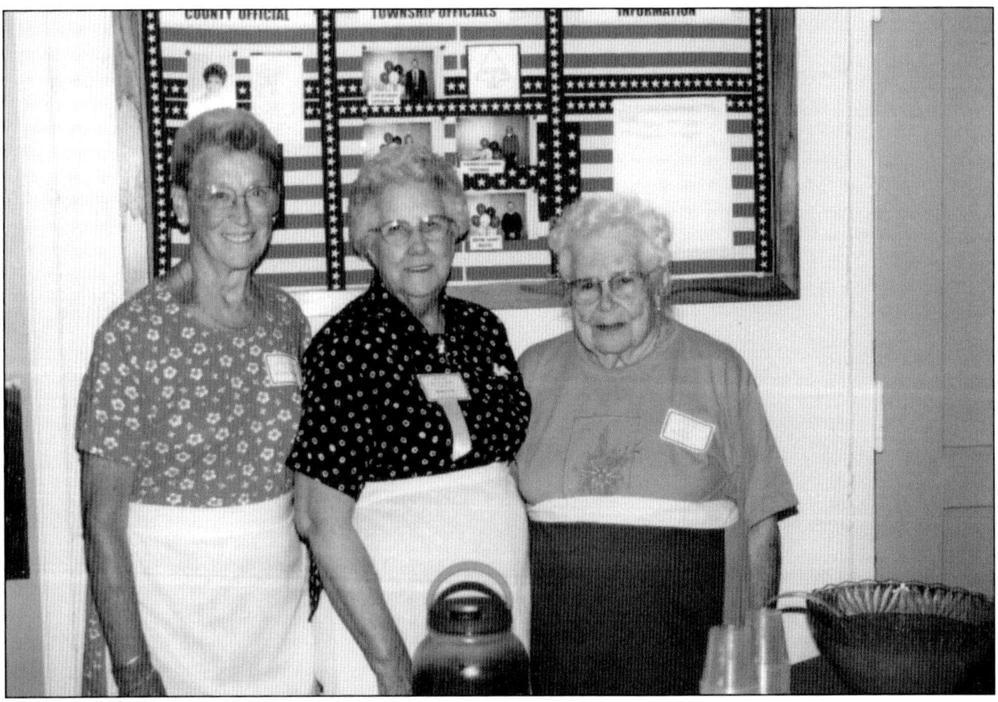

Pictured from left to right, Winifred "Winnie" Knight, Eloise Covey, and Lorraine Pennington were intrinsic in setting up the sesquicentennial celebrations for Algoma Township. They found sponsors and created events, and they served up some cake at the potluck dinner on the second day of the celebration. Without their help, the celebration would have been far less enjoyable.

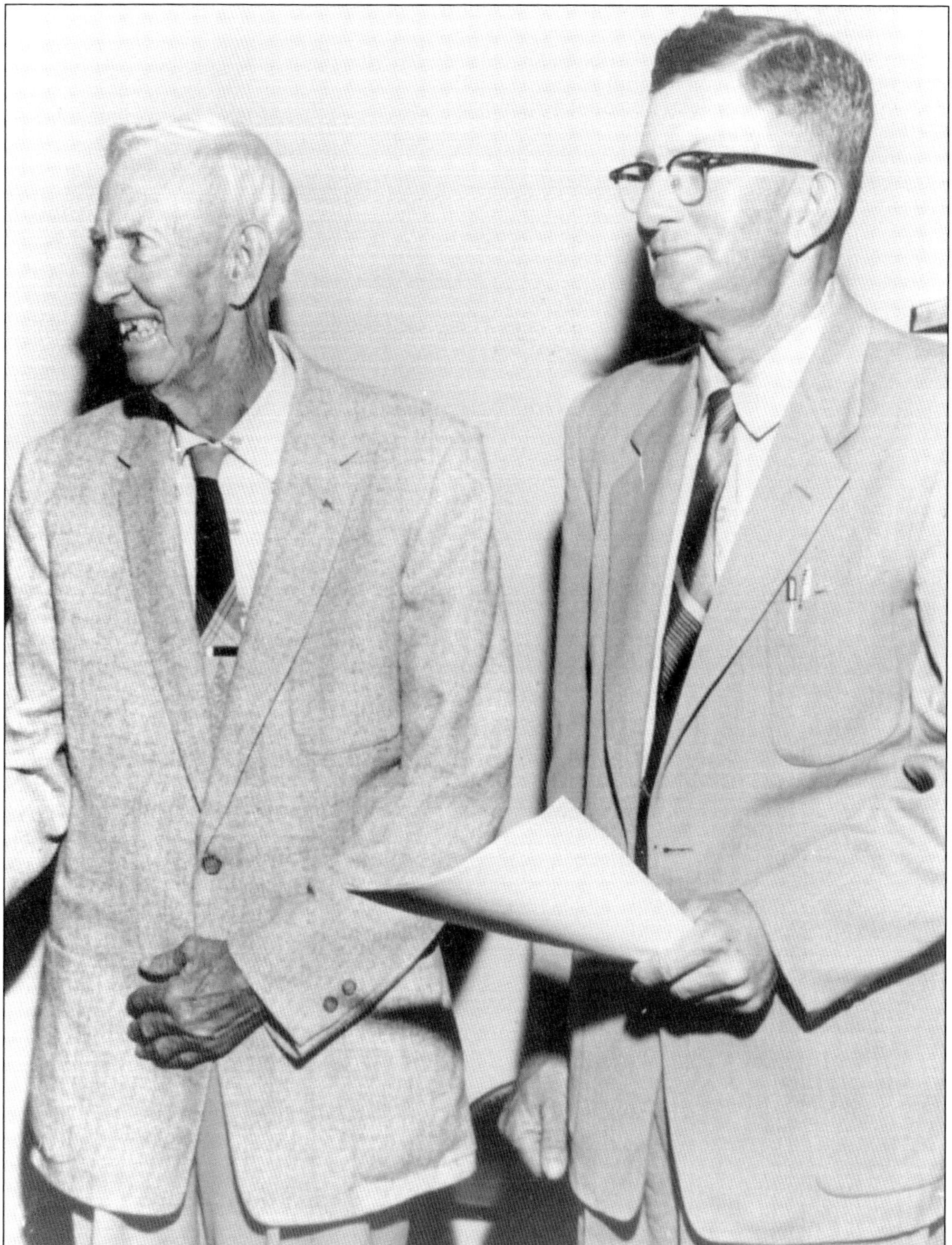

Maurice Post (left) served as Algoma Township supervisor from 1919 to 1933. From 1934 to 1949, he served in the Michigan House of Representatives for the Third District, or all of Kent County outside of Grand Rapids city limits. He was speaker of the house for two years and speaker pro-tem for several others. His son Lynne Post (right) followed in his footsteps and was supervisor of the township for one term.

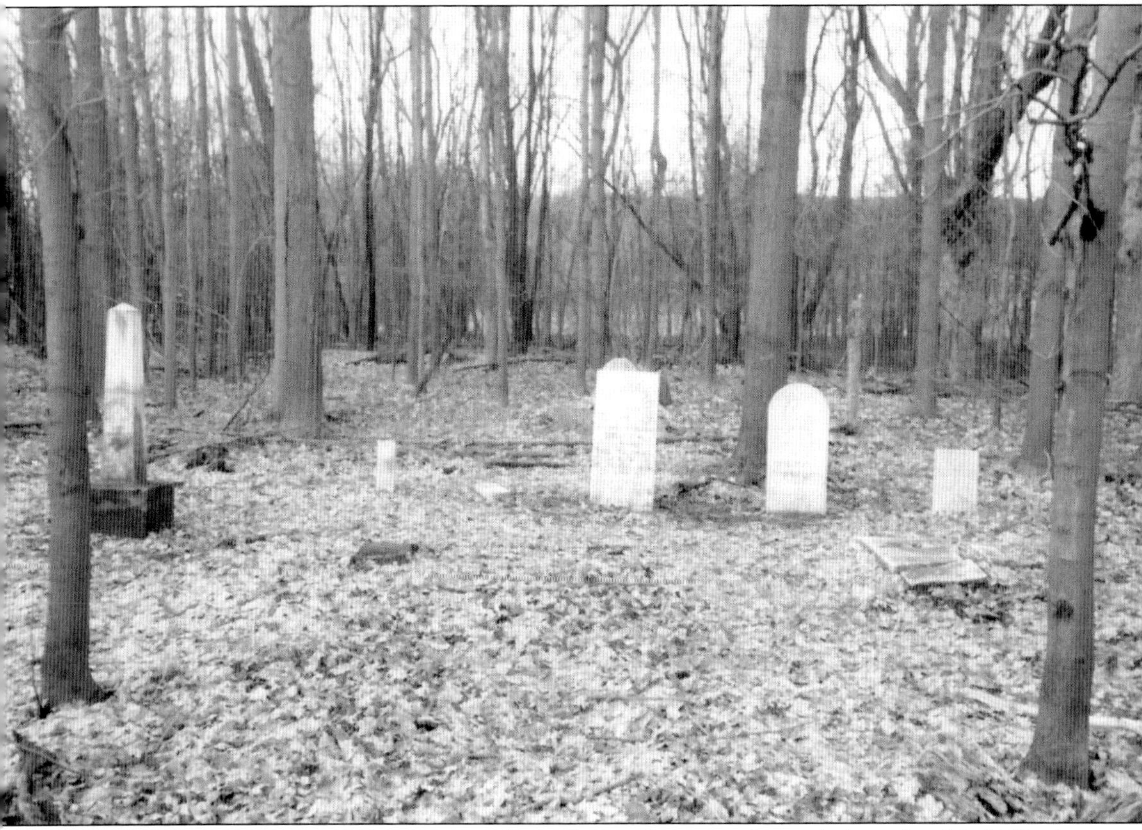

The oldest cemetery in Algoma Township is Briggs Cemetery. Records from April 9, 1929, place five people in the cemetery, the oldest stone bearing the name Johan J. Stone, who died in 1853. The cemetery is located just north of Rockford on the west side of Northland Drive between 11 Mile Road and 12 Mile Road.

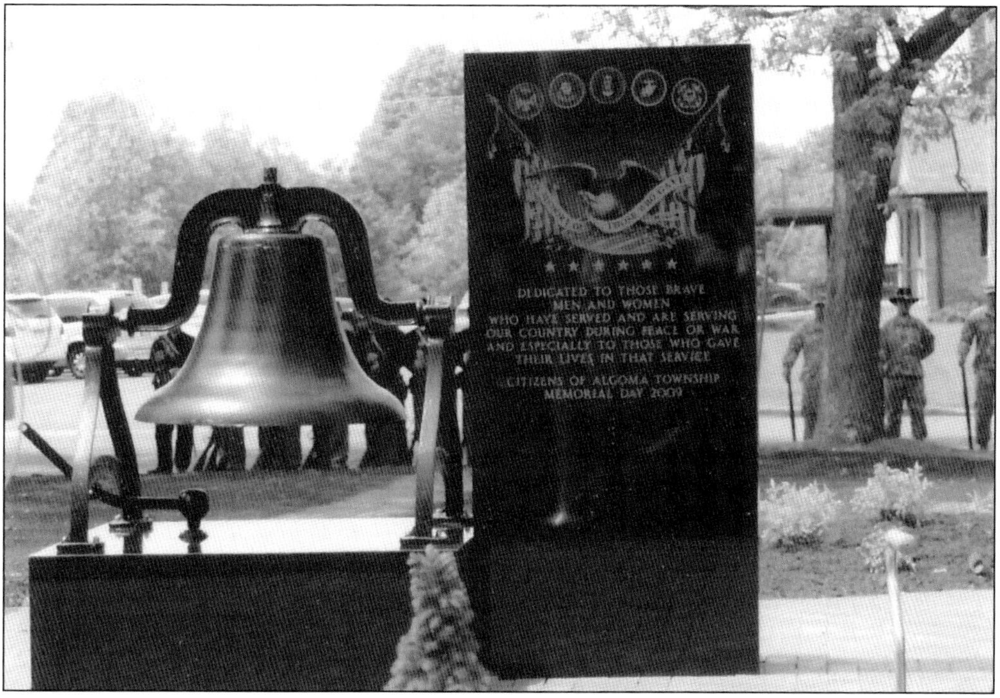

An annual Memorial Day service is held at the Memorial Park. The park was dedicated on Monday, May 25, 2009. The American Legion Rockford post presented arms and the 21-gun salute, and "Taps" was trumpeted. Harold "Hap" Teesdale and Russell Powell, World War II veterans, laid the memorial wreath. Hap served in the 80th Infantry Division, 317th Infantry Regiment, Company K. Russell was in the 87th Infantry Division ("Golden Acorn"), 346th Infantry Regiment. The memorial was erected in honor of the men and women who serve and have served in any branch of the US military. Located near Algoma Cemetery on Grange Avenue, south of 13 Mile Road, the park is paved with memorial bricks etched with names of service members from Algoma Township.

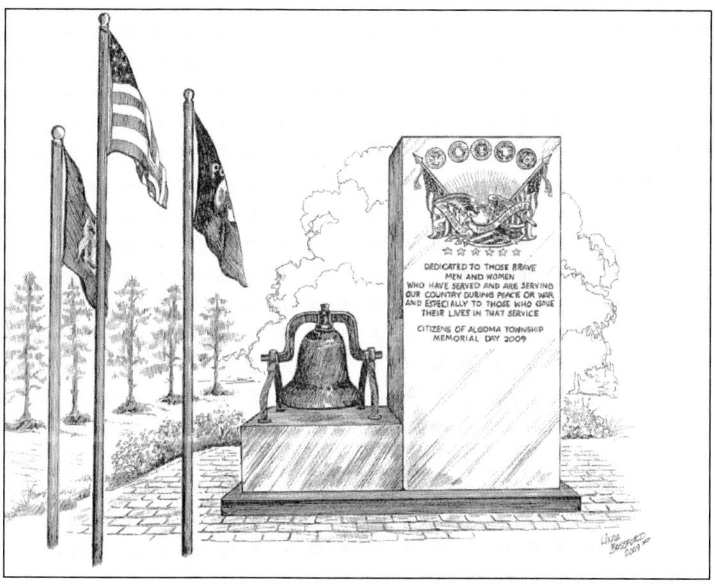

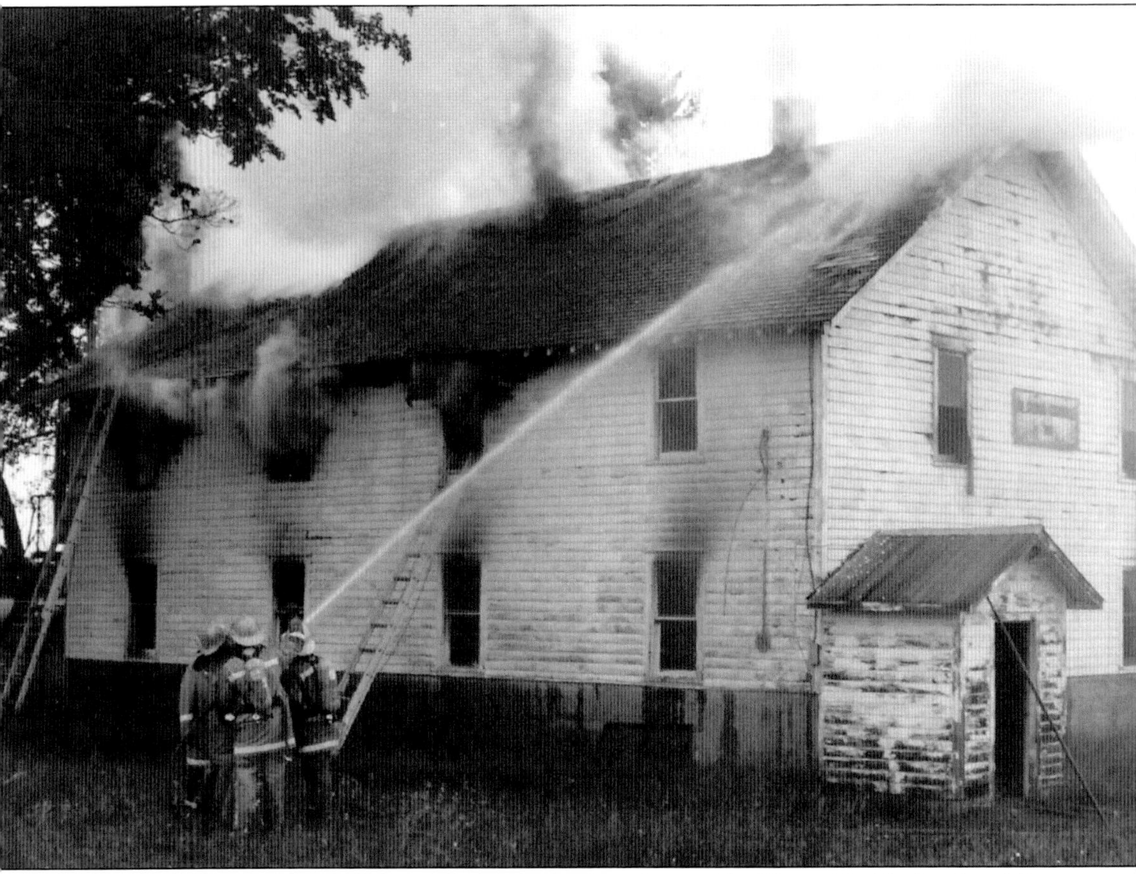

The only known photographs of Algoma Township Grange No. 751, at 13 Mile Road and Grange Avenue, were taken during a fire department practice burn. Township Granges were typically two stories, with a first-floor kitchen, dining room, and facilities and a second-floor meeting room. There are recorded minutes from January 1903, but it is believed No. 751 formed before that date. The Algoma Grange Hall was used by the Algoma Township Fire Department as part of a firefighting training session, with the help of the Solon Township Fire Department. Two of the firefighters seen here are Bill Gross and Ed Rounds.

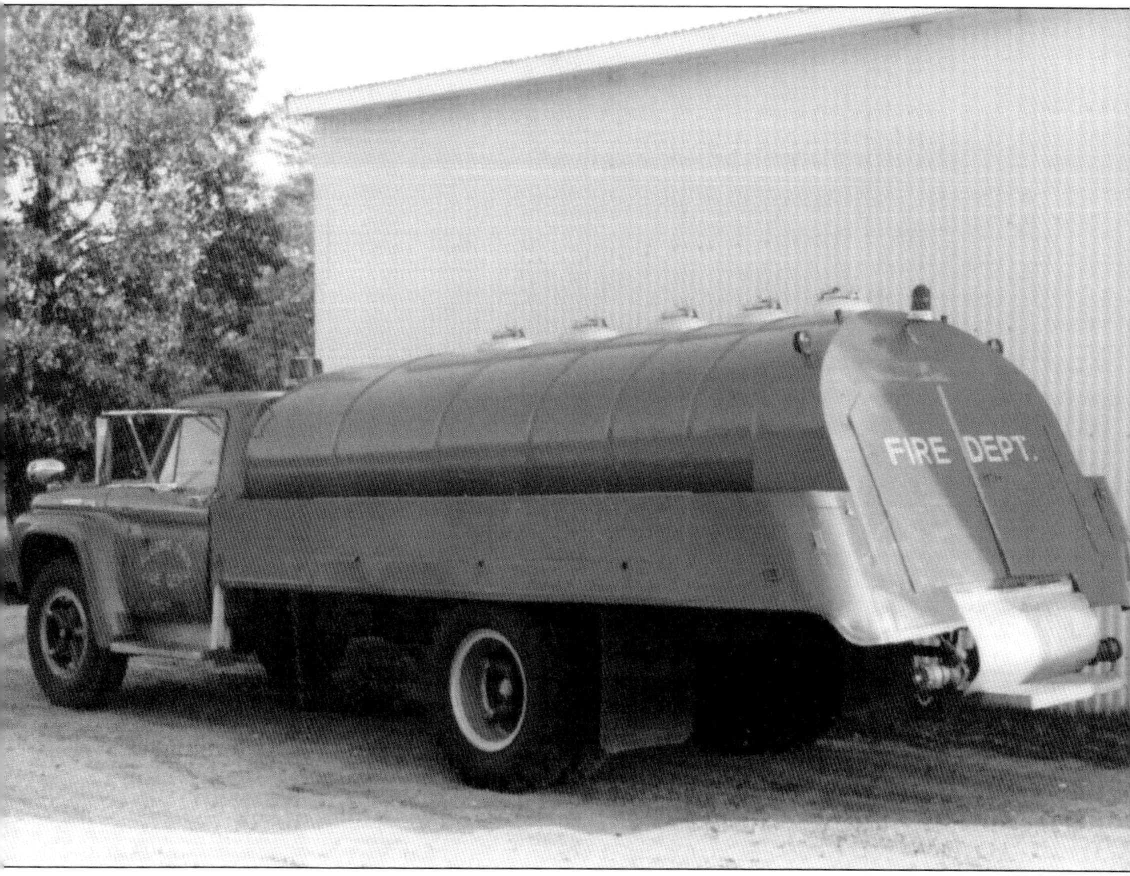

This fire truck was the first major piece of equipment purchased by Algoma Township for its fire department. The 1,500-gallon tanker was mounted on the chassis of a 1953 Ford truck. The two portable pumps carried on the truck were capable of pumping up to 250 gallons per minute.

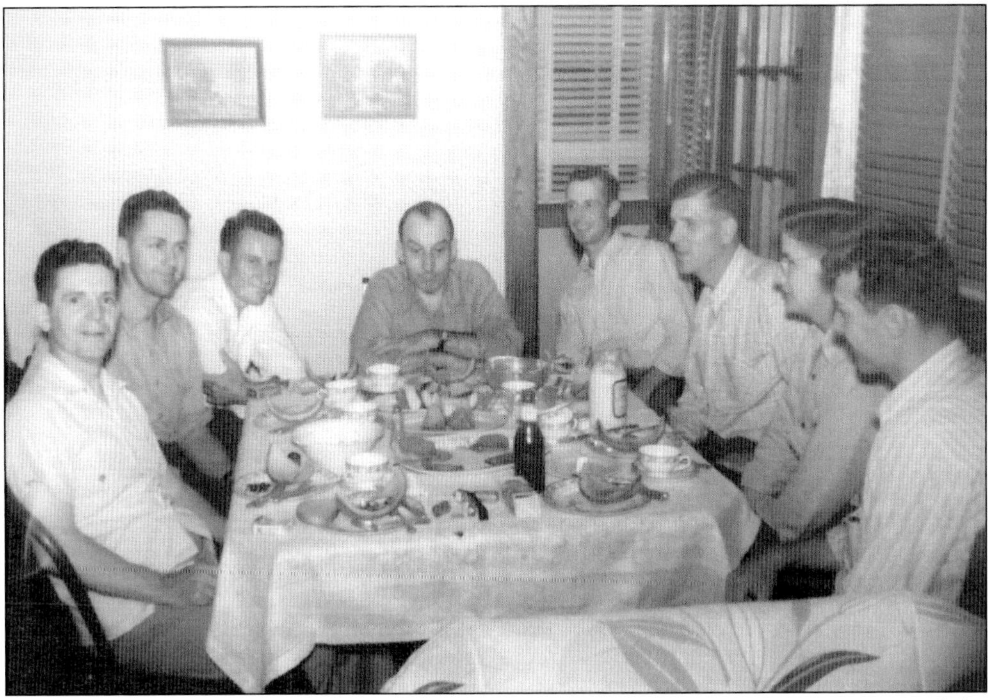

Pausing for the camera are Algoma Township firemen. Camp Lake Fire Station No. 2 and the main Algoma Township fire station, located in the former Chalmers School building from 1968 until 2012, quickly expanded their equipment and training between 1968 and 1972, by which point they had 24 volunteers and five major pieces of firefighting equipment.

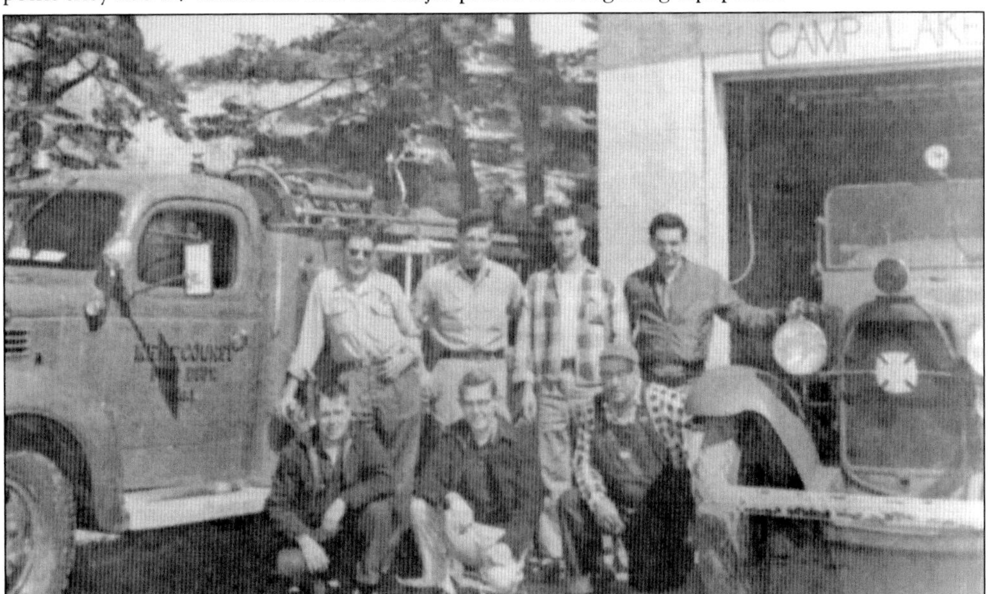

This photograph of Camp Lake Fire Department firemen was taken during Don Swanson's term as fire chief. Pictured from left to right are (first row) Jim Keech Don Swanson and (presumably) Bill Held; (second row) Walton Gold, Clair DeYoung, Ralph Williams, and Larry Welch. It is believed the Camp Lake Fire Department was the first volunteer fire department in Kent County.

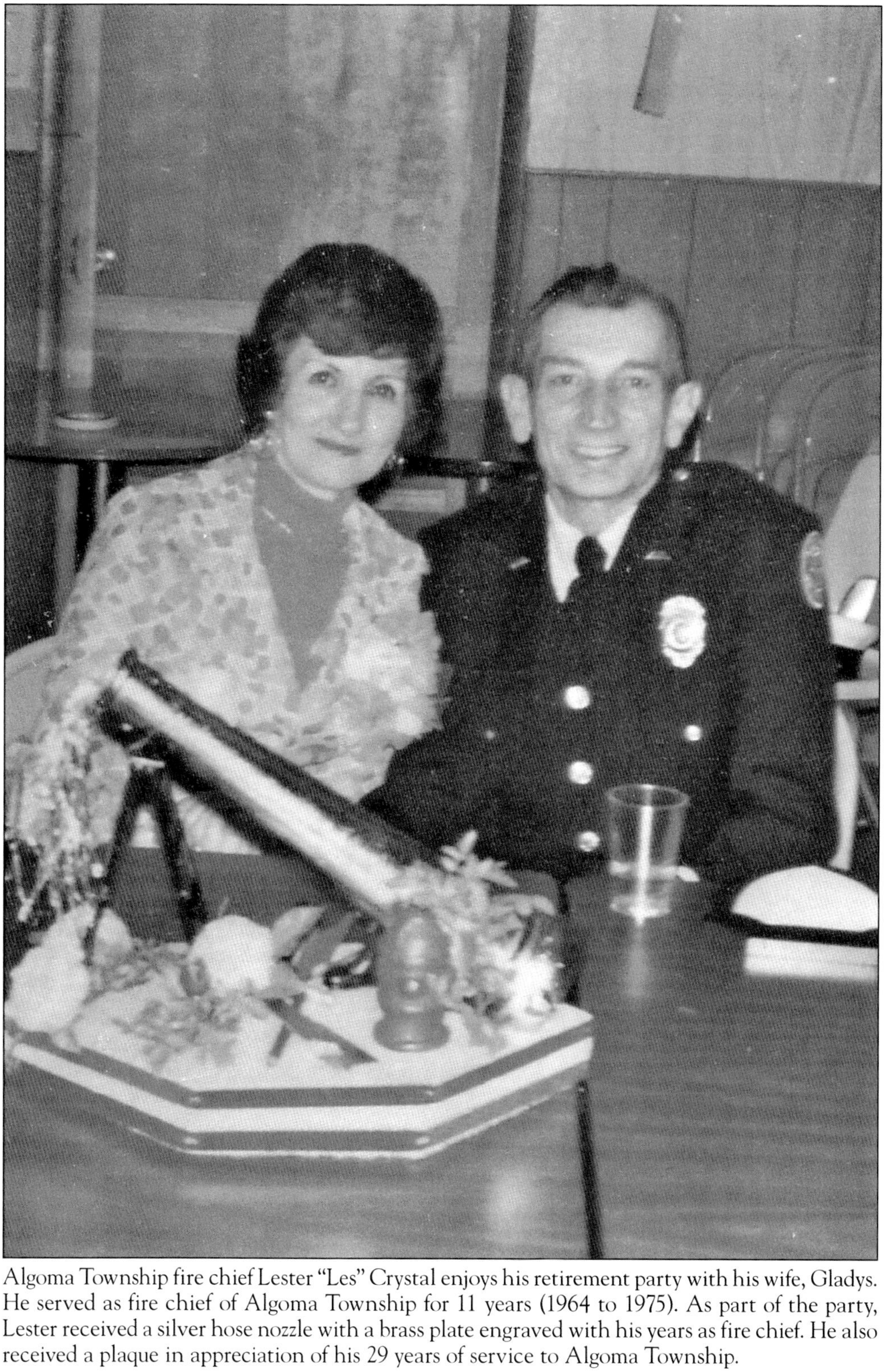

Algoma Township fire chief Lester "Les" Crystal enjoys his retirement party with his wife, Gladys. He served as fire chief of Algoma Township for 11 years (1964 to 1975). As part of the party, Lester received a silver hose nozzle with a brass plate engraved with his years as fire chief. He also received a plaque in appreciation of his 29 years of service to Algoma Township.

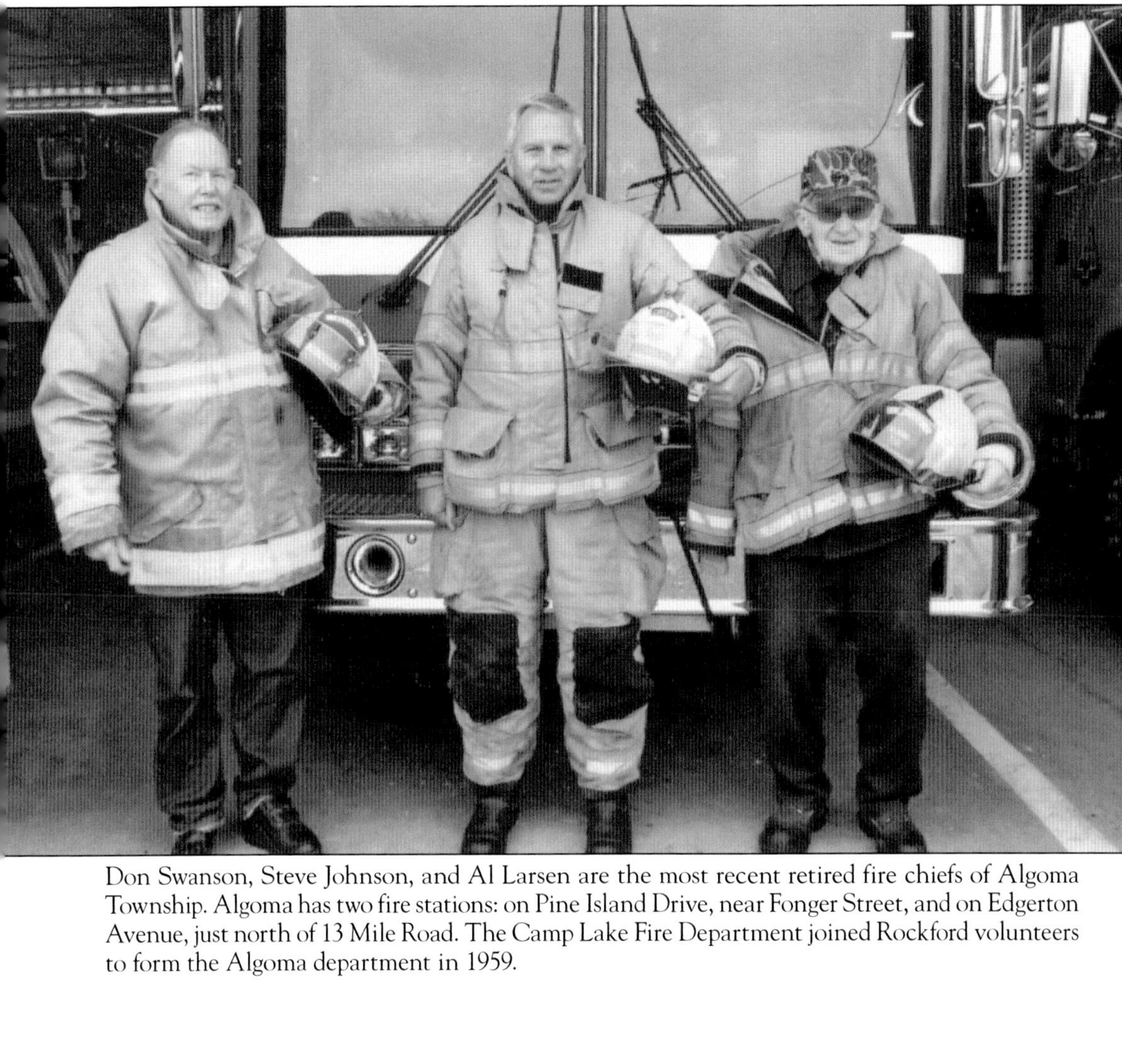

Don Swanson, Steve Johnson, and Al Larsen are the most recent retired fire chiefs of Algoma Township. Algoma has two fire stations: on Pine Island Drive, near Fonger Street, and on Edgerton Avenue, just north of 13 Mile Road. The Camp Lake Fire Department joined Rockford volunteers to form the Algoma department in 1959.

Five

Filling in the Gaps

There are so many people, places, and events to discuss about Algoma Township that it is hard to fit them all within one book. There are also topics to discuss that do not fall within the other chapter topics. In the end, the photographs in this chapter were included to enhance the snapshot of history in Algoma Township that may not necessarily fit into a perfect category.

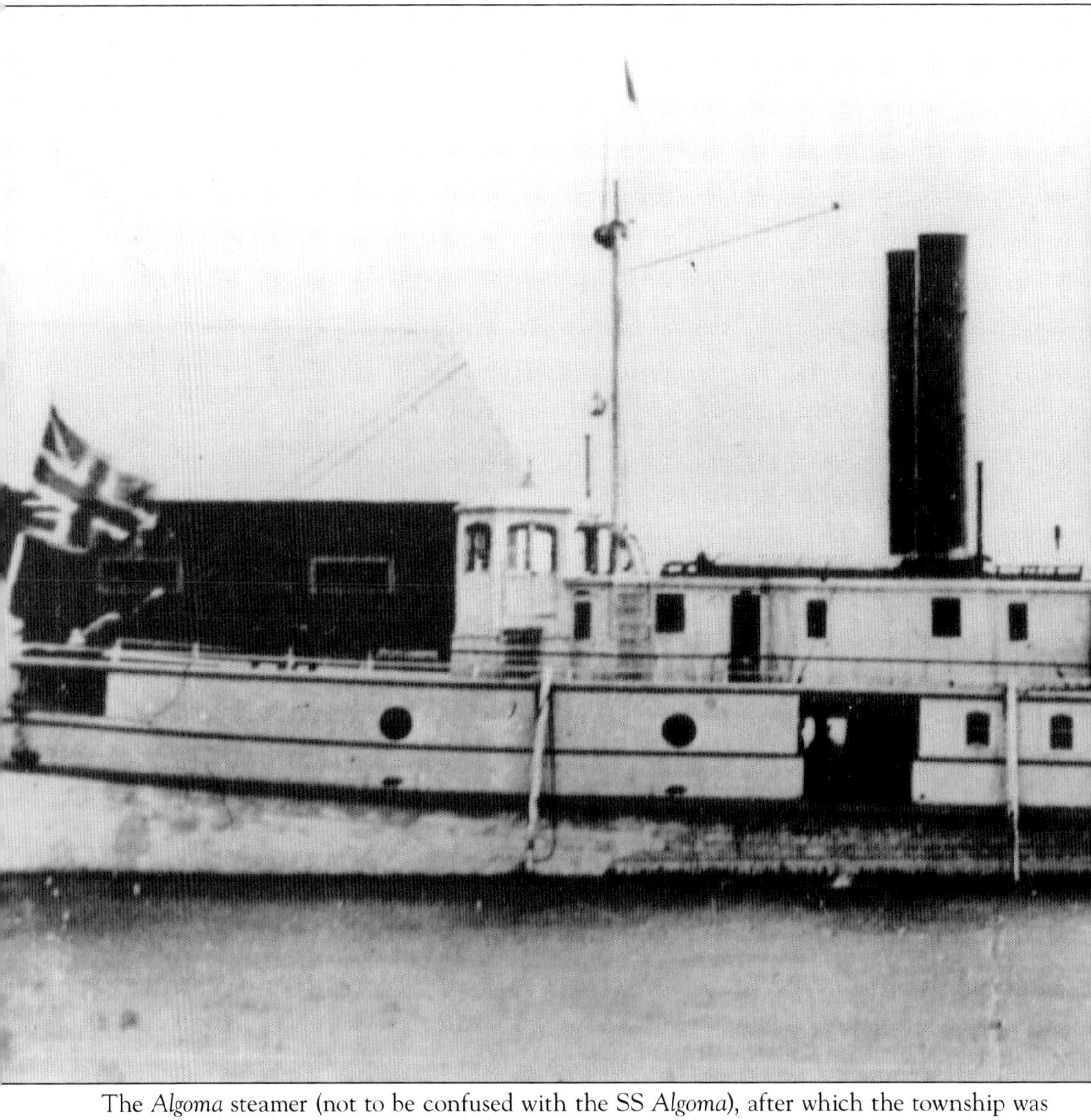

The *Algoma* steamer (not to be confused with the SS *Algoma*), after which the township was named, was launched in 1845. It traveled the Grand River and carried both passengers and freight.

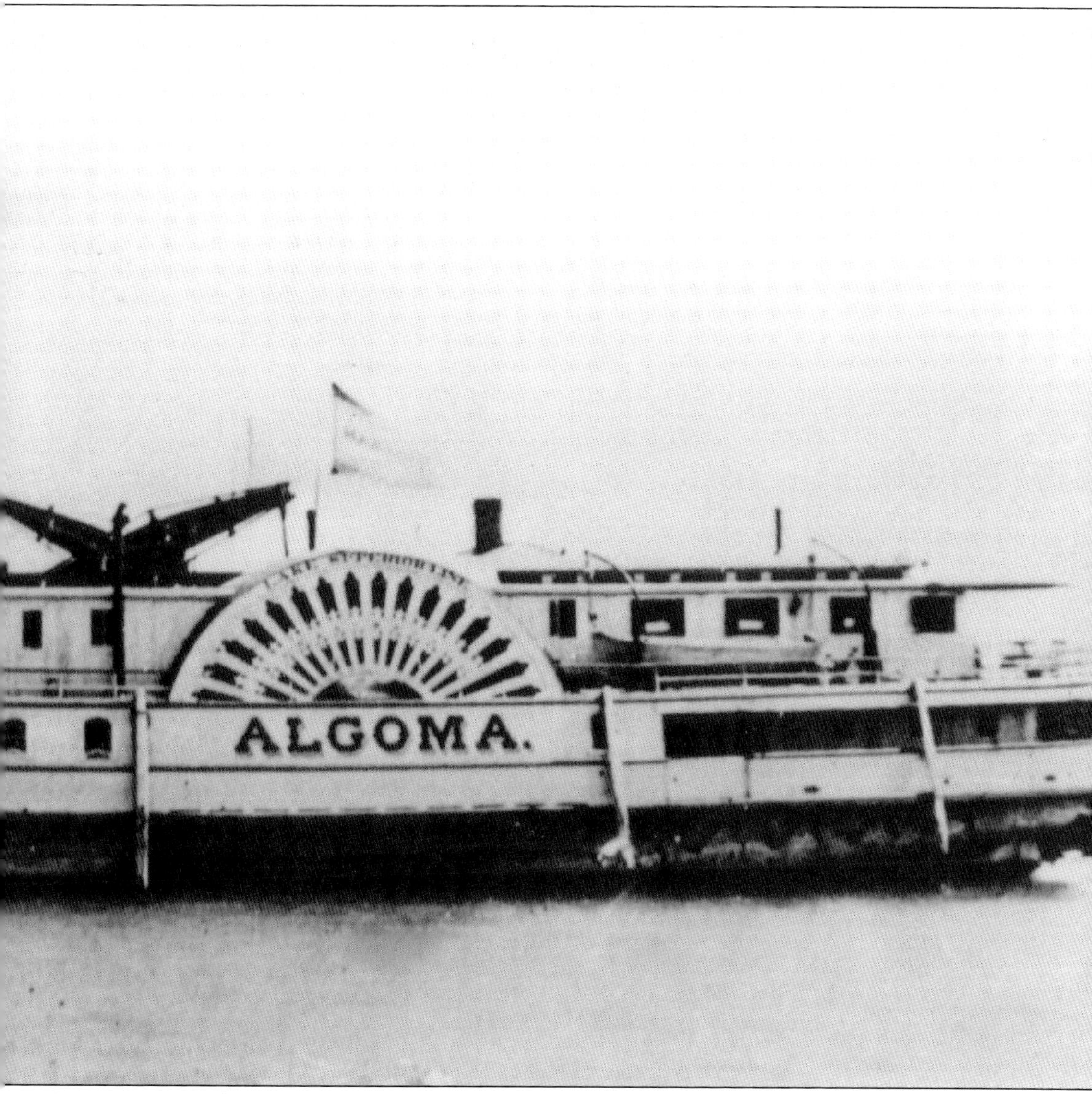

At times, it was also known as the *Racine* and *City of Toronto*.

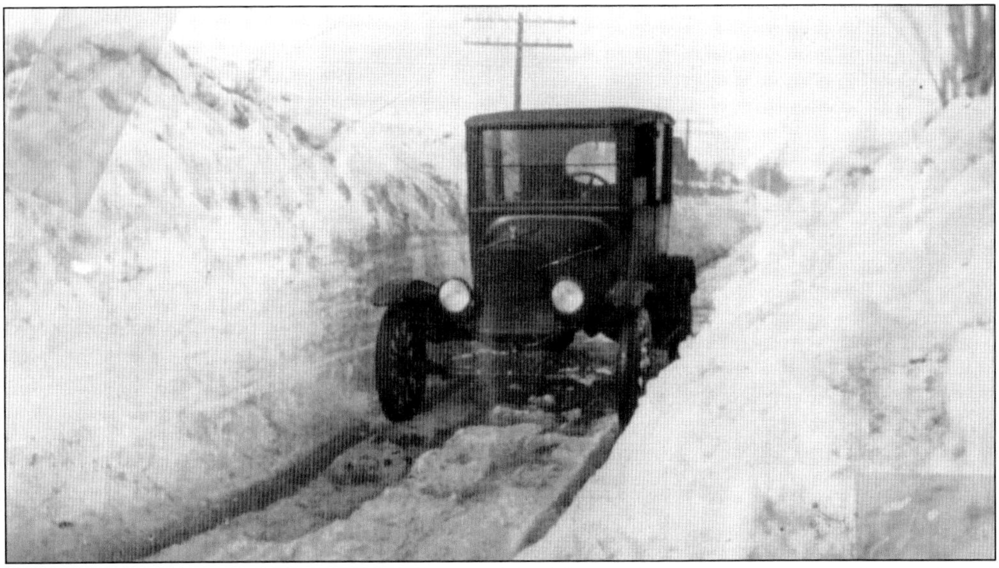

In January 1936, snow made roads barely passable. The road commission was only capable of plowing one lane. It was difficult to even find the road due to the amount of snow. Drivers who ventured out easily became stuck and had extreme difficulty exiting their vehicles due to the snowbanks.

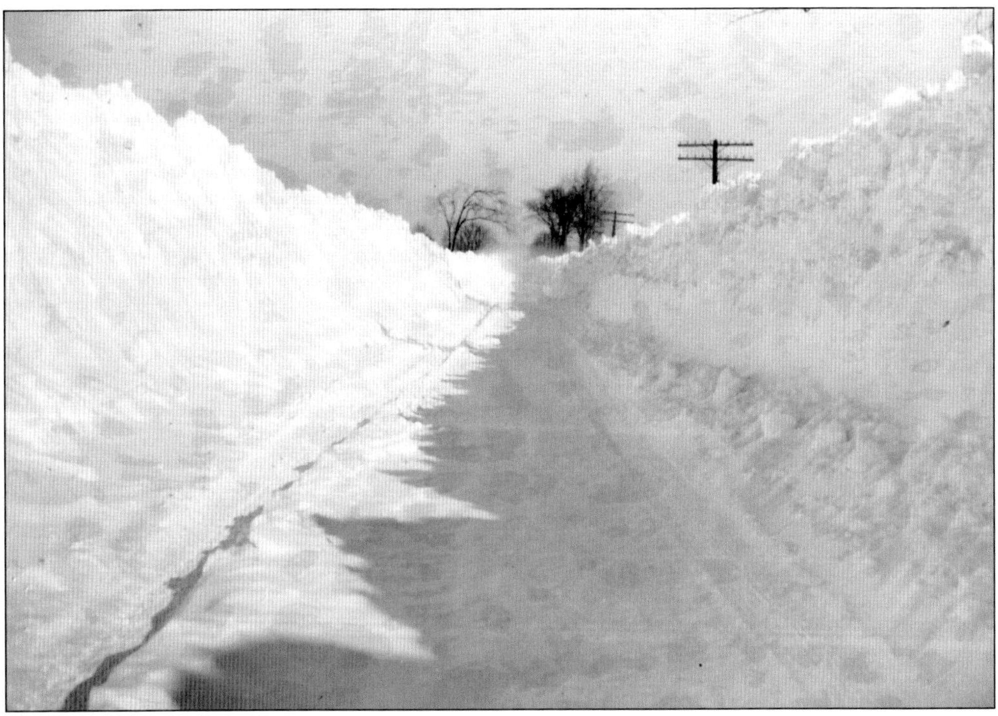

By February 1936, it was nearly impossible for single plows to clear a path for vehicles. One truck could not push through the drifts, so between two and four plows would work together as one. Even with more vehicles, they often had to ram forward 100 feet, back up, and try again. There was also the worry of running into abandoned vehicles that were buried. Even after being plowed, the snowdrifts would cover the roads within hours.

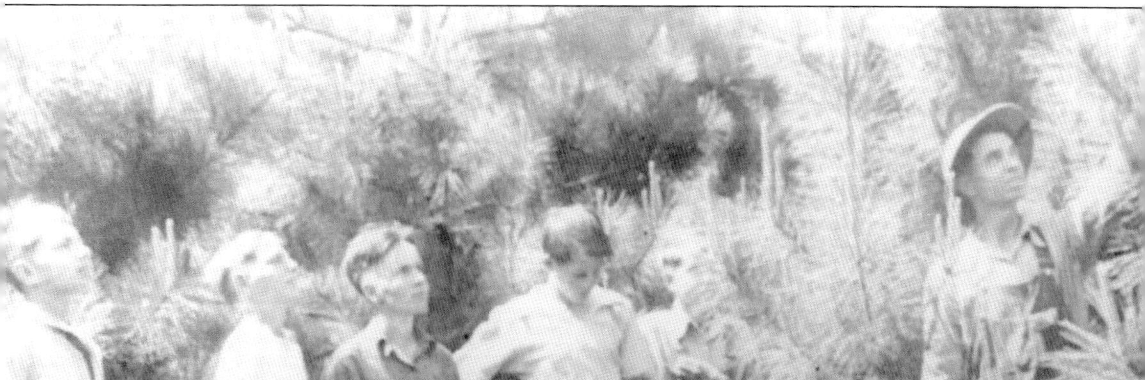

From left to right, Gordon Smith, Harry Jones, Arden Ives, Jim Sweeny, and Hollis Dunn of the Edgerton 4-H Forest Patrol listen to Ward Smith (far right) explain pine tree growth on the Smith farm in Edgerton in the mid-1930s. K.K. Vining, country agent of Kent County, ran the forest patrol.

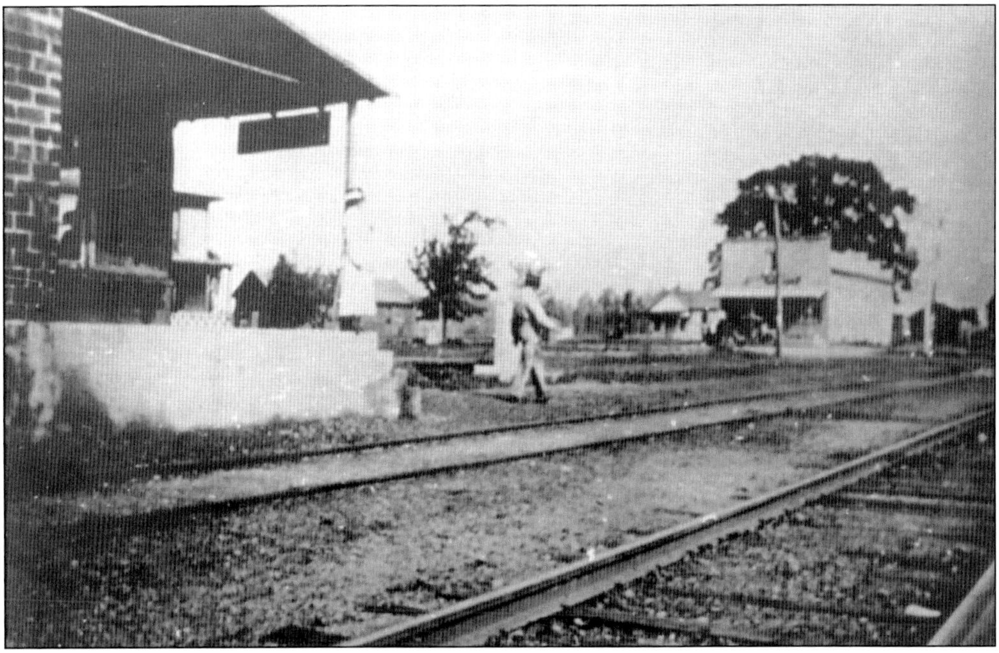

This photograph of the Edgerton train depot was taken in about 1925. The station was on the Pennsylvania Railroad line. Standing on the platform is Agnes Newman. In the background is one of the Edgerton stores north of 13 Mile Road with a Ford vehicle in front of it. (Donated to the ATHS by Robert and Bertha Norman.)

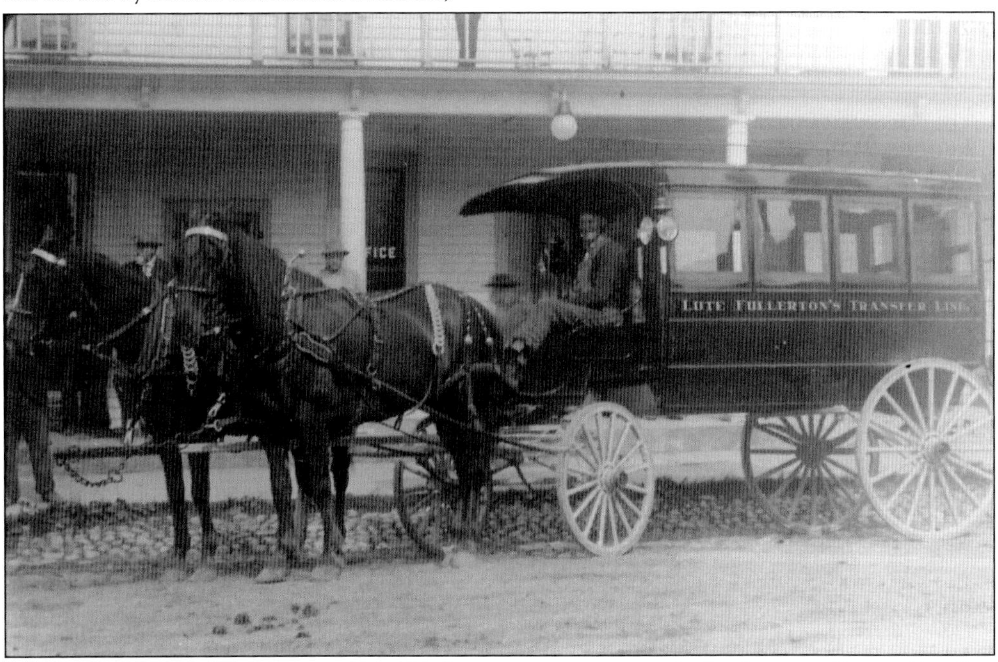

The Lute Fullerton Transfer Line was the livery taxi service in Cedar Springs. Burton Bradley, an Algoma Township farmer and businessman, is driving the team of horses. In the late 1800s, railroads were the primary means of transportation. Horse-drawn taxis took passengers from the railroads to their hotel accommodations or downtown for business and shopping.

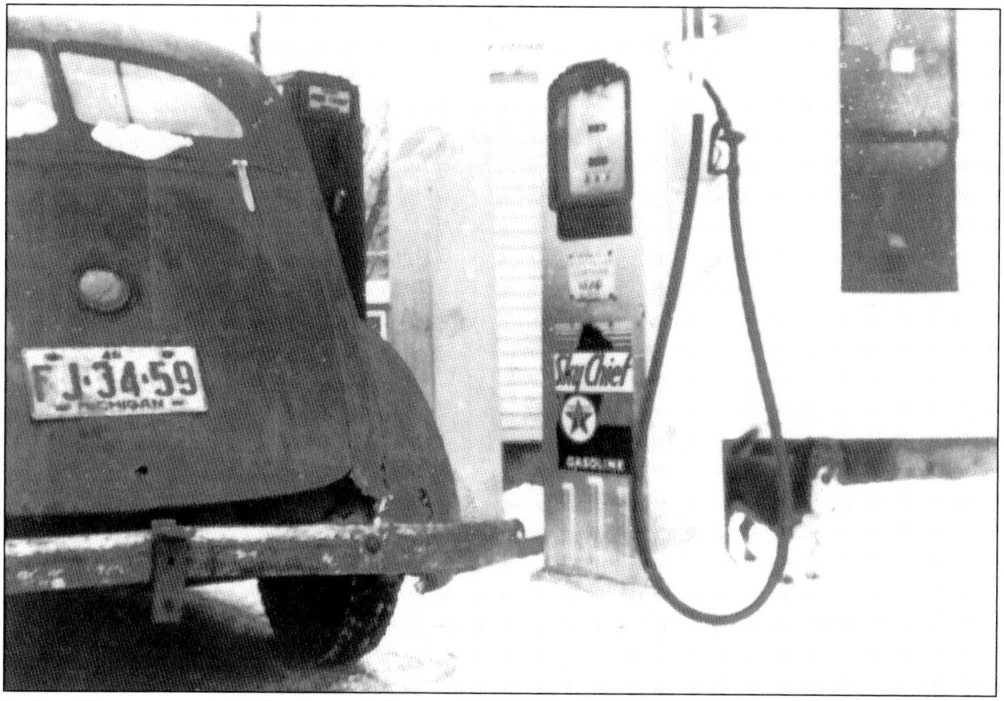

Robert Fonger married Charlotte Culver in 1922. That same year, they bought the general store on the corner of Pine Island Drive and Fonger Street, which had an attached living area. The family both farmed and ran the store, which also sold Texaco gasoline. Early gas pumps, seen above, required one to hand pump gasoline into a glass cylinder with increments on it, up to five gallons. The tank on the vehicle was then filled by gravity pulling the gas through hoses. Robert and Charlotte had three children: Reva, Ruth, and Carl. Ruth passed away at age four. Reva is pictured below next to a gas pump. The store and home burned completely in 1960 and were never rebuilt.

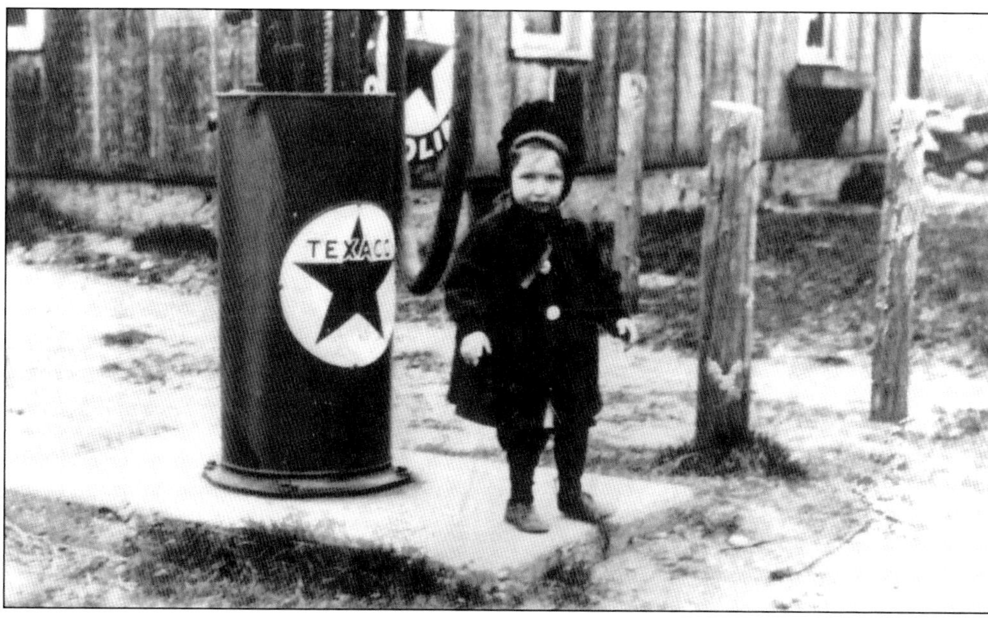

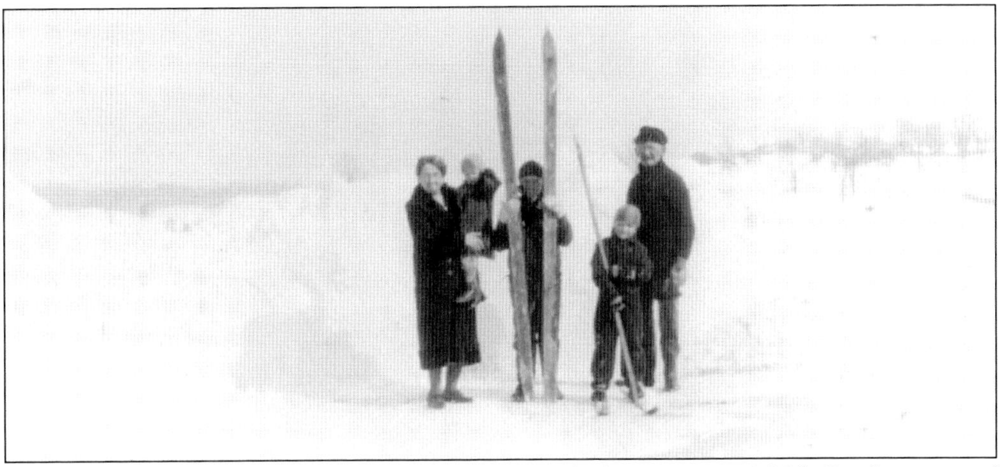

This is Fred Bennett's driveway in the winter of 1937, looking east up 10 Mile Road just east of Algoma Avenue. The home was where US Route 131 and 10 Mile Road now intersect. From left to right are Anna Johnson holding Lyle Bloom, Bill Bloom, Audley Bloom, and Fred Bennett.

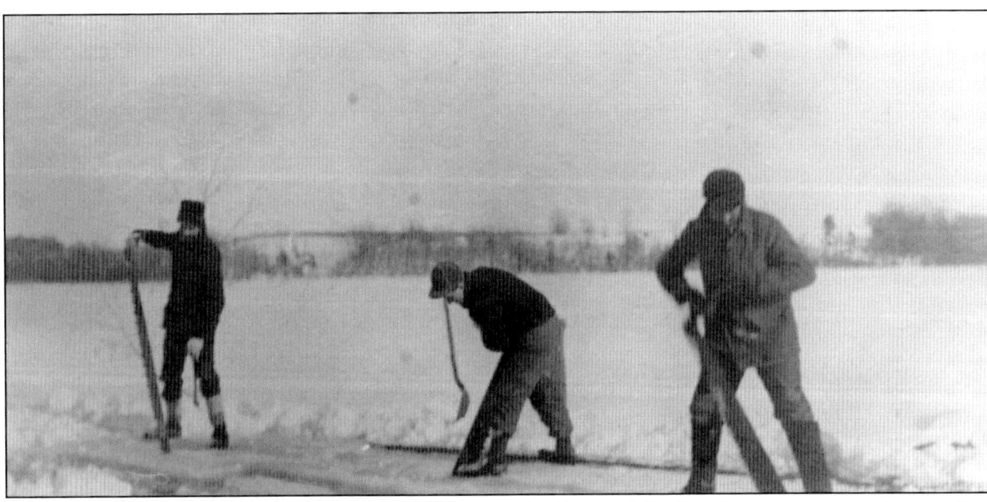

An unidentified team of ice cutters works Camp Lake for ice. Blocks of ice were typically one foot square and weighed at least 25 pounds. Clear ice, when properly insulated, could stay frozen for several years. Insulation was made from a combination of hay and sawdust. Farmers used icehouses to prevent milk and cream from spoiling and to water cows in the winter.

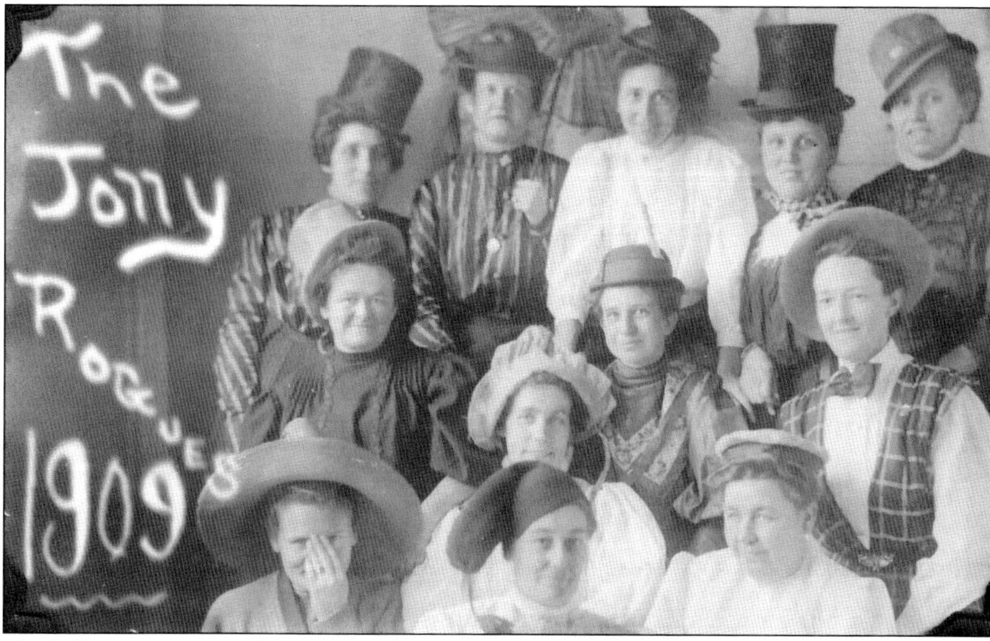

The Jolly Rogues was a club of ladies from Edgerton. They would meet socially in area homes for fun and a "jolly good time" of gossip. They also put on fashion shows and dances at the Maccabee Hall in Edgerton. Known members of the group included Daisy and Fanny Rector, Frankie Morningstar, Hattie House, Maude Peterson, and Ida Robinson.

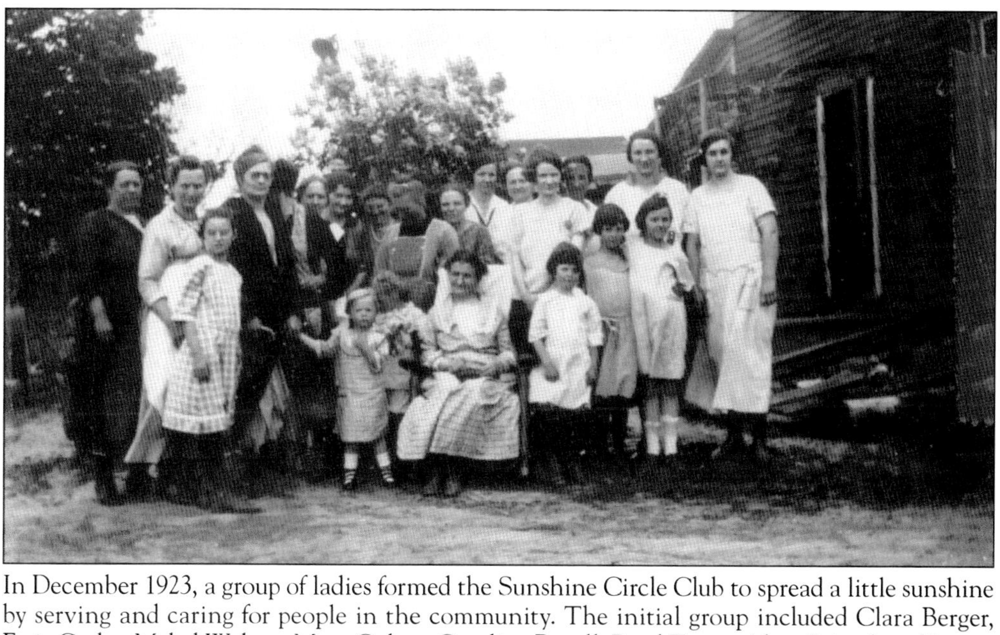

In December 1923, a group of ladies formed the Sunshine Circle Club to spread a little sunshine by serving and caring for people in the community. The initial group included Clara Berger, Essie Casler, Mabel Walton, Mary Culver, Caroline Rosell, Pearl Truax, Alma Bristol, and Lottie Fonger, with Olive Olsen and Ellen Dufort joining at the second meeting. This image depicts a 1924 meeting at the Fields' home.

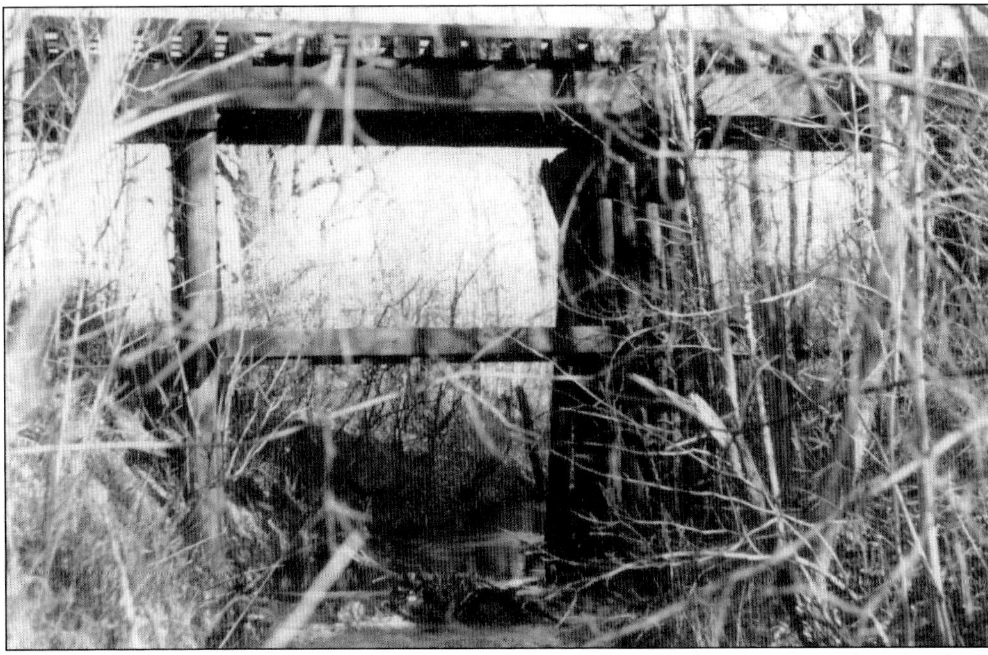

A wooden trestle allowed the Michigan Northern Railway, part of the Grand Rapids and Indiana Railroad line, to cross Shaw Creek. The trestle was located in section 25 of Algoma Township. The Michigan Northern Railway line was abandoned in July 1985 after the last train crossed the tracks.

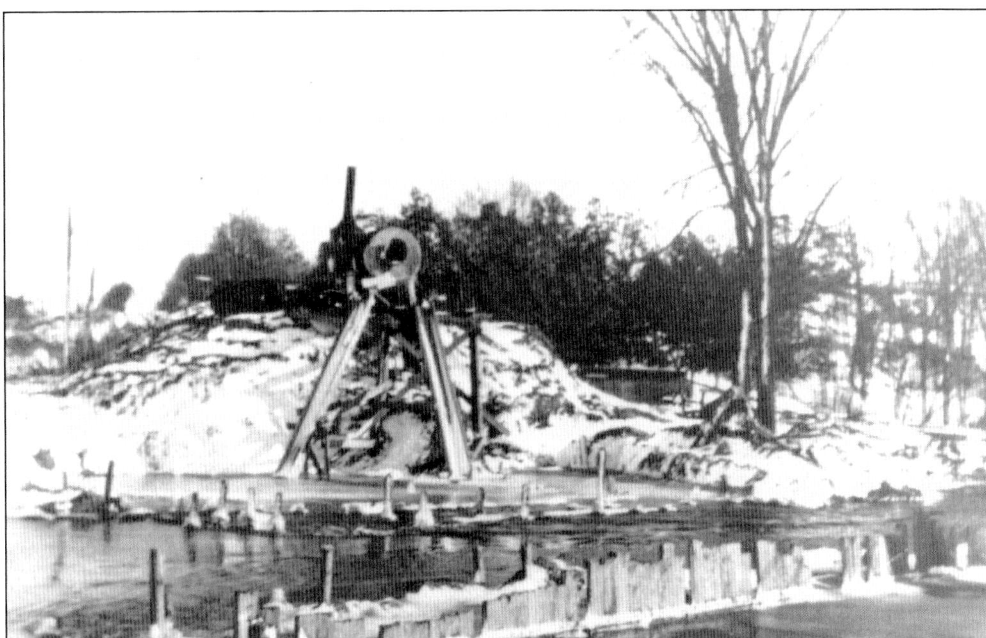

A storm during the winter of 1920–1921 halted road and bridge construction at the Cedar Creek crossing of 13 Mile Road. The grading had been completed and footing foundations were set for new piers. A steam donkey is at the top of the grade. Trees are sparse downstream (to the right) due to logging and construction.

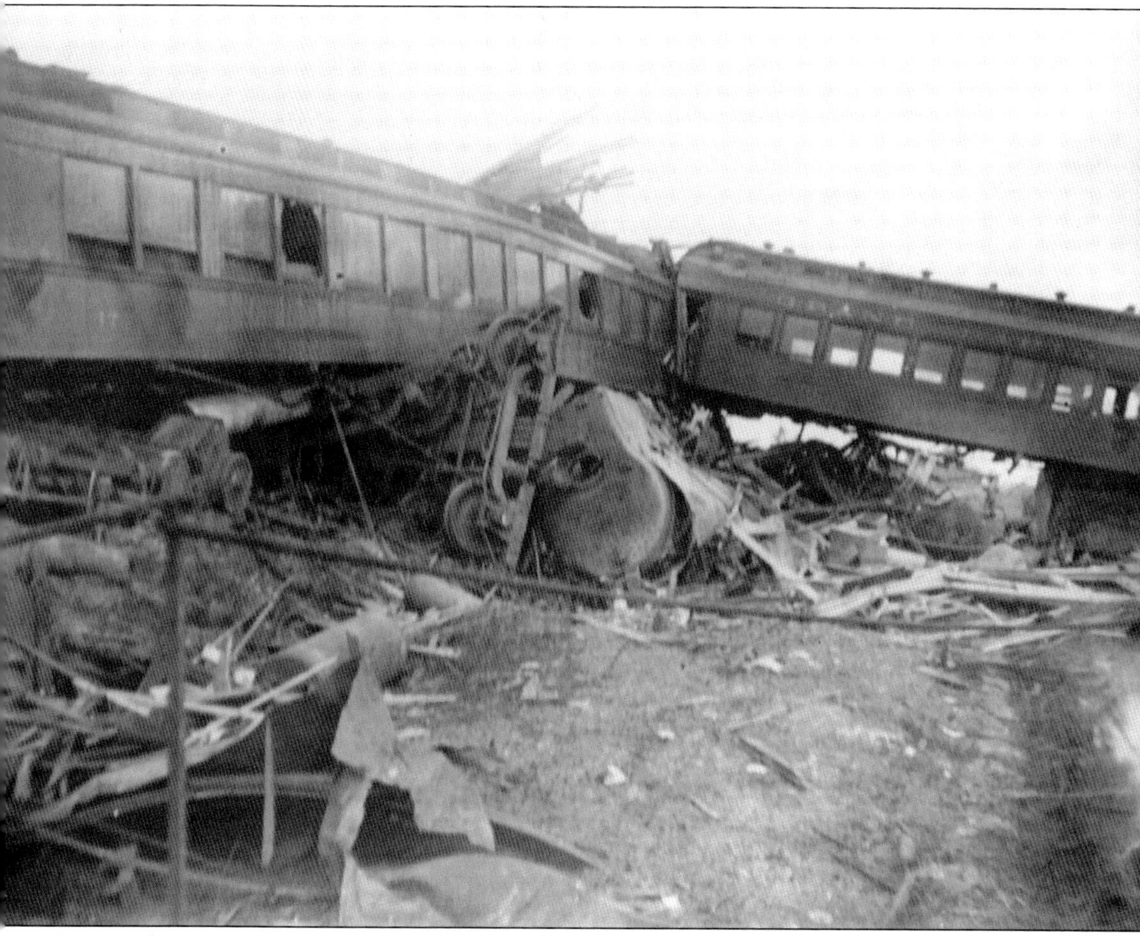

On Monday, November 8, 1943, a train derailed on its way into Algoma Township at about 8:00 p.m. It caused the tanker car to explode, and the resulting fire consumed several cars. The local fire department had difficulty putting out the blaze, and it continued to reignite until late Wednesday. Nearby homes were scorched, and 38 cars containing coal, furniture, and other merchandise were destroyed.

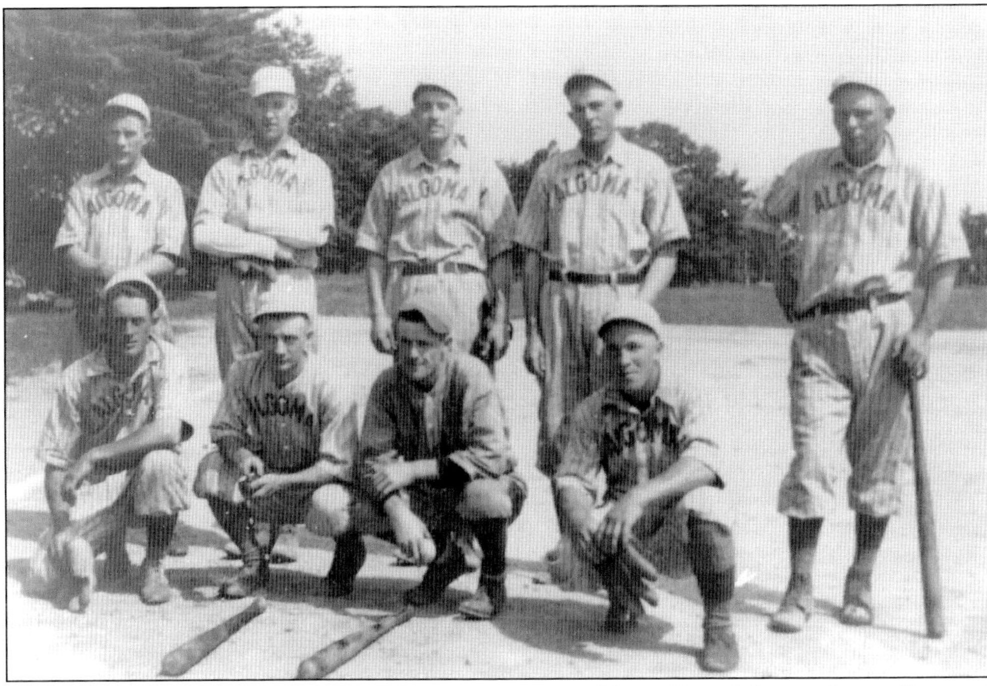

Members of a 1920s baseball team in Algoma are pictured here. From left to right are (first row) Jack Pennington, J.D. MacTavish, Rocky Allen, and Ray Traxler; (second row) Fred Pennington, ? Coleman, Stub Colby, Irvie Pennington, and Mervin Finch.

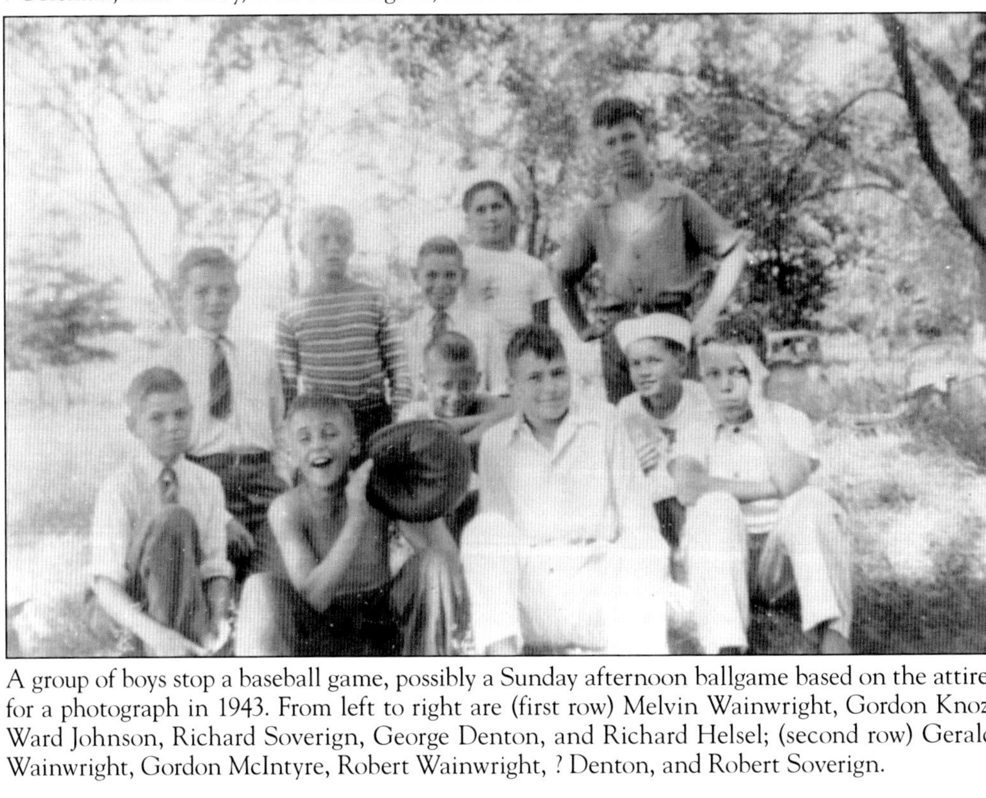

A group of boys stop a baseball game, possibly a Sunday afternoon ballgame based on the attire, for a photograph in 1943. From left to right are (first row) Melvin Wainwright, Gordon Knoz, Ward Johnson, Richard Soverign, George Denton, and Richard Helsel; (second row) Gerald Wainwright, Gordon McIntyre, Robert Wainwright, ? Denton, and Robert Soverign.

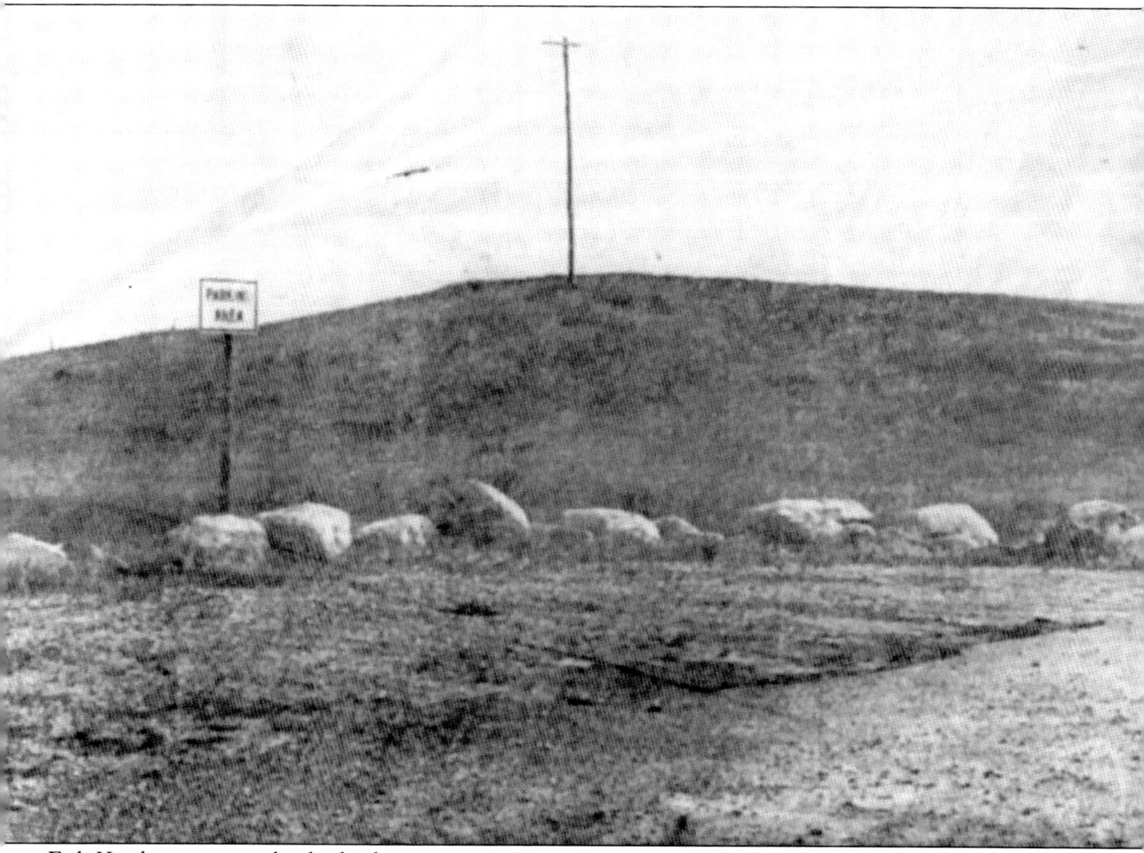

Fisk Knob county park, the highest point in Kent County at 1,075 feet above sea level, is a part of Algoma Township. There is a concrete pedestal nearby the telephone visible in the above photograph, indicating the highest point. A barn and house were located there for many years before it became a park.

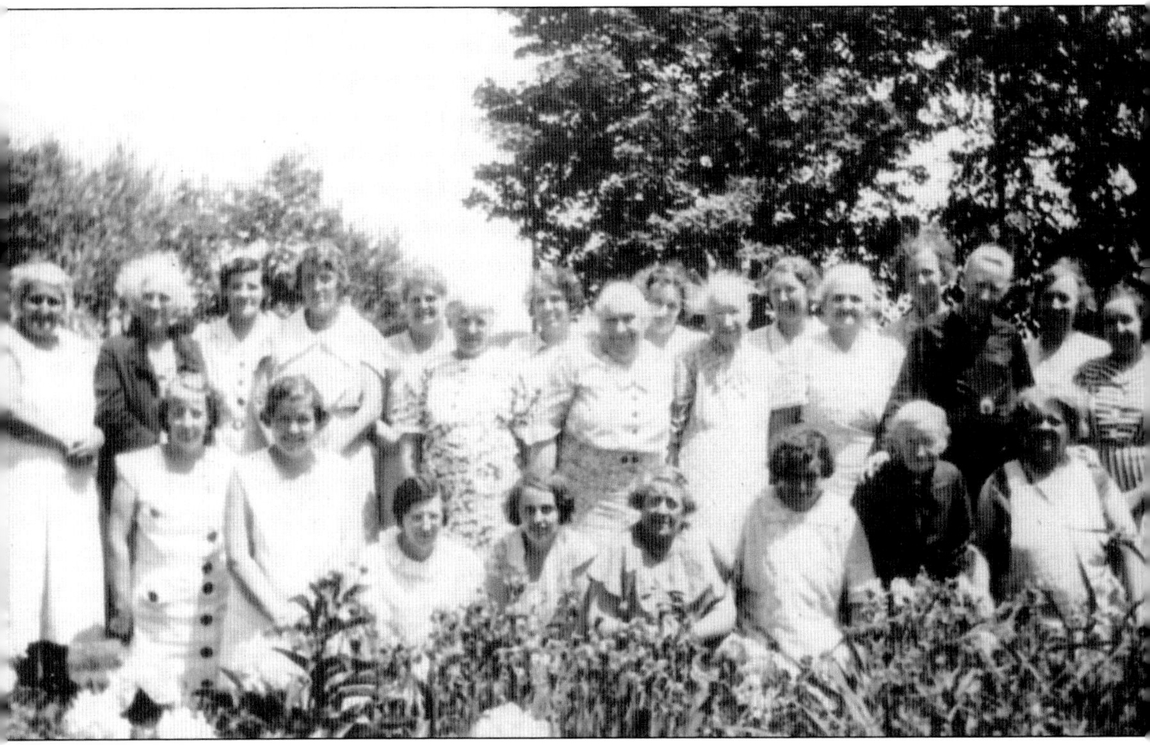

The ladies of the Foxville Friendship Club pose for a photograph in 1925. The Reyburn, VandenBrock, Bradely, Bowler, Magoon Armstrong, and Woodhull families are represented here. The Foxville Friendship Club was responsible for many entertainments in the Foxville neighborhood. It hosted events at Foxville School one Friday per month, including plays, skits, socials, and special music.

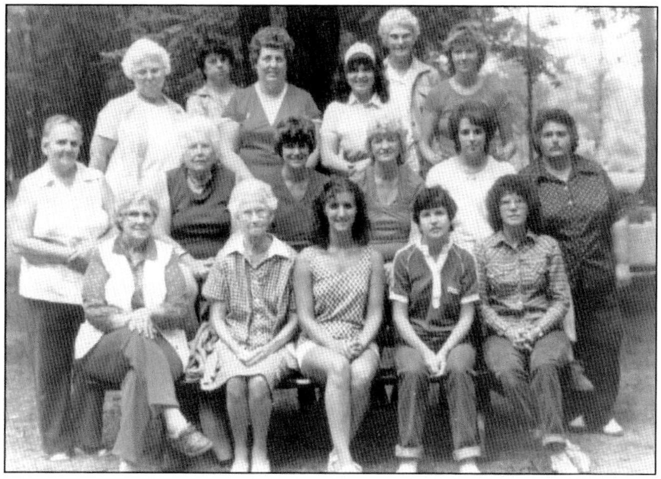

Foxville Friendship Club members pose for the camera sometime in the 1980s. They are, from left to right, (first row) Eloise Covey, Mabel Canter, unidentified, Karen VanVels, and Dawn Heim; (second row) Violet Kleibusch, Loraine Pennington, Karen Rowland, Bev Emmory, Alice Jones and Loraine Roberts; (third row) Stella White, Ruth Stump, Barb Pennington, Bonnie Crobot, Wanda Reyburn, and Retha Schellest.

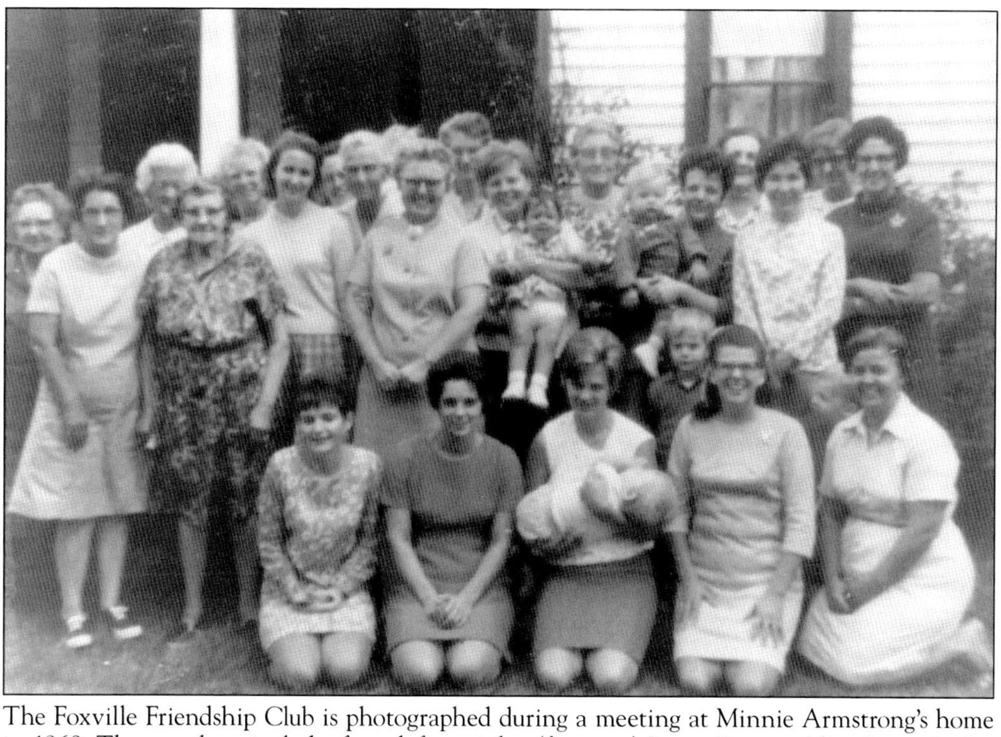

The Foxville Friendship Club is photographed during a meeting at Minnie Armstrong's home in 1968. The members include, from left to right, (first row) Laura Brown, Alice Jones, Lasha Kawalski and baby, Dawn Heim, and Marian Christian; (second row) Florence Mason, Minnie Armstrong, Lois Rhoades, Stella White, Paulette Fitzpatrick, Missy Heim, Carol Magoon and baby, and Margaret Ferrick and son; (third row) Lorna Deboar, Ada Stoops, unidentified, Bernice Armstrong, Wanda Reyburn, Hattie Bigney, Violet Teesdale, and Macil Magoon.

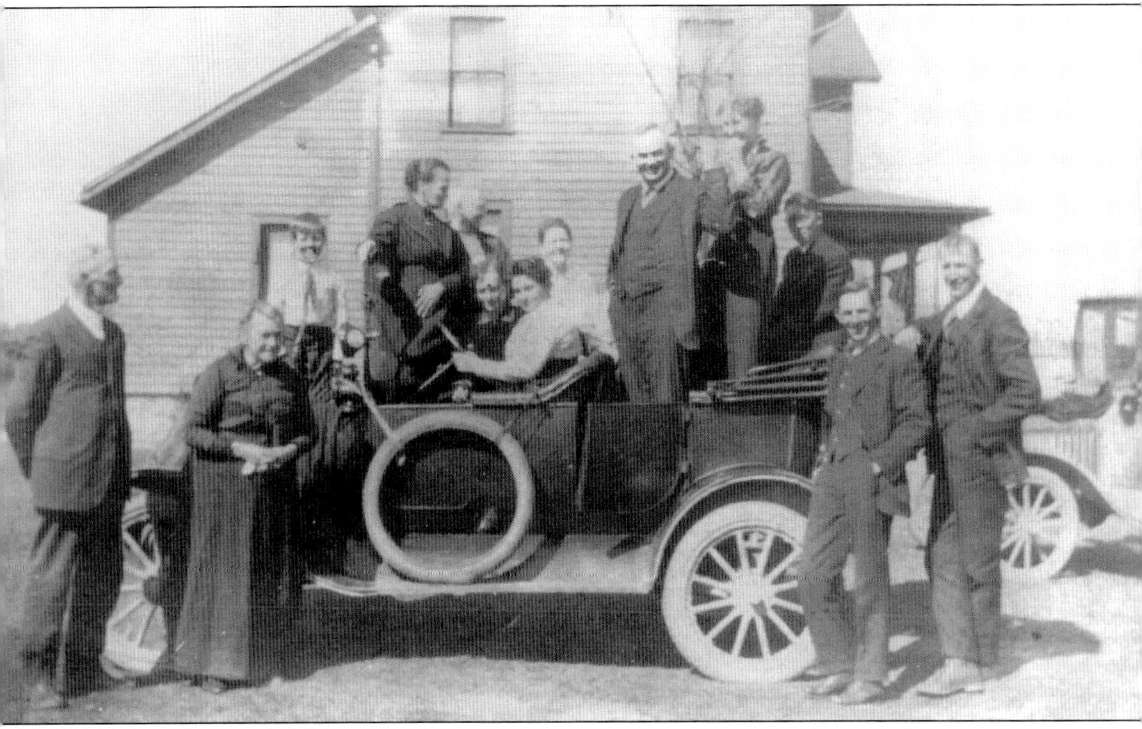

Before the Grange Meeting Hall was built, the Grange met at member homes. This image captures one such in-home meeting. From left to right are Mr. and Mrs. Earl Weston, unidentified, Mrs. Tom Whittle, Tom Whittle, unidentified, Bessie Seeley, Pearl Truax, Dena Rosell Bloom, Floyd Seeley, Irvin Moxon, Abe DeWilde, and Cassius Dillie.

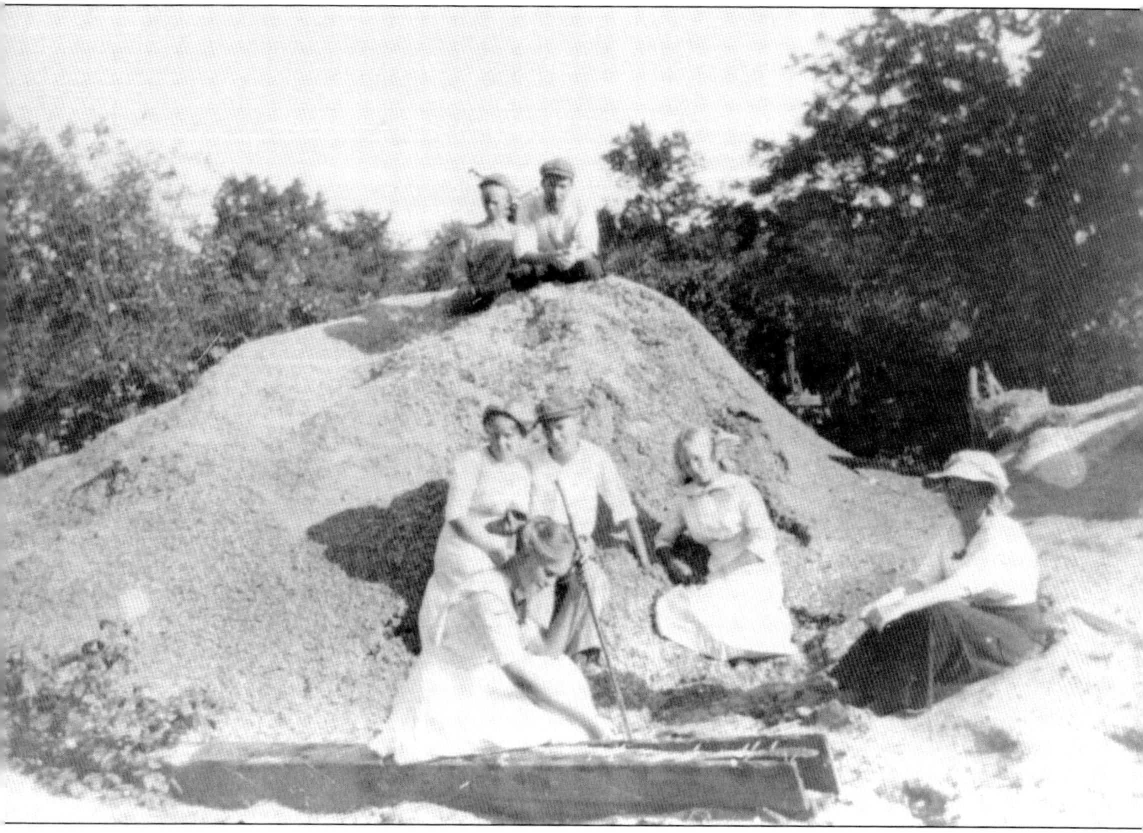

A group of people sits on old sawdust piles of Curtis's Mill in an area called Curtisstown, on the west side of Cedar Creek near the Friske Bridge, in 1913. Curtisstown was named in honor of George S. Curtis, owner of the mill. (Courtesy of Gertrude Lundin Sprik.)

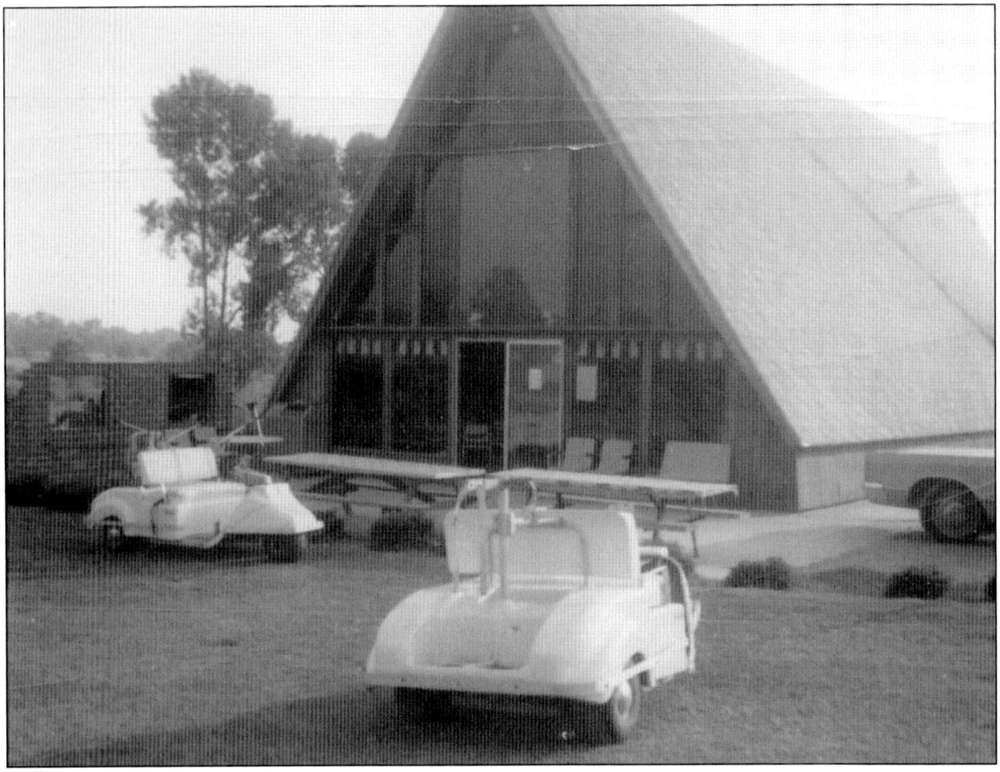

Grand Rapids Moose Lodge No. 50 moved from downtown Grand Rapids to Camp Lake Golf Course in Algoma Township in 1973. The lodge would be unable to retain the chapter number if the name changed, so a compromise, Grand Rapids–Sparta Moose Lodge, was chosen. Wyoming Moose Lodge No. 763 split off from Grand Rapids Moose Lodge No. 50. In 1975, the building (pictured) burned and was fought by Algoma, Sparta, Kent City, and Solon firefighters.

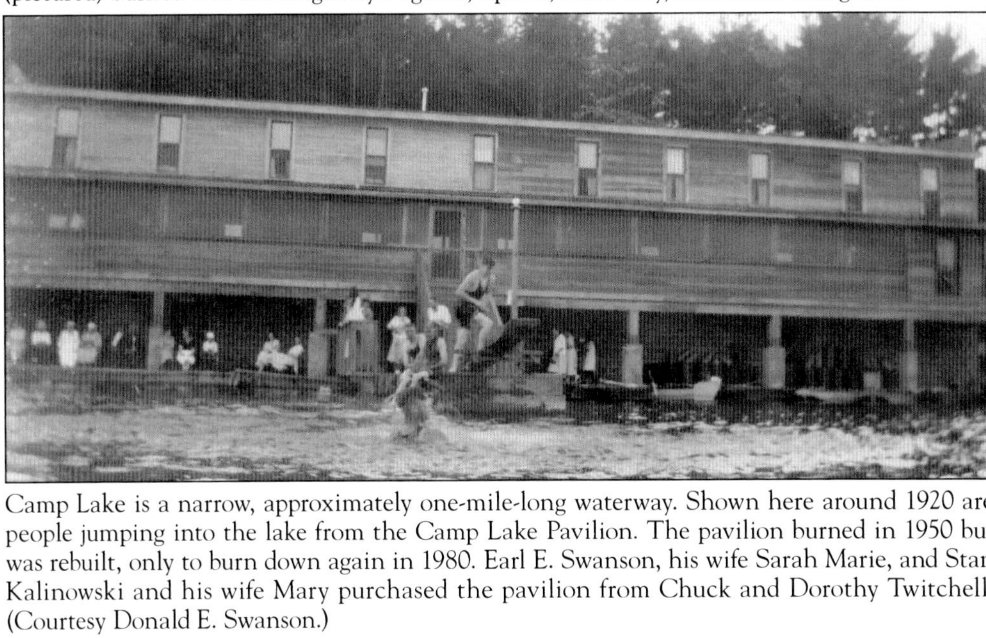

Camp Lake is a narrow, approximately one-mile-long waterway. Shown here around 1920 are people jumping into the lake from the Camp Lake Pavilion. The pavilion burned in 1950 but was rebuilt, only to burn down again in 1980. Earl E. Swanson, his wife Sarah Marie, and Stan Kalinowski and his wife Mary purchased the pavilion from Chuck and Dorothy Twitchell. (Courtesy Donald E. Swanson.)

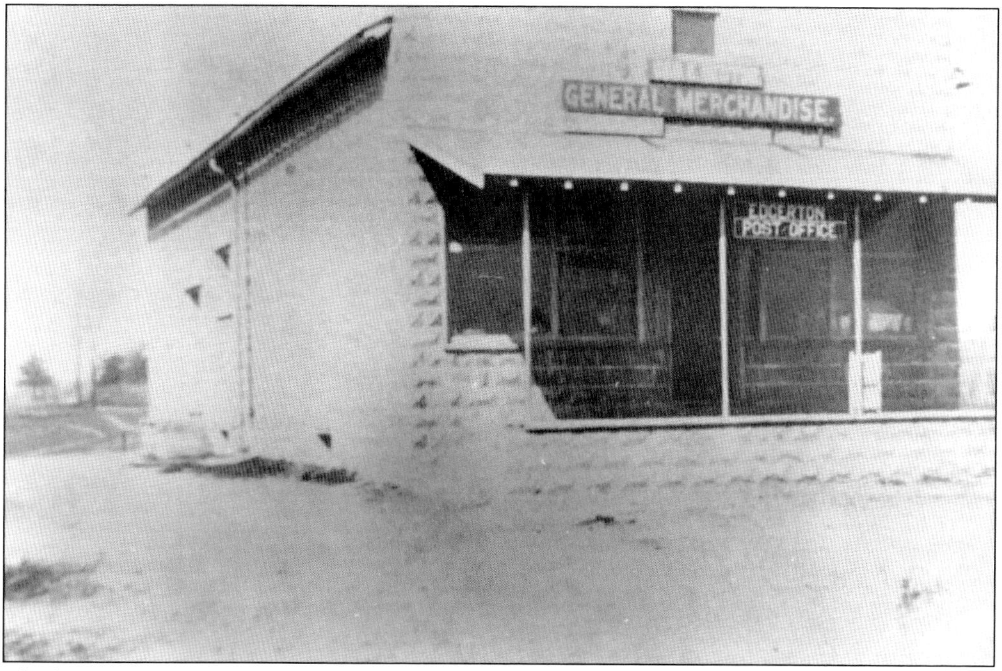

The first store and post office in Edgerton was built in 1869. E.F. Tyron owned the store and sold it to George Tompsett in 1877. Some years later, David Munro, owner of the Munro Mill, purchased the store. He sold produce out of the store and was postmaster for nine years.

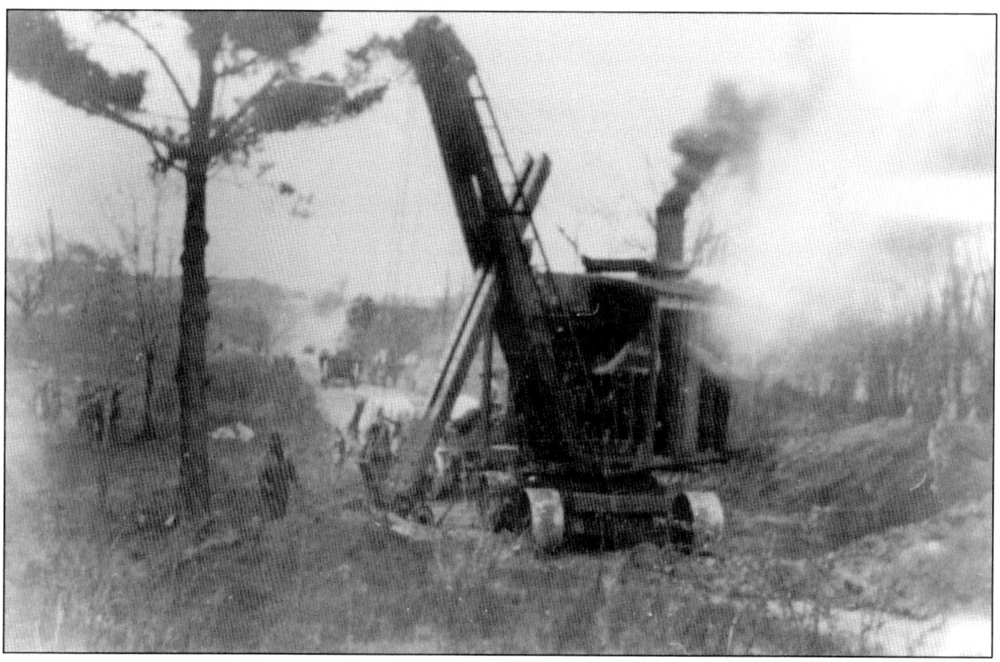

Seen in the fall of 1920, this steam shovel is loading horse-drawn wagons with earthen fill and stones in an effort to widen 13 Mile Road. The view is looking east form the Lundin farm. Just beyond, where the two wagons are passing each other, is the junction of Friske and 13 Mile Roads.

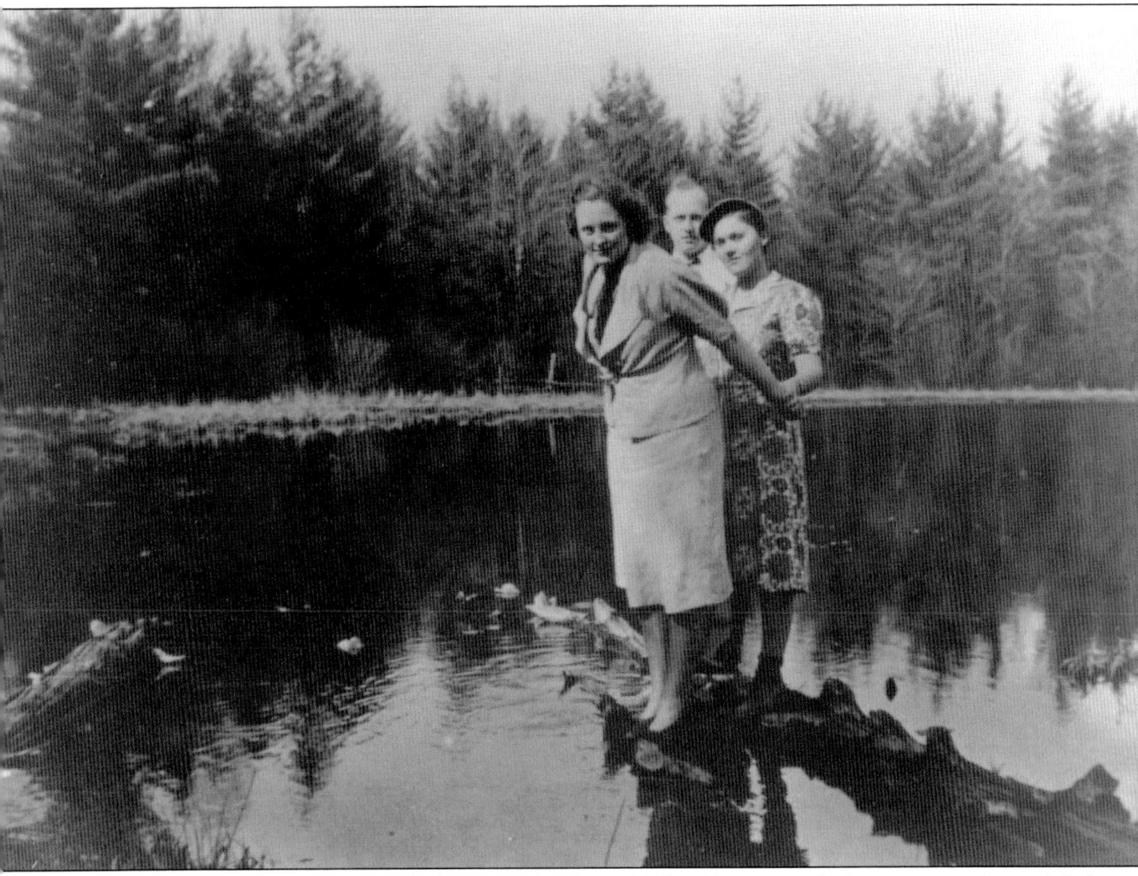

From left to right, Eleanor Helsel, Henry Sprik, and Edna Rector are balancing on a log in Mud Lake around 1935.

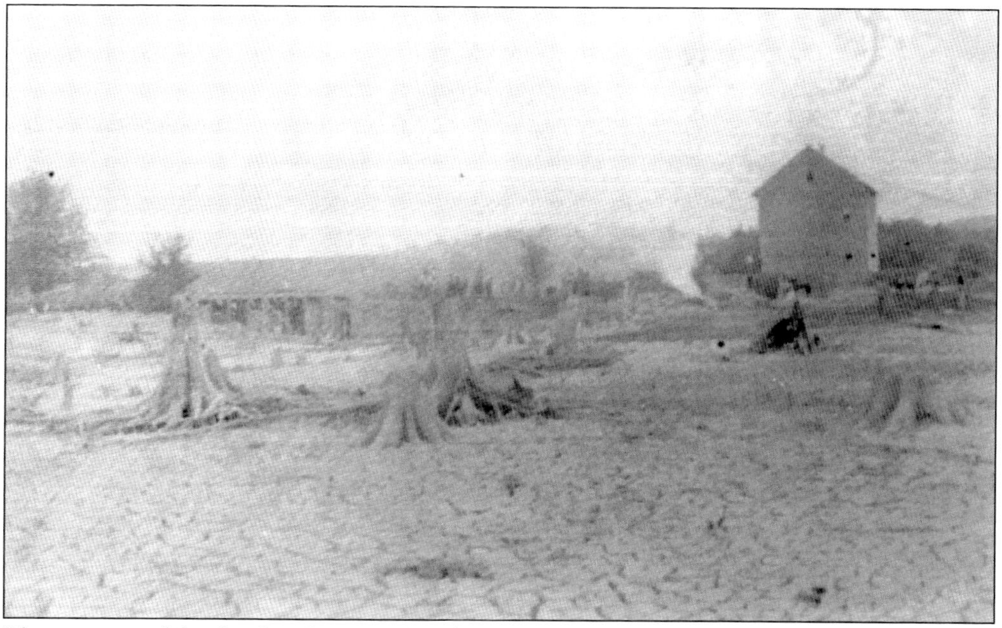

This is a view of the dried-up Stegman Creek impoundment east of David Munro's gristmill. The old stumps probably originate from the time the first dam was built in 1854 by Seth Porter. The railroad grade is visible behind and across the top of the dam. It must have been a hot summer when the photograph was taken, since the cracked bottom of the pond when filled has a depth of up to 12 feet.

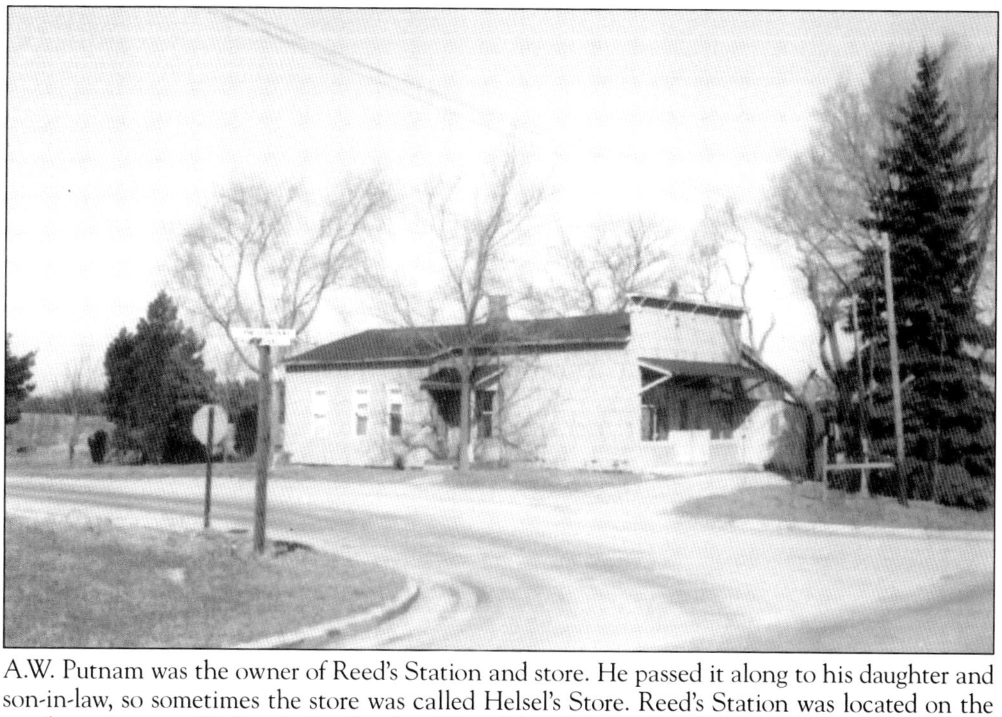

A.W. Putnam was the owner of Reed's Station and store. He passed it along to his daughter and son-in-law, so sometimes the store was called Helsel's Store. Reed's Station was located on the northwest corner of Indian Lakes Road and Pine Island Drive. The Toledo, Saginaw & Muskegon Railroad passed north of the store, running from east to west.

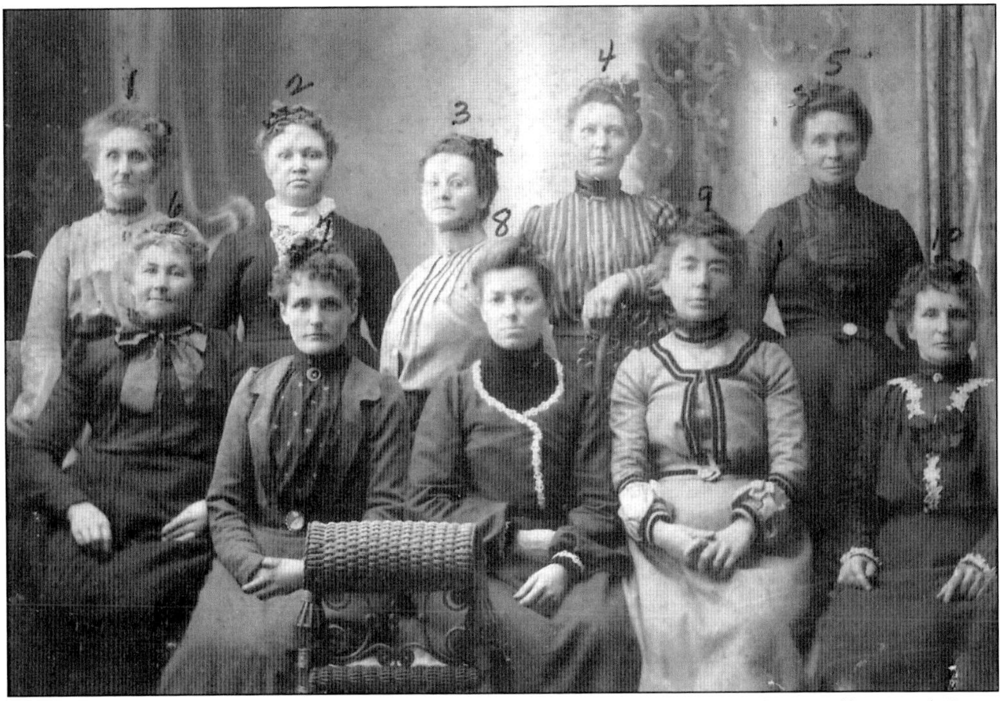

The Algoma Aid Society is seen here in 1905. Pictured from left to right are (first row) Dora Pennington, Armanda Stauffer, Della Pope, Cinthia Burgett, and Betty Hull; (second row) Libby Lemunyon, Kittie Reyburn, Alta Fitch, Claudia Pope, and Eva Colby. The society later changed its name and became the Algoma Community Club.

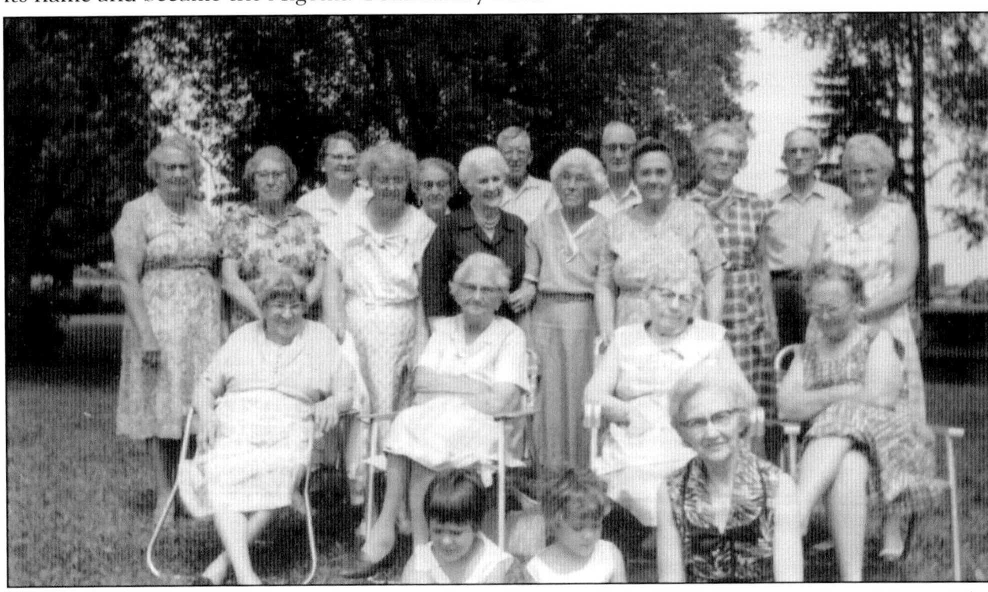

Algoma Community Club members pause for a photograph in 1965. They are, from left to right, (sitting) Maude Allington, Jasie Putman, Mary Atkinson, Tressie Bowler, Retta Norman, and Rena VandenBroeck's granddaughters; (standing) Cora Palmer, Libby Burgett, Edith Couturier Reyburn, Rena VandenBroeck, Lettie Burgett, Verda Caine, Andrew Norman, Lottie Reyburn, Dick Bowler, Marie Pennington Colby, Margaret DeYoung, Jack Pennington, and Lois Bowers.

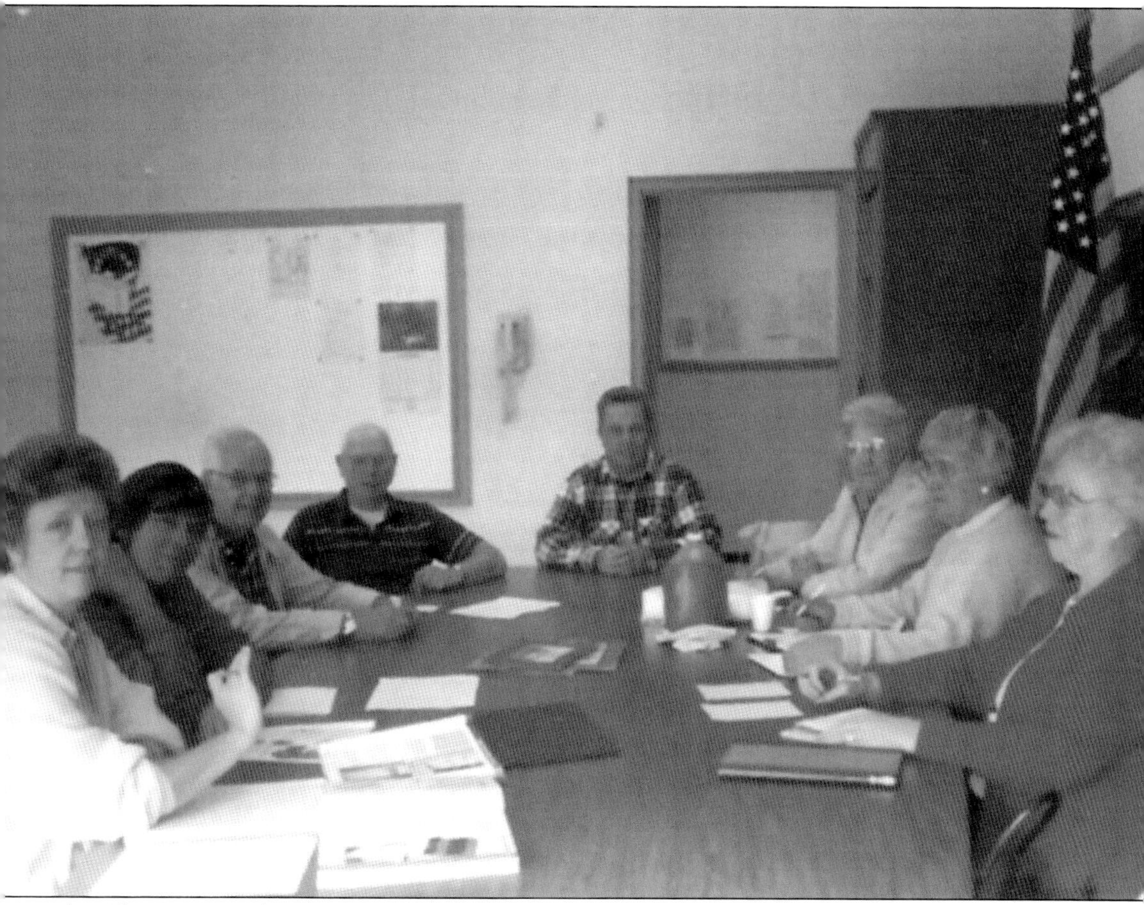

The Algoma Township Historical Society was established in 1986 and gathers and catalogs historical artifacts and archives for the purpose of displaying and preserving the history of the township. The first officers were, from left to right, Candis Bronkema, Richard Geldhof, Lyle Squires, Robert Peck, Carl Friske, Eloise Covey, Irene Lamphear, and Lela Peck.

Consistent with our mission to preserve history on a local level, this book was printed in South Carolina on American-made paper and manufactured entirely in the United States. Products carrying the accredited Forest Stewardship Council (FSC) label are printed on 100 percent FSC-certified paper.

MADE IN THE USA